T0256120

Agricultural Informatics

Scrivener Publishing
100 Cummings Center, Suite 541J
Beverly, MA 01915-6106

Advances in Learning Analytics for Intelligent Cloud-IoT Systems

Series Editor: Dr. Souvik Pal and Dr. Dac-Nhuong Le

The role of adaptation, learning analytics, computational Intelligence, and data analytics in the field of cloud-IoT systems is becoming increasingly essential and intertwined. The capability of an intelligent system depends on various self-decision-making algorithms in IoT devices. IoT-based smart systems generate a large amount of data (big data) that cannot be processed by traditional data processing algorithms and applications. Hence, this book series involves different computational methods incorporated within the system with the help of analytics reasoning and sense-making in big data, which is centered in the cloud and IoT-enabled environments. The series publishes volumes that are empirical studies, theoretical and numerical analysis, and novel research findings.

Submission to the series:
Please send proposals to Dr. Souvik Pal, Department of Computer Science and Engineering, Global Institute of Management and Technology, Krishna Nagar, West Bengal, India.
E-mail: souvikpal22@gmail.com

Publishers at Scrivener
Martin Scrivener (martin@scrivenerpublishing.com)
Phillip Carmical (pcarmical@scrivenerpublishing.com)

Agricultural Informatics

Automation Using the IoT and Machine Learning

Edited by
**Amitava Choudhury,
Arindam Biswas, Manish Prateek
and Amlan Chakrabarti**

Scrivener
Publishing

WILEY

This edition first published 2021 by John Wiley & Sons, Inc., 111 River Street, Hoboken, NJ 07030, USA and Scrivener Publishing LLC, 100 Cummings Center, Suite 541J, Beverly, MA 01915, USA
© 2021 Scrivener Publishing LLC
For more information about Scrivener publications please visit www.scrivenerpublishing.com.

Wiley Global Headquarters
111 River Street, Hoboken, NJ 07030, USA

For details of our global editorial offices, customer services, and more information about Wiley products visit us at www.wiley.com.

Library of Congress Cataloging-in-Publication Data

ISBN 978-1-119-76884-5

Cover image: Pixabay.Com
Cover design by Russell Richardson

Set in size of 11pt and Minion Pro by Manila Typesetting Company, Makati, Philippines

Contents

Preface   **xiii**

1 A Study on Various Machine Learning Algorithms and Their Role in Agriculture   **1**
Kalpana Rangra and Amitava Choudhury
1.1 Introduction   1
     1.1.1 Machine Learning Model   2
         1.1.1.1 Artificial Neural Networks   2
         1.1.1.2 Information Fuzzy Network   4
         1.1.1.3 Decision Trees   5
         1.1.1.4 Regression Analysis   6
         1.1.1.5 Principal Component Analysis   8
         1.1.1.6 Bayesian Networks   8
         1.1.1.7 Time Series Analysis   8
         1.1.1.8 Markov Chain Model   9
1.2 Conclusions   9
     References   10

2 Smart Farming Using Machine Learning and IoT   **13**
Alo Sen, Rahul Roy and Satya Ranjan Dash
2.1 Introduction   14
     2.1.1 Smart Farming   14
     2.1.2 Technology Involvement in Smart Agriculture   14
2.2 Related Work   15
     2.2.1 Monitoring Soil, Climate and Crop   15
     2.2.2 Pesticide Control   15
     2.2.3 Proper Fertilizer Uses   21
     2.2.4 Intrusion Detection   21
     2.2.5 Weed Control   21
     2.2.6 Water Supply Management   21
2.3 Problem Identification   22

2.4 Objective Behind the Integrated Agro-IoT System   23
2.5 Proposed Prototype of the Integrated Agro-IoT System   23
    2.5.1 Pest or Weed Detection Process   25
    2.5.2 Fire Detection Process   26
2.6 Hardware Component Requirement for the Integrated
    Agro-IoT System   26
    2.6.1 Sensors   26
    2.6.2 Camera   26
    2.6.3 Water Pump   27
    2.6.4 Relay   27
    2.6.5 Water Reservoir   28
    2.6.6 Solar Panel   28
    2.6.7 GSM Module   28
    2.6.8 Iron Railing   28
    2.6.9 Beaglebone Black   28
2.7 Comparative Study Between Raspberry Pi vs
    Beaglebone Black   30
    2.7.1 Raw Comparison   30
    2.7.2 Ease of Setup   30
    2.7.3 Connections   31
    2.7.4 Processor Showdown   31
    2.7.5 Right Choice for Projects   31
2.8 Conclusions   31
2.9 Future Work   32
    References   32

3 **Agricultural Informatics vis-à-vis Internet of Things (IoT):
    The Scenario, Applications and Academic Aspects—
    International Trend & Indian Possibilities**   35
    P.K. Paul
3.1 Introduction   36
3.2 Objectives   36
3.3 Methods   37
3.4 Agricultural Informatics: An Account   37
    3.4.1 Agricultural Informatics and Environmental
        Informatics   38
    3.4.2 Stakeholders of Agricultural Informatics   39
        3.4.2.1 Technology   39
        3.4.2.2 Digital Content   40
        3.4.2.3 Agricultural Components   40
        3.4.2.4 Peoples   40

3.5   Agricultural Informatics & Technological Components: Basics & Emergence   40

3.6   IoT: Basics and Characteristics   41

3.7   IoT: The Applications & Agriculture Areas   43

3.8   Agricultural Informatics & IoT: The Scenario   45

     3.8.1   Weather, Climate & Agro IoT   46

     3.8.2   Precision Cultivation With Argo IoT   47

     3.8.3   IoT in Making Green House Perfect   47

     3.8.4   Data Analytics and Management by IoT in Agro Space   47

     3.8.5   Drone, IoT and Agriculture   48

     3.8.6   Livestock Management Using AIoT   48

     3.8.7   Environmental Monitoring & IoT, Environmental Informatics   48

3.9   IoT in Agriculture: Requirement, Issues & Challenges   49

3.10   Development, Economy and Growth: Agricultural Informatics Context   50

3.11   Academic Availability and Potentiality of IoT in Agricultural Informatics: International Scenario & Indian Possibilities   51

3.12   Suggestions   60

3.13   Conclusion   60

     References   61

4   Application of Agricultural Drones and IoT to Understand Food Supply Chain During Post COVID-19   67

Pushan Kumar Dutta and Susanta Mitra

4.1   Introduction   68

4.2   Related Work   69

4.3   Smart Production With the Introduction of Drones and IoT   72

     4.3.1   Real-Time Surveyed Data Collection and Storage Utilizing an IoT System   73

         4.3.1.1   Efficient Control of Distributed Networks of Services (Using the Integrated Networks Sensors Provided)   73

         4.3.1.2   Human Participation in Surveillance and Monitoring can be Identified to Take the Following Roles   74

4.4   Agricultural Drones   75

4.5   IoT Acts as a Backbone in Addressing COVID-19 Problems in Agriculture   77

     4.5.1   Implementation in Agriculture—Drones   77

     4.5.2   Communication and Networking Mechanisms   79

4.5.3 Managing Agricultural Data Safety and Security
of Individual Farmers 81
4.6 Conclusion 81
References 82

5 IoT and Machine Learning-Based Approaches for Real Time
Environment Parameters Monitoring in Agriculture:
An Empirical Review 89
Parijata Majumdar and Sanjoy Mitra
5.1 Introduction 90
5.2 Machine Learning (ML)-Based IoT Solution 90
5.3 Motivation of the Work 91
5.4 Literature Review of IoT-Based Weather and Irrigation
Monitoring for Precision Agriculture 91
5.5 Literature Review of Machine Learning-Based Weather
and Irrigation Monitoring for Precision Agriculture 92
5.6 Challenges 112
5.7 Conclusion and Future Work 113
References 114

6 Deep Neural Network-Based Multi-Class Image Classification
for Plant Diseases 117
Alok Negi, Krishan Kumar and Prachi Chauhan
6.1 Introduction 117
6.2 Related Work 119
6.3 Proposed Work 121
6.3.1 Dataset Description 122
6.3.2 Data Pre-Processing and Augmentation 122
6.3.3 CNN Architecture 123
6.4 Results and Evaluation 124
6.5 Conclusion 127
References 128

7 Deep Residual Neural Network for Plant Seedling Image
Classification 131
Prachi Chauhan, Hardwari Lal Mandoria and Alok Negi
7.1 Introduction 131
7.1.1 Architecture of CNN 133
7.1.1.1 Principles of ConvNet 133
7.1.2 Residual Network (ResNet) 134
7.2 Related Work 136
7.3 Proposed Work 139

	7.3.1	Data Collection	139
	7.3.2	Data Pre-Processing	139
	7.3.3	Data Annotation and Augmentation	141
	7.3.4	Training and Fine-Tuning	142
7.4	Result and Evaluation		142
	7.4.1	Metrics	142
	7.4.2	Result Analysis	143
		7.4.2.1 Experiment I	143
		7.4.2.2 Experiment II	143
7.5	Conclusion		144
	References		145

8 Development of IoT-Based Smart Security and Monitoring Devices for Agriculture   **147**
Himadri Nath Saha, Reek Roy, Monojit Chakraborty and Chiranmay Sarkar

8.1	Introduction		148
8.2	Background & Related Works		150
8.3	Proposed Model		155
	8.3.1	Raspberry Pi 4 Model B	156
	8.3.2	Passive Infrared Sensor (PIR Sensor)	157
	8.3.3	pH Sensor	158
	8.3.4	Dielectric Soil Moisture Sensor	158
	8.3.5	RGB-D Sensor	159
	8.3.6	GSM Module	159
	8.3.7	Unmanned Aerial Vehicle (UAV)	160
8.4	Methodology		160
8.5	Performance Analysis		165
8.6	Future Research Direction		166
8.7	Conclusion		167
	References		168

9 An Integrated Application of IoT-Based WSN in the Field of Indian Agriculture System Using Hybrid Optimization Technique and Machine Learning   **171**
Avishek Banerjee, Arnab Mitra and Arindam Biswas

9.1	Introduction		172
	9.1.1	Contribution in Detail	173
9.2	Literature Review		175
9.3	Proposed Hybrid Algorithms (GA-MWPSO)		177
9.4	Reliability Optimization and Coverage Optimization Model		179

9.5   Problem Description   181
9.6   Numerical Examples, Results and Discussion   182
       9.6.1   Case Example   182
       9.6.2   Theoretical Approach to Make Machine
               Learning Model   183
9.7   Conclusion   183
       References   184

10 Decryption and Design of a Multicopter Unmanned Aerial
Vehicle (UAV) for Heavy Lift Agricultural Operations   **189**
Raghuvirsinh Pravinsinh Parmar
10.1   Introduction   190
       10.1.1 Classification of Small UAVs   190
10.2   History of Multicopter UAVs   192
10.3   Basic Components of Multicopter UAV   193
       10.3.1 Airframe   194
               10.3.1.1   Fuselage   195
               10.3.1.2   Landing Gear   196
               10.3.1.3   Arms   196
               10.3.1.4   Selection of Material for UAV Airframe 196
       10.3.2 Propulsion System   197
               10.3.2.1   Lithium Polymer (LiPo) Battery   197
               10.3.2.2   Propeller   198
               10.3.2.3   Brushless DC (BLDC) Motor   199
               10.3.2.4   Electronic Speed Controller (ESC)   200
       10.3.3 Command and Control System   201
               10.3.3.1   Remote Controlled (RC) Transmitter
                          and Receiver   201
               10.3.3.2   Flight Controller Unit (FCU)   202
               10.3.3.3   Ground Control Station (GCS)   203
               10.3.3.4   Radio Telemetry   204
               10.3.3.5   Global Positioning System (GPS)   204
10.4   Working and Control Mechanism of Multicopter UAV   207
       10.4.1 Upward and Downward Movement   207
       10.4.2 Forward and Backward Movement   208
       10.4.3 Leftward-and-Rightward Movement   209
       10.4.4 Yaw Movement   209
10.5   Design Calculations and Selection of Components   210
       10.5.1 Fuselage Configuration   210
       10.5.2 Propeller Selection   211
       10.5.3 Motor Selection   212

10.5.4   Maximum Power and Current Requirement   214
10.5.5   Thrust Requirement by Motor   215
10.5.6   Thrust Requirement by the Propeller   216
10.5.7   Endurance or Flight Time   217
10.5.8   Maximum Airframe Size   217
10.6   Conclusion   218
References   219

11 IoT-Enabled Agricultural System Application, Challenges
and Security Issues   223
Himadri Nath Saha, Reek Roy, Monojit Chakraborty
and Chiranmay Sarkar
11.1   Introduction   224
11.2   Background & Related Works   226
11.3   Challenges to Implement IoT-Enabled Systems   232
         11.3.1   Secured Data Generation and Transmission
                  and Privacy   232
         11.3.2   Lack of Supporting Infrastructure   233
         11.3.3   Technical Skill Requirement   233
         11.3.4   Complexity in Software and Hardware   234
         11.3.5   Bulk Data   236
         11.3.6   Disrupted Connectivity to the Cloud   236
         11.3.7   Better Connectivity   237
         11.3.8   Interoperability Issue   238
         11.3.9   Crop Management Issues   238
         11.3.10 Power Consumption   239
         11.3.11 Environmental Challenges   239
         11.3.12 High Cost   239
11.4   Security Issues and Measures   240
11.5   Future Research Direction   243
11.6   Conclusion   244
References   245

12 Plane Region Step Farming, Animal and Pest Attack Control
Using Internet of Things   249
Sahadev Roy, Kaushal Mukherjee and Arindam Biswas
12.1   Introduction   250
         12.1.1   Possible Various Applications in Agriculture   252
         12.1.2   Cayenne IoT Builder   254
12.2   Proposed Work   254
         12.2.1   Design of Agro Farm Structure   254

12.3	Irrigation Methodology		257
	12.3.1	Irrigation Scheduling	258
	12.3.2	Two Critical Circumstances Farmers Often Face	259
	12.3.3	Irrigation Indices	259
12.4	Sensor Connection Using Internet of Things		259
	12.4.1	Animal Attack Control	261
	12.4.2	Pest Attack Control	262
	12.4.3	DHT 11 Humidity & Temperature Sensor	262
	12.4.4	Rain Sensor Module	262
	12.4.5	Soil Moisture Sensor	263
12.5	Placement of Sensor in the Field		263
12.6	Conclusion		267
	References		268
Index			**271**

Preface

The emergence of automation in agriculture has become an important issue for every country. The world population is increasing at a very fast rate, and along with this increase in population the need for food is also increasing at a brisk pace. Traditional methods used by farmers are no longer sufficient to serve this increasing demand, resulting in the intensified use of harmful pesticides. This in turn has had a profound effect on agricultural practices, which in the end can render the land barren. This book discusses the different automation practices, including the internet of things (IoT), wireless communications, machine learning, artificial intelligence, and deep learning, currently being employed to address this problem. There are some areas of concern in the field of agriculture, such as crop disease, lack of storage, weed and water management, pesticide control, and lack of irrigation, all of which can be solved using the different techniques mentioned above.

From the earliest civilizations up till now, clothing, shelter and food have been the three primary needs of human beings that have remained constant. And even though we have become quite advanced in addressing issues related to housing and clothing, despite the increasing population (as per the Food and Agriculture Organization of the United Nations, 70% more food will need to be produced in 2050 than was produced in 2006), issues related to food production have yet to be completely addressed. In recent years, the IoT began to be used to address different industrial and technical challenges to meet this growing need. Therefore, now is the time to meet the future demands of farming which can only be accomplished by smart Agro-IoT tools. This will in turn boost productivity and minimize the pitfalls of traditional farming, which is the backbone of the world's economy. Aided by the IoT, continuous monitoring of fields will provide useful information to farmers, ushering in a new era in farming. The IoT can be used as a tool to combat climate change; monitor and manage water, land, soil and crops; increase productivity; control insecticides/pesticides; detect plant diseases; increase the rate of crop sales; etc. This book will focus on some case studies that involve monitoring of climate conditions, greenhouse automation, crop management, cattle monitoring and management for smart farming with IoT devices, which will give a clear indication as to why these techniques should be used in agriculture rather than some of the previously developed agricultural tools currently in use.

Organization of the Book

We are delighted to present this book, which was made possible with the support and contributions from academicians from various highly reputable institutions. It is a manifestation of various interesting and important aspects of theoretical and applied research covering complementary facets of innovative algorithms and applications in the fields of agriculture and cultivation processes, including:

- Machine learning algorithm and its role in agriculture
- Smart farming using machine learning and the IoT
- Agricultural informatics vis-à-vis the IoT
- Application of agricultural drones
- Real-time monitoring of environmental parameters in agriculture
- Deep neural network-based multiclass image classification of plant diseases
- Decryption and design of a multicopter unmanned aerial vehicle (UAV) for heavy lift agricultural operations

The 12 chapters of the book are briefly summarized below.

Chapter 1 discusses various state-of-the-art machine learning algorithms and their role in agriculture. The domain of crop production is very important for organizations, firms, and products related to agriculture. Data is collected from different sources for crop forecasting, and may vary in shape, size and type depending upon the source of collection. Agricultural data may be collected from metrological instruments, soil-sensors that are remotely installed, agricultural statistics, etc. Marketing, storage, transportation and decisions pertaining to crops have a high requirement for accurate data produced in a timely manner that can be used for predictions.

Chapter 2 describes how IoT tools are effective in smart farming. This chapter focuses on case studies like climate conditions monitoring, greenhouse automation, crop management, cattle monitoring, and smart farming management with IoT devices, which will provide a clear idea as to why this technique is preferable in agriculture rather than some previously developed agricultural tools.

Global aspects of agriculture automation through the IoT are discussed in Chapter 3. In this chapter, a case study on the IoT is highlighted which briefly discusses its basic and current applications. Also highlighted are aspects of IoT application in agriculture and related fields, and its importance in promoting agricultural informatics practice. The chapter focuses on the academic programs available in the field of agricultural informatics and related areas. Agricultural informatics programs are also proposed in concert with IoT and related fields in an international context and the potential fields in agricultural informatics are discussed as well.

In Chapter 4, the role that gathering information plays in productive crop management in smart farming is discussed. Current advances in data management for smart farming enabled by using sensor-based data-driven architecture have been found to increase efficiency in generating both qualitative and quantitative approaches in a range of challenges that will shake up existing agriculture methodologies. The chapter highlights the potential of wireless sensors and the IoT in agriculture and similar techniques which are feasible for surveillance and monitoring from sowing to harvesting and similar packaging operations. In this chapter, the authors focus on IoT technologies by highlighting the design of a novel drone concept with 3D mapping and address post COVID-19 issues in agriculture and proposed monitoring in comparative analysis. This chapter reviews an artificial intelligence-based decision-making system that will create supplementary benefits as a result of precision agriculture. Machine learning also plays a critical role in farming in terms of nutrients management. It is further found that automation in agriculture via the IoT is a proven technology that can work even for small farms such as those in India.

The study in Chapter 5 discusses real-time monitoring of environmental parameters in agriculture. The main objective of this chapter is real-time visualization and on-demand access of weather parameters even from remote locations and intelligent processing using IoT-based solutions like machine learning (ML). Ever-augmenting technologies like ML pave the way for identifying and adapting changes in crop design and irrigation patterns by taking into account a large variety of multidimensional weather data to accurately predict climate conditions suitable for crop irrigation. Hence, this chapter offers a detailed review of IoT-based ML solutions for precision agriculture depending on weather and irrigation schedules. It also highlights security solutions based on ML, which are capable of handling illegal data access by intruders during cloud data storage.

The immensely difficult challenge of recognizing plant disease in an agriculture farming field is discussed in Chapter 6. An effective management strategy will enable faster and more accurate prediction of leaf diseases in plants, which will help to improve crop production and market value and also dramatically reduce environmental damage. Since recognizing diseases in plants requires a lot of knowledge about all plant diseases, it can be a time-consuming and labor-intensive process. Hence, plant disease recognition is the most promising approach in agriculture, which is attracting significant attention in both the farming and computer communities. In order to help grow healthy plants, a deep convolutional neural network (CNN) model described in this chapter aids farming by identifying leaf disease. The CNN techniques are applied to a large agricultural plant dataset for accurate detection of plant leaf diseases.

In Chapter 7, deep residual neural network for plant seedling image classification is discussed. Weed conservation within the first six to eight weeks after planting is critical because during this time weeds compete aggressively with crops for nutrients and water. In general, yield losses will range from 10 to 100 percent depending on the degree of weed control practiced. Since yield losses are caused by weeds interfering with the growth and production of crops, successful weed control is imperative. The first vital prerequisite to enact successful control is accurate identification and classification of weeds. In this research, a detailed experimental study has been conducted on a residual neural network (ResNet) to tackle the problem of yield losses. The authors used the Plant Seedlings Dataset to train and test the system. The use of ResNet to classify images with a high accuracy rate can ultimately change how weeds affect the current state of agriculture.

Smart farming technologies continue to empower farmers, which helps them address the significant problems they face through much better remedies. The growth pattern and environmental parameters of crop growth provide scientific guidance and optimum countermeasures for agricultural production. A proposed system is presented in Chapter 8 that uses a Raspberry Pi board and an array of sensors, i.e., PIR sensor, pH sensor, and capacitance dielectric soil moisture sensor, which was proven to be more robust and accurate than existing systems in tracking soil content and security of the crops. If soil nutrients, pH, or moisture of the soil is not up to par with the requirements for a given crop the user is notified to take action via an alarm buzzer with an LED indicator light. A monitoring system consisting of an unmanned aerial vehicle (UAV) equipped with an RGB-D sensor is deployed to regularly check the status of the crops, so that in cases where pests attack crops or when crop health begins to degrade, it can be efficiently noted and the necessary steps can be taken to correct the problem. The various data generated is stored in the cloud and is sent to user websites and mobile applications, which will be used for further study to enhance the agricultural process.

An integrated application of IoT-based wireless sensor network (WSN) in India's agriculture system that uses the hybrid optimization technique is discussed in Chapter 9. A new hybrid algorithm, i.e., GA-MWPSO, has been used for solving nonlinear constrained optimization problems. To test the competence of the proposed algorithms, a set of test problems has been considered, solved and compared with the existing literature.

Chapter 10 discusses multicopter unmanned aerial vehicles (UAVs) designed for heavy lift agricultural operations. The knowledge of flying multicopter UAVs and the workings of other components should be strong while developing UAVs; otherwise, the design and assembly of UAVs leads to poor performance or even design fails. Configuration of UAVs includes the size and shape of the UAV and the proper matching of brushless DC electric (BLDC) motors and propellers. Therefore, it is essential to have a deep knowledge about each and every component and its design and selection requirements. In this chapter, information about several UAV systems and components and basic principles of design are presented.

Chapter 11 describes various security challenges in IoT-enabled agricultural system applications. The challenges facing these systems are software simplicity, secure data generation and transmission, and lack of supporting infrastructure. But at present the biggest obstacle is lack of smooth integration with the agricultural industry and lack of an optimally skilled human workforce. In addition to the need for sensors to work wirelessly and consume low power, they should have better connectivity and remote management, and the complexity and security of software should be rectified. There is also a high demand for fail-safe systems to mitigate the risk of data loss in any faults occurring during operation.

Chapter 12 looks at optimized crop treatment, such as watering, pesticide application, accurate planting, and harvesting, directly affects crop production rates. Using an organized fashion of field structure and proper irrigation scheduling and providing early prediction of weather conditions directly on the mobile devices of farmers may save thousands of lives, since this technique enables farmers to effectively produce crops in all growing seasons and losses will be minimized, ultimately decreasing the death toll due to lack of food in growing populations. For pest control, various ultrasound frequencies are used. When any pest interacts with any part of the plant, a capacitive touch shield can be used to detect its presence, generating an alert signal via an ultrasonic signal generator. For the supply of constant and continuous energy to the sensor, a solar cell powered battery needs to be set up in the field. To reduce power consumption of the battery, some logic needs to be set up to activate the sensor network at a particular time, with the sensor network otherwise remaining idle. A small exhaust fan is incorporated as a heat sink to protect the sensor devices or drive circuitry from the excess heat of the sun so that the longevity of the sensor devices and circuitry will increase. The IoT enables plane region step farming and animal and pest attack control, which truly enhances crop production rate.

In summary, at present there is a genuine need for agriculture upgradation and this book provides a technological overview that will open new dimensions which may be useful in discovering solutions to aid in the current growth in agricultural processes. The editors of this book are thankful to the all authors whose valuable contributions made this book as complete.

Editors
Amitava Choudhury
University of Petroleum and Energy Studies, Dehradun, India
Arindam Biswas
Kazi Nazrul University, Asansol, India
Manish Prateek
University of Petroleum and Energy Studies, Dehradun, India
Amlan Chakrabarti
University of Calcutta, Kolkata, India
January 2021

1

A Study on Various Machine Learning Algorithms and Their Role in Agriculture

Kalpana Rangra and Amitava Choudhury*

School of Computer Science, University of Petroleum and Energy Studies, Dehradun, India

Abstract

The term machine learning indicates empowering the machine to gain knowledge and process it for decision making. The domain of crop production is very important for organizations, firms, products related to agriculture. Data collection is done from different sources for crop forecasting. The collected data may vary in shape, size and type depending upon the source of collection. Agricultural data may be collected from metrological sources, agricultural and metrological, soil, sensors that are remotely installed, agricultural statistics, etc. Marketing, storage, transportation and decisions pertaining to crops have high requirement of accurate data that should be produced timely and can be used for predictions.

Keywords: Agriculture, machine learning, smart farming, decision tree, crop prediction, automated farming, ML models for agriculture

1.1 Introduction

Machine learning can be studied under two vast categories called supervised and unsupervised learning. Supervised learning pertains to fact that data and process is supervised by supervisor. The process of training data is controlled to find the conclusions for new data. Some of the most commonly used techniques for supervised learning are Artificial neural network, Bayesian network, decision tree, support vector machines, ID3, k-nearest

Corresponding author: a.choudhury2013@gmail.com

Amitava Choudhury, Arindam Biswas, Manish Prateek and Amlan Chakrabarti (eds.)
Agricultural Informatics: Automation Using the IoT and Machine Learning, (1–12) © 2021 Scrivener Publishing LLC

neighbor, hidden Markov model, etc. For unsupervised learning enormous volume of data is given as input to program for which the program generates patterns and identify the relations among them. Unsupervised learning can be used to discover the hidden patterns. K-nearest neighbor algorithm, self-organizing map methods, and partial based clustering techniques, hierarchical clustering approaches, k-means clustering, etc., belong to class of unsupervised learning. Predictive power of computers can be increased by integrating machine with statistics. Data scientists and analysts use this integration to predict trends from raw data that is fed into the system. The amount of data obtained in agricultural field is increasing enormously so the machine learning techniques can be applied to agricultural production for predicting crop related queries. Decisions regarding crop production can be made by using several available machines learning techniques. All such techniques use mathematics and stats for algorithm generation.

1.1.1 Machine Learning Model

1.1.1.1 Artificial Neural Networks

The artificial neural network is a collaboration of artificial neurons based on human brains biological architecture. They replicate the behavior of the human brain for processing the data. Artificial neural network belongs to the category of supervised learning where a part of data is used for model training and the remaining is tested on the trained model. Once the neural net is trained, the similar patterns can be generated for obtaining efficient and solutions to problems and predictive analysis. The trained neural network can produce solutions even if the input data is incomplete or incorrect. Adding more layers and data increases the accuracy of the ANN. The ANN is capable of adopting their complexity without the need to know the underlying principles. The relationship among input and output for any process can be derived using ANN. Authors used [1] ANN to predict potato yield in Iran. Figure 1.1 shows the basic architecture of artificial neural network.

Input energy was taken as the input parameter. The work intended to design output energy and greenhouse gas emission for production forecast. The data collection was done from 260 farmers by taking inputs from them. Multiple ANNs were designed and utilized to forecast. The forecast efficiency was assessed from quality aspect. The prediction results. Electricity, chemical fertilizer and seed were identified as most important factors affecting production rate. Literature [3] quotes ANN systems are

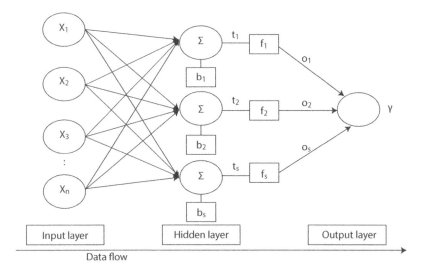

Figure 1.1 Layers and connection of a feed-forward back propagation ANN [2].

the results of inspiration of the human brain. Each node in neural net represents neurons and each link is the representation of interaction among two associated neurons. Execution of simple tasks is the responsibility of single neuron while the network performs more complex tasks that are aggregations of all the neuron groups in network. There exists an interconnected set of input and output that has weighted connections. The testing phase of network enables them to earn to predict the input sampled by performing weight tuning. Flood forecast uses neural networks to model rainfall and runoff relationships for predicting flood situations. Neural networks have better performance over conventional computing methods. ANN finds suitability for the time consuming problem solutions such as pest prediction. Research [4] found that validation of the symptoms of tomato crop can be done using a web-based expert system that utilized applied artificial learning and machine learning algorithms particularly for the identification task. In crop expert system applicant is advised with crop related information. The farmer gets insight for crop varieties, pest affecting the crop production and diseases symptoms on the crop, cultural practice for good yield, mosaic of tomato fruits and plant. Client is also facilitated for communicating with the system online. The query put forward by the client is responded by the expert system that advises and informs client regarding all the hazards and control measures. The knowledge expert system provides data about disease recognition, pest and varieties of tomato crop.

Machine learning algorithms are reliable for decisions and can be integrated with statistics for implementation in applied machine learning [5]. Machine Learning is an emerging subject to expedite the release of new genotypes. There exist several uses of Machine Learning in maize breeding. Few of them can be enlisted as loci mapping based on quantitative traits, heterotic group assignment and selections based on genomes. Authors [6] implemented ANN to predict crop production. The parameters used for the task were related to soil properties such as pH, nitrogen, phosphate, potassium, organic carbon, calcium, magnesium, and sulfur, manganese, copper, iron, depth and climate parameters such as temperature, rainfall, humidity. Cotton, Sugarcane, Jawar, Bajara, Soybean, Corn, Wheat, Rice and Groundnut were the crops taken for experiment.

1.1.1.2   Information Fuzzy Network

Research experiments analyzed parameters for predicting crop yield. The study used aggressive neural network for prediction. Remote sensing was one among the used parameters for the work [7, 8]. The experiments implemented the flexible Neuro-fuzzy Inference system (ANFIS). The inputs to the ANFIS were moisture content available in soil, biomass information of the ground and repository organ. Yield was the output node for result. Limited data was used for designing the network to predict values for future. This is the challenge in prediction. Rearrangement of data was done by eliminating one year and using the remaining data. The estimation deviation was calculated and compared to the yield of the year that is left out. The procedure was applied recursively to all the years and averaged efficiency for prediction was obtained

Experiments used Refs. [10–12] as stated in Figure 1.2. Hellenic sugar Industry used FINKNN for sugar production forecast based on the population of assessment. FINKNN is studied as K-nearest neighbor classifier that performs over the metric lattice of traditional convex fuzzy set.

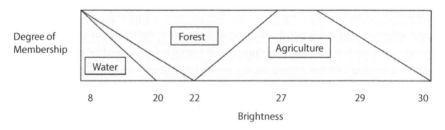

Figure 1.2 Fuzzy cluster membership function representation in various field [9].

Results proved that FINKNN showed improved results for efficiency in forecasting.

1.1.1.3 Decision Trees

Decision trees are the supervised learning techniques used in machine learning. The Decision Tree model is comprised of nodes, branches, leaf, terminal value, payoff distribution, rollback and certain equivalent and method. Decision trees have three variants of nodes and two variants of branches. Square is used to represent one of the decision points. The decision node is a point of choice for the tree. The decision nodes extend decision branches. Each node toward the end of the tree is called terminal node. There is an associated value associated with terminal node commonly referred to as payoff, outcome value. The terminal value is the measure of sequences of decisions or the resultant of the scenario in the tree. The construction of Decision tree algorithm is a two-step process that includes growth of tree and pruning. In the growth step the large decision tree is created, reduced and overfitting is removed. The second step does the tree pruning to reach a decision. The classification tree used for decision making is the obtained pruned tree [13].

Prediction is influenced by various factors in agricultural explorations [14]. Variables associated with agronomics, application of nitrogen and weed control were used for machine learning and decision tree for yield forecasting and development of yield mapping. Both decision trees and ANN were implemented and results showed that greater accuracies were obtained from ANN results.

Authors [15] modeled productivity of soybean using decision trees. Data for climate in Bhopal district was collected for since 1984 to 2003 considering the climatic factors of evaporation, minimum and maximum temperature, humidity, and rainfall. The factors were studied for the production of soybean crop. Interactive Dichotomizer3 (ID3) algorithm was implemented on data. ID technique is based on information and two assumptions. Relative humidity was found to be a major parameter that affected soybean crop yield. Few rules were generated that helped know the lowest and highest prediction of soybean. The only one limitation of the model was that, the amount of yield production cannot be predicted [4, 16], as shown in Figure 1.3.

The vast climatic diversity of India impacts the agricultural production in several parts of the country .Convenient decisions can be made by the farmers and policy inventors if the production can be forecasted in advance.

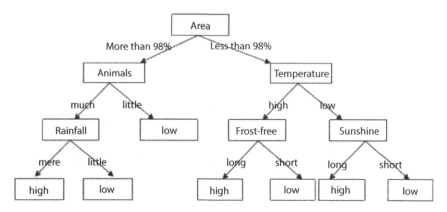

Figure 1.3 Decision tree structure for crop details prediction [4].

Crop Advisor is one of the advancement in this area. It is a user friendly webpage that identified the impact of weather parameters on the yield of crops. Crop Advisor implements C4.5 algorithm. The most effective parameter of the climate on the yields of specified crops in selected region of Madhya Pradesh was ascertained using C4.5. There is boom in cloud based decision and support system for agriculture these days. There exists a Decision support and Automation system (DSAS) to assist farmers and growers. Users of the application have controls for different features in web portal. There are different stages in DSAS. DSAS provides farmer with real time data via interconnection of several devices. The farmer had right to monitor the real time data and control the machine through software. Few another systems like spray controller will spray defined amount of pesticide in fields, irrigation controller manage irrigation and fertilizer controller takes care of fertilizer. The data to DSAS is given by different sensors of climate and soil [17].

1.1.1.4   Regression Analysis

There exist several statistical techniques for crop production. One of the most widely used is regression analysis [18, 19]. Regression models were developed as a technique for prediction of response variable called yield and weather, soil properties were addressed as explanatory variables [20]. Several yield forecasting models used parametric regression by taking known functional forms of the predictor variables [21]. Authors [22] described the linear regression as commonly used models for crop production. Researchers also found the use of polynomial regression models in nonlinear regression models in for agricultural applications [23]. The influence of temperature on Jowar crop was forecasted in Jowar production system. The production, minimum and maximum temperatures were the parameters of the experiment [4]. The significance was tested where 2-tailed test approach and Pearson correlation coefficients were used. The results obtained were significant at 0.01 level. Then regression analysis was carried out for yield of crop and measures of temperature. Results showed that that the Jowar yields were very less dependent on the temperature yield was highly affected by some other factors. The reduced temperature increased the yield of Jowar crops. Experiments used functional liner regression analysis to relate yield with rainfall and temperature as predictor variable [4, 24].

Correlation analysis was done taking the yield as output variable and temperature and precipitation as prediction parameters. Stepwise regression technique was used to select best predictors [4, 25]. The crop production changes with the changes in climate. This effect of changing climatic variables on crop production was studied under anticipated seasonal climate change conditions. Daily weather data was obtained from weather generator and authors used the multiple linear regression models. The parameters referencing the climate such as measures of minimum and maximum temperature, density of rainfall, humidity and precipitation rate, speed of wind and solar radiation were used for analysis. These factors were used to predict the corn yield they have results implied that climate variability *significantly* affects crop yields [4].

The process of identifying similar objects that are different from individuals in other groups is called Cluster analysis or clustering. Clustering finds wide usage in data analysis and many other fields such as machine learning, recognition patterns, analyzing images, retrieval of information and agriculture, etc. Clustering can be studied with several algorithms such as k-means, k-medoid, etc. K-means is most common and widely used clustering algorithm [26]. Demonstration of modified k-Means clustering algorithm in prediction of crop was done in Ref. [4]. Comparison of results for modified k-Means over k-Means and -Means++ clustering algorithms was done and it was found that the modified k-Means had the maxi-mum number of highly differentiable good quality clusters, highly correct results of crop prediction and maximum count for accuracy.

A weather forecast model was developed for classifying the metrological data. The model was based on the frequency of variables. Patterns associated to severe convective activity were identified for the task. Brazilian regions were spot for collection of features during summer of 2007. A fairly good classification performance was seen in results [27].

1.1.1.5   Principal Component Analysis

Principal component analysis is one of the data mining processes that ensures correct forecast by the arrangement and familiarity in data. Monsoon rainfall is important parameter for variable for crop yield. The amount of rainfall varies periodically during monsoons depending upon the region selected for experiments. Rainfall information is considered important area where water storage from rainfall had been carried out, particularly for flood observant methods. Broad range prediction of Indian monsoon rainfall is based on statistical methods. Indian economy is highly impacted by the limited variation in the periodic rainfall. Evaluation of high spatial datasets like temperature of sea surface and rainfall periods is done using weather and water assets analysis that used component derivation method. Prediction of monsoon rainfall in India is obtained using the principal component analysis [4, 28, 29].

1.1.1.6   Bayesian Networks

A Bayesian network also known as Bayes network or belief network or Bayesian model is probabilistic directed acyclic graphical that uses statistical model. Effect of climate change on potato production was assessed using a belief network [4]. The change in climate (uncertainty) and the variability of current weather parameters were collaborated in the belief network. The parameters studied were such as temperature conditions, radiation, rainfall data and the potato development information. The network was developed to support the policy makers in agriculture. Synthetic weather scenarios were used for tests and then, comparison of the results with the conventional mathematical model was done. The belief network proved efficient for the experiment.

1.1.1.7   Time Series Analysis

Meaningful statistics can be extracted from a series data that can be analyzed on time based parameters. This is commonly termed as Time series Analysis and predicts future values based on previously obtained data. Time series analysis can be an important tool used in forecasting the crop yield. The dependent variable yield is time function that can establish the relation between yield and time. Frequency and time domain, parametric or non-parametric methods, linear or nonlinear approaches, univariate and multivariate models are few variants of time series analysis. Spectral analysis are used in frequency domain and wavelet analysis, time domain includes auto-correlation and cross-correlation, parametric approaches use autoregressive or moving average model, non-parametric [30] approaches have covariance or spectrum of the process in the core. A new concept of crop yield under average climate conditions was used in Ref. [31]. The time series techniques was used on the past yield data to set up a forecasting model. The moving average method was used first then regression equation was applied thereafter and finally the difference of the yield and impact of climate on yield was found. Moving average model was concluded as better model for yield forecasting. The model used a small dataset and useful results were obtained.

1.1.1.8 Markov Chain Model

Markov chain model is mathematical model in a probabilistic manner. It uses a stochastic process in which Markov chain of output of an experiment depends only on the results of the initial experiments. Alternately, present state determines next state. Markov chains derived the name from the mathematician who belonged to Russian origin (1856–1922). He initiated the theory of stochastic processes. Markov chain approach was used for prediction of cotton yield from pre-harvest data of crops [32]. The application of the Markov chain approach in predicting crop yields was investigated along with the analysis of data for yield of cotton crop for two leading states for cotton crop production. California and Texas were the states of study. Data was taken for the four-year period from 1981 to 1984. Probability distribution was estimated using Markov chain. Selection of key variables for the key within each period for the baseline data was done using multiple linear regressions and multiple rank regressions. Means of these predicted yield distributions was used for yield forecast. Sugarcane yield forecast was obtained from the model that implemented second order Markov chain. Results concluded that the second order Markov chain model can be preferred over other models of regression and first order Markov chain model for crop yield forecasting [33].

1.2   Conclusions

There exist a number of applications in agriculture that use machine learning techniques for prediction and analysis. The article discusses some of the commonly used approaches in research. Large amount of data can be collected from various resources for performing analysis on crop yield forecast. Integrating machine learning into agricultural processes is a vastly growing research area these days. The collaborative model of computer science with agriculture can help in exploring various domains of agronomics and forecasting agricultural crops. The merger of the two approaches can be helpful in pre-harvest crop forecasting and the traditional forecasting method can be out ruled by using computational statistical approaches.

References

1. Khoshnevisan, B., Rafiee, S., Omid, M., Mousazadeh, H., Rajaeifar, M.A., Application of artificial neural networks for prediction of output energy and GHG emissions in potato production in Iran. *Agric. Syst.*, 123, 120–127, 2014.
2. Bejo, S., Mustaffha, S., Wan Ismail, W., Application of artificial neural network in predicting crop yield: A review. *J. Food Sci. Eng.*, 4, 1, 1–9, 2014.
3. Patel, H. and Patel, D., A Brief survey of Data Mining Techniques Applied to Agricultural Data. *Int. J. Comput. Appl.*, 9, 95, 6–8, 2014.
4. Mishra, S., Mishra, D., Santra, G.H., Applications of machine learning techniques in agricultural crop production: A review paper. *Indian J. Sci. Technol.*, 9, 38, 1–14, 2016.
5. Ornella, L., Cervigni, G., Tapia, E., Applications of machine learning in breeding for stress tolerance in maize, in: *Crop Stress and its Management: Perspectives and Strategies*, 2012.
6. Dahikar, M.S. and Rode, D.V., Agricultural Crop Yield Prediction Using Artificial Neural Network Approach. *Int. J. Innovat. Res. Electr. Electron. Instrum. Contr. Eng.*, 2, 684–686, 2014.
7. Stathakis, D. and Savin, I., Networks, F.N., Neuro-Fuzzy Modelling For Crop Yield Prediction. *Int. Arch. Photogramm. Remote Sens. Spat. Inf. Sci.*, 34, 1–4, 2006.
8. Qaddoum, K., Hines, E., Illiescu, D., Adaptive neuro-fuzzy modeling for crop yield prediction, *AIKED'11: Proceedings of the 10th WSEAS international conference on Artificial intelligence, knowledge engineering and data bases*, 199–204, February, 2011.
9. Murmu, S. and Biswas, S., Application of Fuzzy Logic and Neural Network in Crop Classification: A Review. *Aquat. Procedia*, 4, Icwrcoe, 1203–1210, 2015.
10. Hartati, S. and Sitanggang, I.S., A fuzzy based decision support system for evaluating land suitability and selecting crops. *J. Comput. Sci.*, 6, 417–424, 2010.
11. Qureshi, M.R.N., Singh, R.K., Hasan, M.A., Decision support model to select crop pattern for sustainable agricultural practices using fuzzy MCDM. *Environ. Dev. Sustain.*, 6, 417–424, 2018.
12. Petridis, V. and Kaburlasos, V.G., FINkNN: A fuzzy interval number k-nearest neighbor classifier for prediction of sugar production from populations of samples. *J. Mach. Learn. Res.*, 41, 539–545, 2004.

13. Uno, Y. *et al.*, Artificial neural networks to predict corn yield from Compact Airborne Spectrographic Imager data. *Comput. Electron. Agric.*, 47, 2, 149–161, 2005.

14. Veenadhari, S., Bharat Mishra, D., Singh, D.C., Soybean Productivity Modelling using Decision Tree Algorithms. *Int. J. Comput. Appl.*, 27, 7, 11–15, 2011.

15. Veenadhari, S., Misra, B., Singh, C.D., Machine learning approach for forecasting crop yield based on climatic parameters, *2014 International Conference on Computer Communication and Informatics*, Coimbatore, pp. 1–5, 2014.

16. Bitouk, D., Verma, R., Nenkova, A., Class-level spectral features for emotion recognition. *Speech Commun.*, 52, 7–8, 613–625, 2010.

17. Tan, L., Cloud-based Decision Support and Automation for Precision Agriculture in Orchards. *IFAC-PapersOnLine*, 49, 330–335, 2016.

18. Horie, T., Yajima, M., Nakagawa, H., Yield forecasting. *Agric. Syst.*, 40, 1–3, 211–236, 1992.

19. Basso, B., Cammarano, D., Carfagna, E., Review of Crop Yield Forecasting Methods and Early Warning Systems. *First Meet. Sci. Advis. Comm. Glob. Strateg. to Improv. Agric. Rural Stat*, 2013.

20. De La Rosa, D., Cardona, F., Almorza, J., Crop yield predictions based on properties of soils in Sevilla, Spain. *Geoderma*, 25, 3–4, 267–274, May, 1981.

21. Kaspar, T.C. *et al.*, Relationship between six years of corn yields and terrain attributes. *Precis. Agric.*, 4, 87–101, 2003.

22. Shibayama, M. and Akiyama, T., Estimating grain yield of maturing rice canopies using high spectral resolution reflectance measurements. *Remote Sens. Environ.*, 36, 1, 45–53, 1991.

23. Wilcox, A., Perry, N.H., Boatman, N.D., Chaney, K., Factors affecting the yield of winter cereals in crop margins. *J. Agric. Sci.*, 135, 4, 335–346, 2000.

24. Lee, H., Bogner, C., Lee, S., Koellner, T., Crop selection under price and yield fluctuation: Analysis of agro-economic time series from South Korea. *Agric. Syst.*, 148, 1–11, 2016.

25. Selvaraju, R., Meinke, H., Hansen, J., Approaches allowing smallholder farmers in India to benefit from seasonal climate forecasting. *Crop Sci.*, 2004.

26. Groenendyk, D., Thorp, K., Ferré, T., Crow, W., Hunsaker, D., A k-means clustering approach to assess wheat yield prediction uncertainty with a HYDRUS-1D coupled crop model, *7th International Congress on Environmental Modelling and Software, iEMSs 2014* - San Diego, United States Duration: Jun 15, 2014 to Jun 19, 2014.

27. Teixeira de Lima, G.R. and Stephany, S., A new classification approach for detecting severe weather patterns. *Comput. Geosci.*, 52, 34, 2013.

28. Challinor, A.J., Slingo, J.M., Wheeler, T.R., Craufurd, P.Q., Grimes, D.I.F., Toward a combined seasonal weather and crop productivity forecasting system: Determination of the working spatial scale. *J. Appl. Meteorol.*, 175–192, 2003.

29. Singh, C.V., Pattern characteristics of Indian monsoon rainfall using principal component analysis (PCA). *Atmos. Res.*, 79, 3–4, 317–326, 2006.
30. Canale, A. and Ruggiero, M., Bayesian nonparametric forecasting of monotonic functional time series. *Electron. J. Stat.*, 10, 2, 3265–3286, 2016.
31. Hong-ying, L., Yan-lin, H., Yong-juan, Z., Hui-ming, Z., Crop Yield Forecasted Model Based on Time Series Techniques. *J. Northeast Agric. Univ. (Engl. Ed.)*, 6, 4, 298–304, 2012.
32. Matis, J.H., Birkett, T., Boudreaux, D., An application of the Markov chain approach to forecasting cotton yields from surveys. *Agric. Syst.*, 1989.
33. Jain, R. and Ramasubramanian, V., Forecasting of crop yields using second order Markov Chains. *J. Indian Soc. Agric. Stat.*, 52, 2, 61–72, 1998.

2

Smart Farming Using Machine Learning and IoT

Alo Sen[1], Rahul Roy[1*] and Satya Ranjan Dash[2]

[1]ei2 Classes and Technologies, Durgapur, India
[2]School of Computer Application, KIIT University, Bhubaneswar, India

Abstract

From the early civilization till the date, three things: Shelter, Garment and Food are main mantra of a human being. People are quite advanced with modern houses and dresses. But with increased population of Earth, As per UN Food and Agriculture Organization, people will have to produce 70% more food in 2050 rather than it did in 2006. In recent years IoT had been used to meet the challenge of different industrial and technical purposes. Now it is the time to meet the demand of future farming which can only be accomplished by smart Agro-IoT tool. There is a need to boost the productivity and minimize the pitfalls of traditional farming which is the main backbone of World's Economical growth. IoT will help in continuous monitoring of the field to give useful information to the farmers which will add a new era in future farming. IoT tool can be implemented for monitoring climate change, water management, land monitoring, increasing productivity, monitoring crops, controlling insecticides and pesticides, soil management, detecting plant diseases, increasing the rate of crop sale etc. In this book chapter we will focus on some case studies like *monitoring of climate conditions, greenhouse automation, crop management, cattle monitoring and management for smart farming* with IoT device which will provide a clear idea why to use the technique in agriculture rather than some pre existing agricultural tool developed earlier.

Keywords: Smart farming, agro-IoT, agricultural tool, efficiency, productivity, IoT

*Corresponding author: rahul.aec1@gmail.com

Amitava Choudhury, Arindam Biswas, Manish Prateek and Amlan Chakrabarti (eds.)
Agricultural Informatics: Automation Using the IoT and Machine Learning, (13–34) © 2021
Scrivener Publishing LLC

2.1 Introduction

The word "smart" means intelligent, clever, wise, etc. Now, when the word sits as a prefix with farming and built the word "smart farming", obviously it is different from the traditional farming. In the past years, farmers had to monitor all the necessary things in field themselves or by hiring other labor for the same. Firstly, it requires manual checking of all the things associated with farming as well as it is time consuming. Secondly, it acquires a huge loss due to damage of growing crops in the field if continuous monitoring is not done. Thus traditional farming is not a good option due to major pitfalls. It also cannot fulfill the upcoming demand of food for upcoming years. Thus here is the need of smart farming system which will overcome all the shortcomings by taking the decision on their own in complex situations. Different sensors are embedded in the autonomous system to collect the data instant and support on time decision making process.

2.1.1 Smart Farming

In this section, researchers have shown the different applications of Agro-IoT through Figure 2.1. Figure 2.2 illustrates the flow chart of step by step process of Agro-IoT farming.

2.1.2 Technology Involvement in Smart Agriculture

Table 2.1 illustrates the technology which are used in smart agriculture.

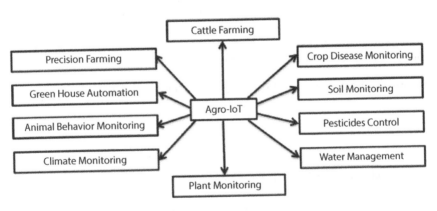

Figure 2.1 Applications of agro-IoT.

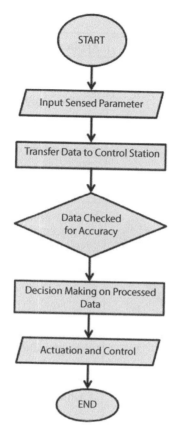

Figure 2.2 Flow chart of step by step process of agro-IoT farming.

2.2   Related Work

Researchers have identified the following major problems like climate, crop, soil monitoring, water management, pest, weed management which are discussed in the following section and researchers have found out efficient solutions for the same.

2.2.1   Monitoring Soil, Climate and Crop

Table 2.2 illustrates the technology for monitoring soil, climate and crop in smart agriculture.

2.2.2   Pesticide Control

Table 2.3 illustrates the technology for controlling pest in smart agriculture.

Table 2.1 Hardware for smart farming.

Hardware	Figure	Application	Utilization
Moisture sensor		It can measure the percent of water in soil. It measure dielectric permittivity of soil.	Farmers get alert of the growing condition of the plants.
Humidity sensor		It can measure the accurate air humidity level.	Farmers get alert of the growth of leaf, change in photosynthesis level of the plants.
PH sensor		It can measure the ph value of soil. It determines which nutrient is available in the soil.	Farmers get alert of the particular crop to grow in the field to get best production in terms of quality and quantity.
Spoiled crop detection sensor		It can detect the disease in crop in early phase by detecting the chemical compound released by an infected plant.	Farmers get alert of quick and timely crop protection.
Fertility sensor		It can measure the fertility of the soil.	Farmers get alert of the quality of the soil and accordingly choose the crop to plant.

(Continued)

Table 2.1 Hardware for smart farming. (*Continued*)

Hardware	Figure	Application	Utilization
Climate sensor		It can provide climate condition by measuring the CO2 level in air. Also monitor any faulty condition.	Farmers get the data about the environment like wind speed, humidity etc.
Temperature sensor		It can measure the temperature of the soil up to a certain depth from the surface of the soil.	Farmers get alert of the change in absorption of soil nutrients by plants.
Pressure sensor		It can measure the air pressure in a particular area depending on which rainfall on that particular area can be guessed.	Farmers get alert of the higher or lower level of rainfall and accordingly plan to monitor the plants.
Microcontroller		It detects signal from other devices and respond according to the process.	Many works of farmers can be automated by it.

Table 2.2 Technology of monitoring soil, climate and crop.

Authors	Parameters	Technology	Advantage
Liqiang et al. [1] Zhua et al. [2] Jaishetty et al. [3]	Image Temperature Humidity	Wireless sensor network	Low power consumption
Keerthi.v et al. [4]	Light Temperature Humidity Soil moisture	Cloud Computing, IoT	Collection of periodic data, Online storage
Srisruthi et al. [5]	Temperature Humidity Soil moisture Fertility	Sensors	Energy efficient, Low maintenance cost, also controls supply of waters and fertilizers
Swarup et al. [6]	Temperature Humidity Soil moisture	Wireless protocol, Serial protocol, Microcontroller, Wireless Bluetooth module	Uses of gateway
Channe et al. [7]	PH value Humidity Temperature	Sensors, Cloud computing, IoT, Mobile-Computing, Big-Data Analysis	Increase in crop production rate
Satyanarayana et al. [8]	Temperature Humidity	Sensors, Zigbee protocol, GPS	
Sakthipriya [9]	Crop leaf condition	Wireless Sensor network	Increase in production of rice plant

(Continued)

Table 2.2 Technology of monitoring soil, climate and crop. (*Continued*)

Authors	Parameters	Technology	Advantage
Kumar [10]	Temperature downfall	Sensors	The system can measure crop loss amount, Increase in crop production
Baggio [11]	Temperature Humidity	Sensors	Identify and reduce potato crop disease
Kavitha *et al.* [12]		Sensors	Automatic detection of fire accidents
ICT [13]	Climate condition Soil Fertility	Internet, Wireless communication, remote monitoring system, short messaging service	Collected climate, soil pattern, pest and disease change pattern help farmer to plan for the next crop plantation
Entekhabi *et al.* [14]	Radar and radiometer information	Optimization, minimization, Extensive Monte Carlo numerical simulations	Efficient soil moisture, roughness estimation
Nandurkar *et al.* [15]	Temperature Humidity	Sensors, GPS	With controlling temperature and humidity, detection of theft is also possible

(*Continued*)

Table 2.2 Technology of monitoring soil, climate and crop. (*Continued*)

Authors	Parameters	Technology	Advantage
Liqiang *et al.* [16]	Temperature Humidity Soil moisture	Green energy, sensors.	The motor have both facility auto and manual, Increase in productivity, Water management

Table 2.3 Technology of controlling pest.

Authors	Parameters	Technology	Advantage
Thulasi Priya *et al.* [17]	Image.	GSM, Image sensor, Aspic, Wireless sensor network	Farmers get aware of the pests inside the field.
Shalini *et al.* [18]		Real-time system.	Automatic pesticide sprayer in the field.
Baranwal *et al.* [19]	Image, sensed data.	Python scripts, sensors, Integrated electronic device, Image processing.	Identification of pest, detection of crop disease, Increase in production.
Kapoor *et al.* [20]	Image of lattice leaf.	Matlab, Image processing.	Determine pesticide or fertilizer which prevent growth of plant.
Rajan *et al.* [21] Sladojevic *et al.* [22]	Image.	Image processing, Machine Learning Approach.	Detect pest, determine pesticide which prevent growth of plant. Also determine the disease in plant leaf.

2.2.3   Proper Fertilizer Uses

Table 2.4 illustrates the technology for using proper fertilizer in smart agriculture.

2.2.4   Intrusion Detection

Table 2.5 illustrates the technology for monitoring intrusion in smart agriculture.

2.2.5   Weed Control

Table 2.6 illustrates the technology for monitoring weed in smart agriculture.

2.2.6   Water Supply Management

Table 2.7 illustrates the technology for water management in smart agriculture.

Table 2.4 Technology of using proper fertilizer.

Authors	Parameters	Technology	Advantage
Rajesh *et al.* [23]	Different soil property	IoT with Cloud storage	The system can analyze the proper fertilizer needed for specific crop.

Table 2.5 Technology of monitoring intrusion.

Authors	Parameters	Technology	Advantage
Borgia *et al.* [24]	Anonymous object	Map reduce IoT with Mobile application	Detect intruder efficiently.

Table 2.6 Technology of monitoring weed.

Authors	Parameters	Technology	Advantage
Hariharan *et al.* [25]	Image of crop.	At mega 2560 Microcontroller Bluetooth Wi-Fi H-bridge driver	Detect weed as well as control weed efficiently.

Table 2.7 Technology for water management.

Authors	Parameters	Technology	Advantage
Rajalakshmi *et al.* [26]	Sensed data	Sensors, Wireless transmission, Web server database.	Farmers can monitor field efficiently. Irrigation system is automated. Farmers can remotely control the reduction in waste of water.
Kaur *et al.* [27]	Water level with other sensed data	Android mobile application, Water level sensor, other sensors.	Farmers can also monitor the crop field remotely.
Parameswaran *et al.* [28] Amel *et al.* [29] Hemalatha *et al.* [30]	Sensed data	Sensors Generic IoT border Router wireless.	Measurement of humidity and water level is possible.
Joaquín Gutiérrez *et al.* [31]	Digital image	Irrigation sensor, smartphone.	Farmers can monitor crop area, also measure the water level.
Saraswati Dept. of Electr. Eng. *et al.* [32]	Water level	Sensors Cloud storage Mobile phone Mobile application.	Farmers can control the water level by using a mobile phone.

2.3   Problem Identification

As the researchers discussed in the previous section about variety of exciting methods developed which are very advantageous in modern agricultural field, still it lacks maximum level of efficiency. Different researchers have tried to capture one or two problems associated with agriculture and figured out the solution for the same. But the actual need is to have such a system which will combine solution of all the problems associated with agriculture in a single system. Thus the future system will be more acceptable to the farmers.

2.4   Objective Behind the Integrated Agro-IoT System

Researchers have built a prototype model for the above said problem by keeping the followings points in mind:

- Increase in crop production value.
- Minimizing activities of a farmer. He should have to do the basic field work only.
- The cost of the integrated system to be nominal as much as possible.
- Utilization of solar energy to get clean source of energy and emits lower amount of GFGs.
- Cultivation process should be efficient with less human interfere.

Thus the work of the integrated Agro-IoT is as follows:

1. Humidity Monitoring.
2. Soil fertility Monitoring.
3. Low water level detection and automatic water level Management.
4. Climate Condition Monitoring.
5. Detection of Pest and control it by spraying pesticide automatically.
6. Detection of Weed and give a notice to farmer for cutting.
7. Fire Accident Detection and automatic control of fire.
8. Intrusion Detection (e.g. goat, cow, etc.) within a certain limit and automatic control.
9. Temperature Monitoring.

2.5   Proposed Prototype of the Integrated Agro-IoT System

Figure 2.3 illustrates the proposed prototype model of the field with Agro-IoT system.

A total of 6 types of sensors have been used to build the prototype model for the integrated system. The soil condition is getting measured by temperature, moisture, and ph sensor and sends the data to beaglebone black. Ultrasonic sensor senses the water level of the field and when it detects

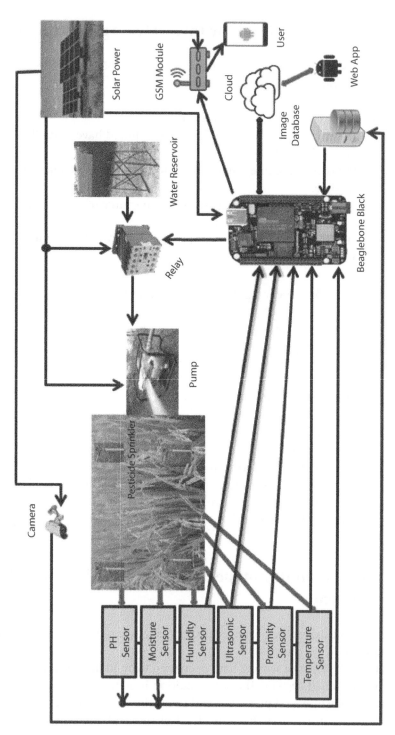

Figure 2.3 Proposed prototype model for integrated Agro-IoT system.

a lower voltage value than the predefined threshold value, then it send a signal to beaglebone black so that automatically the water pump will start to provide water in field. When the water level is enough in field the sensor again send the signal to beaglebone black to stop the water pump automatically.

The camera plays an important role in the prototype model. It captures image of the crop field in every milliseconds and sends the processed data to the image server which is connected to beaglebone black. Through the camera and with our proposed image processing algorithm three most important things i.e. pest, weed and fire can be detected easily. If the proposed image processing algorithm detects the amount of pest is severe, then through beaglebone black the sprinkler for spraying pesticide will get active and spray automatically. So pest can be controlled efficiently by the system without the farmer. When the proposed algorithm detect weed, it sends the signal to beaglebone black and farmer can get the alert via sms to control the weed by themselves only. In case of fire in the field, the proposed algorithm detect the region of fire and send the signal to beaglebone black so that the sprinkler for distributing water to the field gets active and take action to resolve it. Thus pest, weed and fire can be detected and controlled efficiently. Proximity sensor is also playing an important role to find any intruder. In the present of any animal in the field like cow or goat, the sensor sends the signal to beaglebone black and automatically it will send it to the corresponding device to uplift the iron railing from all the four sides of the field. Thus, no animal except bird can enter the field. All the device is getting active by utilizing the eco-friendly energy source of solar panel. Farmers get alert of every above mentioned condition via sms. For future records, the processed data from beaglebone black also get uploaded in cloud storage and an interface can be used by the farmer to get all the records of the field anytime from anywhere.

2.5.1   Pest or Weed Detection Process

The continuous image of the field is captured by the camera in every millisecond and gets processed for any unwilling pattern from known pattern. HOG (Histogram Oriented Gradient) image processing strategy is applied here to distinguish between the known and unknown pattern. The known image pattern like crop leaf are treated as training image set which is input to the image processing algorithm. Then by image comparing technique, classifier classifies the image as known or unknown. If any unknown

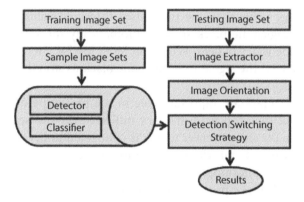

Figure 2.4 Proposed image processing method to detect pest and weed.

pattern is observed moveable then it will be treated as a weed and unknown pattern is observed not movable then it will be treated as pest.

The same image processing method is used in the integrated Agro-IoT system to detect weed and pest and finally store the data in image database.

Figure 2.4 illustrates the internal image process method used in the proposed integrated Agro-IoT system.

2.5.2   Fire Detection Process

The researchers have proposed an image processing technique to detect the flame and detect the fire region. Figure 2.5 illustrates the flow chart of the proposed method which have used in the proposed integrated Agro-IoT system to detect the fire captured through the camera.

2.6   Hardware Component Requirement for the Integrated Agro-IoT System

2.6.1   Sensors

The integrated Agro-IoT system uses different sensors which had been discussed in Table 2.1.

2.6.2   Camera

The integrated Agro-IoT system uses a night vision camera which has zooming capacity and will capture the image of the field in every millisecond.

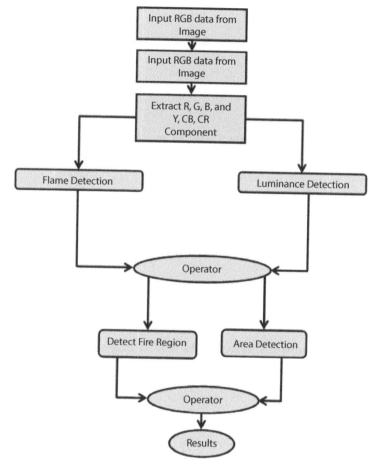

Figure 2.5 Proposed image processing method to detect fire region.

No need of having SD card inside the camera as will transfer the images directly to image databases.

2.6.3   Water Pump

The water pump pumps water from the water reservoir and fill the field with water as need.

2.6.4   Relay

The integrated Agro-IoT system uses a relay to open or close the circuit as per the requirement for different operations. It basically acts as a switch.

2.6.5   Water Reservoir

The Water Reservoir stores water from different sources for watering the field when require.

2.6.6   Solar Panel

The integrated Agro-IoT system uses solar panel to use solar energy for running water pump, camera, beaglebone black and GSM module.

2.6.7   GSM Module

The integrated Agro-IoT system uses a GSM module to establish a connection between beaglebone black and the GSM–GPRS enabled mobile system.

2.6.8   Iron Railing

The integrated Agro-IoT system uses iron railing surrounding the total field to prevent the crops from intruders like goat, cow, etc.

2.6.9   Beaglebone Black

The integrated Agro-IoT system use Beaglebone Black, a small stand-alone linux computer. Here used as an embedded system. Figure 2.6 illustrates the model of beaglebone black.

Figure 2.6 Beaglebone black.

2.7   Comparative Study Between Raspberry Pi vs Beaglebone Black

2.7.1   Raw Comparison

To get Quick Overview of each.

Specification	BeagleBone Black	Raspberry Pi	Result
Processor	1 GHz TI Sitara AM3359 ARM Cortex A8	700 MHz ARM1176JZFS	BeagleBone Black Winner
RAM	512 MB DDR3L @ 400MHz	512 MB SDRAM @ 400MHz	BeagleBone Black Winner
Storage	2 GB on-board eMMC, MicroSD	SD	BeagleBone Black Winner
Operating Systems	Angstrom (Default), Ubuntu, Android, Arch Linux, Gentoo, Minix, RISC OS	Raspbian (Default), Ubuntu, Android, Arch Linux, Fedora, RISC OS	Tie
Power Draw	210–460 mA @ 5V	150–350 mA @ 5V	Raspberry Pi Winner
GPIO Capability	65 Pins	8 Pins	BeagleBone Black Winner
Peripherals	1 USB Host, 1 Mini-USB Client, 1 10/100 Mbps Ethernet	2 USB Hosts, 1 Micro-USB Power, 1 10/100 Mbps Ethernet, RPi Camera Connector	Tie

2.7.2   Ease of Setup

Raspberry Pi bit Laborious whereas BeagleBone Black as simple as it gets.
Winner: BeagleBone Black.

2.7.3 Connections

BeagleBone Black	Raspberry Pi	Result
3 I2C Buses	1 I2C Bus	BeagleBone Black Winner
CAN Bus	1 SPI Bus	
SPI Bus	8 GPIO Pins	
4 Timers	1 UART Interface	
5 Serial Ports		
65 GPIO Pins		
8 PWM O/P		
7 Analog Inputs		

2.7.4 Processor Showdown

BeagleBone Black is nearly 2 times as fast as Raspberry Pi.
Winner: BeagleBone Black.

2.7.5 Right Choice for Projects

BeagleBone Black	Raspberry Pi
1. Projects that need to interface plenty of External Sensors.	1. Multimedia based Projects.
2. High Speed Processing.	2. Community Driven.
3. Commercialization Projects.	3. Graphical Learning Platform
4. Embedded System Learning	4. Internet Connected Projects.

2.8 Conclusions

The proposed integrated Agro-IoT system tends to integrate the earlier problems faced in the previous smart farming as well as tried to find out the solution for the same. Thus all the traditional monitoring problems faced by one farmer get solved by getting together in a one integrated agro-IoT system. The researchers have succeeded in reaching their objective and they made the whole system efficient for the upcoming modern farming era.

2.9 Future Work

The prototype model of the proposed system can be built up in real farming area to replace the traditional monitoring system of farmers in the field. With the advancement of upcoming technology, the agro-IoT system can be more advanced in future.

References

1. Liqiang, Z., Shouyi, Y., Leibo, L., Zhen, Z., Shaojun, W., A crop monitoring system based on wireless sensor network. *Procedia Environ. Sci.,* 11, 558–65, Jan, 2011.
2. Zhu, Y., Song, J., Dong, F., Applications of wireless sensor network in the agriculture environment monitoring. *Procedia Eng.,* 16, 608–14, Jan, 2011.
3. Jaishetty, S.A. and Patil, R., IoT sensor network based approach for agricultural field monitoring and control. *IJRET: Int. J. Res. Eng. Technol.,* 5, 06, Jun, 2016.
4. Keerthi.v and Kodandaramaiah, G.N., Cloud IoT Based greenhouse Monitoring System. *Int. J. Eng. Res. Appl.,* 5, 10, (Part—3), 35–41, 2015.
5. Srisruthi, S., Swarna, N., Susmitha Ros, G.M., Elizabeth, E., Sustainable Agriculture using Eco-friendly and Energy Efficient Sensor Technology. *IEEE International Conference On Recent Trends In Electronics Information Communication Technology,* May 2016.
6. Mathurkar, S.S., Lanjewar, R.B., Patel, N.R., Somkuwar, R.S., Smart Sensors Based Monitoring System for Agriculture using Field Programmable Gate Array. *International Conference on Circuit, Power and Computing Technologies [ICCPCT],* 2014.
7. Channe, H., Kothari, S., Kadam, D., Multidisciplinary model for smart agriculture using internet-of-things (IoT), sensors, cloud-computing, mobile-computing & big-data analysis. *Int. J. Comput. Technol. Appl.,* 6, 3, 374–382, Apr. 2015.
8. Satyanarayana, G.V. and Mazaruddin, S.D., Wireless Sensor Based Remote Monitoring System for Agriculture using ZigBee and GPS. *Conference on Advances in Communication and Control Systems,* 2013.
9. Sakthipriya, N., An Effective Method for Crop Monitoring Using Wireless Sensor Network. *Middle East J. Sci. Res.,* 20, 9, 1127–1132, 2014.

10. Kumar, S. and Somani, V., Social Media Security Risks, Cyber Threats And Risks Prevention And Mitigation Techniques. *Int. J. Adv. Res. Comput. Sci. Manag.*, 4, 4, 125–9, 2018.
11. Baggio, A., Wireless Sensor Networks in Precision Agriculture, in: *ACM Workshop Real-World Wireless Sensor Networks*, 2005.
12. Kavitha, T., Preethi, D.L., Saranya, S., Evert, P.J.A., Realizing IoT based real time monitoring and controlling system. *i-manager's J. Comput. Sci.*, 4, 4, 20–24, 2017.
13. George, T., Bagazonzya, H., Ballantyne, P., Belden, C., Birner, R., Castello, R.D., Castren, T., Choudhary, V., Dixie, G., Donovan, K., Edge, P., ICT in agriculture: Connecting smallholders to knowledge, networks, and institutions. The World Bank, Nov 1, 2011.
14. Entekhabi, D. *et al.*, The Soil Moisture Active Passive (SMAP) mission. *Proc. IEEE*, 98, 5, 704–716, 2010.
15. Nandurkar, S.R., Thool, V.R., Thool, R.C., Design and Development of Precision Agriculture System Using Wireless Sensor Network. *IEEE International Conference on Automation, Control, Energy and Systems (ACES)*, 2014.
16. Liqiang, Z., Shouyi, Y., Leibo, L., Zhen, Z., Shaojun, W., A crop monitoring system based on wireless sensor network. *Procedia Environ. Sci.*, 11, 558–65, Jan, 2011.
17. Priya, C.T., Praveen, K., Srividya, A., Monitoring of pest insect traps using image sensors & dspic. *Int. J. Eng. Trends Tech.*, 4, 9, 4088–93, Sep, 2013.
18. Shalini, D.V., Automatic Pesticide Sprayer for Agriculture Purpose. *IJSART*, 2, 7, July, 2016.
19. Baranwal, T. and Pateriya, P.K., Development of IoT based smart security and monitoring devices for agriculture. In: *2016 6th International Conference-Cloud System and Big Data Engineering (Confluence)*, IEEE, pp. 597–602, Jan, 2016.
20. Kapoor, A., Bhat, S., II, Shidnal, S., Mehra, A., Implementation of IoT and Image Processing in Smart Agriculture. *2016 International Conference on Computational Systems and Information Systems for Sustainable Solutions.*
21. Rajan, P., Radhakrishnan, B., Suresh, L.P., Detection and classification of pests from crop images using Support Vector Machine, in: *Emerging Technological Trends (ICETT), International Conference on*, 2016, October, IEEE, pp. 1–6.
22. Sladojevic, S., Arsenovic, M., Anderla, A., Culibrk, D., Stefanovic, D., Deep neural networks based recognition of plant diseases by leaf image classification. *Comput. Intell. Neurosci.*, 2016, 1–11, May, 2016.
23. Rajesh, D., Application of spatial data mining for agriculture. *Int. J. Comput. Appl.*, 15, 2, 7–9, Feb, 2011.
24. Borgia, E., The Internet of things: Key features, applications and open issues. *Comput. Commun.*, 54, 1–31, Dec. 2014.
25. Manju, M., Karthik, V., Hariharan, S., Sreekar, B., Real time monitoring of the environmental parameters of an aquaponic system based on Internet

of Things. In: *2017 Third International Conference on Science Technology Engineering & Management (ICONSTEM)*, IEEE, pp. 943–948, Mar, 2017.

26. Rajalakshmi, P. and Mahalakshmi, S.D., IOT based crop-field monitoring and irrigation automation. In: *2016 10th International Conference on Intelligent Systems and Control (ISCO)*, IEEE, pp. 1–6, Jan, 2016.

27. Kaur, B., Inamdar, D., Raut, V., Patil, A., Patil, N., A Survey On Smart Drip Irrigation System. *Int. Res. J. Eng. Technol. (IRJET)*, 03, 02, Feb, 2016.

28. Parameswaran, G. and Sivaprasath, K., Arduino based smart drip irrigation system using Internet of Things. *Int. J. Eng. Sci.*, 5518, May, 2016.

29. Amel, B., Mohamed, C., Tarek, B., Smart irrigation system using Internet of Things. *The Fourth International Conference on Future Generation Communication Technologies (FGCT)*, 2015.

30. Hemalatha, R., Deepika, G., Dhanalakshmi, D., Dharanipriya, K., Divya, M., Internet of things (iot) based smart irrigation. *Int. J. Adv. Res. Biol. Eng. Sci. Technol. (IJARBEST)*, 2, 2, 128–32, Feb, 2016.

31. Jagüey, J.G., Villa-Medina, J.F., López-Guzmán, A., Porta-Gándara, M.Á., Smartphone irrigation sensor. *IEEE Sens. J.*, 15, 9, 5122–7, May, 2015.

32. Saraswati, M., Kuantama, E., Mardjoko, P., Design and construction of water level measurement system accessible through SMS. In: *2012 Sixth UKSim/AMSS European Symposium on Computer Modeling and Simulation*, IEEE, pp. 48–53, Nov, 2012.

3

Agricultural Informatics vis-à-vis Internet of Things (IoT): The Scenario, Applications and Academic Aspects— International Trend & Indian Possibilities

P.K. Paul

Raiganj University, Raiganj, West Bengal, India

Abstract

Agricultural Informatics or Agro-Informatics is a combination of Agricultural Sciences and Information Sciences. Agricultural Informatics is the applications of Information Technology in Agriculture and allied fields and thus also known as Agricultural Information Science or Agricultural Information Technology. There are different tools, techniques and technologies are applied in the agriculture and allied fields. In developed nations Agricultural Informatics is an emerging area and applicable in different areas for the betterment of agricultural activities. Apart from traditional latest viz. decision support system, artificial intelligence, remote sensing, image processing computing components are being used in the field. In some countries Agricultural Informatics is become a field of study and research. However in many developing and undeveloped countries Agricultural Informatics field can be seen as a research area instead of field of study/programs. This paper focused on how Internet of Things is applicable in agricultural sectors including the importance for promoting Agricultural Informatics practice. Paper highlighted academic programs available in the field of Agricultural Informatics and allied areas and further proposed about the Agricultural Informatics programs in concentration with IoT and allied fields in international and context. Paper talks about the potential fields in Agricultural Informatics as well.

Email: pkpaul.infotech@gmail.com

Amitava Choudhury, Arindam Biswas, Manish Prateek and Amlan Chakrabarti (eds.)
Agricultural Informatics: Automation Using the IoT and Machine Learning, (35–66) © 2021
Scrivener Publishing LLC

Keywords: Agricultural informatics, ICT in Agriculture, educational innovations, degrees, emerging programs, universities, India, smart agriculture

3.1 Introduction

Agricultural Informatics is the application of IT and Computing in agriculture and allied areas; it is the combination of ideas, techniques and technologies. In general, it can be treated as an information technology applied to the management and analysis of agricultural data. Apart from the basic Information Technology components some areas which incorporated in agriculture include decision support system, artificial intelligence, artificial neural networks, expert system, geographic information system, etc. in respect to agriculture [3, 6, 42]. There are various dimensions of agro-informatics and all these are increasing rapidly. Agricultural Informatics is required in the Strategic intervention of IT regarding the Agricultural affairs viz. Agricultural Input, Production as well as Output systems. Moreover it also required in the integration and facilitation of trade, food management and security using technologies [9, 12, 34]. There are many universities, which have started manpower development in the field of Agriculture Informatics and this list is rising with not only Agriculture Informatics nomenclature but also in others viz.:

- Agricultural Information Science
- Agricultural Information Technology
- Agricultural Information Science and Technology
- Agricultural Information Systems.

The research programs are quite common in Agricultural Informatics/ Information Systems, etc. in the universities and research centers involved in Agriculture and allied fields, IT and Computing and the institutes involved in interdisciplinary research, etc. [1, 2, 14, 42].

3.2 Objectives

This current paper entitled 'Agricultural Informatics vis-à-vis Internet of Things (IoT): The Techno-Academic Potentialities' deals with following aims and objectives:

- To learn about the basics of Agricultural Informatics including its features, characteristics and background.

- To find out the potential stakeholders in Agricultural Informatics and allied fields.
- To get knowledge about the allied and related field of Agricultural Informatics in brief.
- To learn about basic technologies and emerging technologies in current and future Agricultural Informatics practice.
- To get the knowledge on Agricultural Informatics and its importance in agriculture and allied field of study and practice.
- To learn about the available programs on Agricultural Informatics in International and India.
- To know about the proposed programs on Agricultural Informatics and allied field in concentration of IoT and allied technologies.

3.3 Methods

The paper 'Agricultural Informatics vis-à-vis Internet of Things (IoT): The Techno-Academic Potentialities' is an interdisciplinary work and empirical in nature. So, different kinds of tools and methods have been incorporated to do this research work. Secondary sources are used in this research work. To reach and design desirable goal, paper also incorporated and analyzed few basic papers on the Agriculture, Informatics, Agricultural Informatics and allied fields. Similarly web-based and hard copy-based journals also can be treated as an important tool for proper designing of this paper. Further, as it is a kind of policy making work so here in this paper review on primary sources made for the areas of Agricultural Informatics/IoT from the universities and educational institutes to reach the conclusion on current and proposed programs on Agricultural Informatics. Here both Indian and international context are treated and considered valuable.

3.4 Agricultural Informatics: An Account

Agricultural Informatics can be treated as a discipline and combination of two important and interdisciplinary fields of study i.e. Information Science/Information Technology with the Agricultural Science & allied fields [4, 5, 19, 44]. The integration of these technologies and fields not only created Agricultural Informatics but also healthy information system and technology; and results sustainable agricultural systems & development. The skilled manpower in the field may be from both the fields and streams viz.:

- Computer Science/CSE
- Computer Applications/Computing
- Information Technology/ICT
- Information Science/Informatics
- Information Systems & Information Management
- Agricultural Science
- Horticulture
- Environment Science
- Soil Science
- Forest Sciences & Management, etc.

Agricultural System is the core of Agricultural Informatics and can be built-in with effective and healthy ICT-based systems; and thus responsible for the quality delivering services and modeling. Automatically it helps in enhancing following basic benefits of the agricultural systems viz.:

- Agricultural production systems.
- Agricultural productivity and financial benefits.
- Decision making systems.
- Planning and monitoring of agricultural facets.
- Better communication among the stakeholders of agriculture [7, 8, 26, 42].

3.4.1   Agricultural Informatics and Environmental Informatics

Agricultural Informatics is an emerging and interdisciplinary field of study; there are many fields and disciplines which are close with many subjects viz. Geo Informatics, Environmental Informatics, Forest Informatics, Disaster Informatics, and Irrigation Informatics.

However, among these subject most close are two—i.e. Geo Informatics & Environmental Informatics. In respect to subject area, field of study and importance Agricultural Informatics is smaller than Environmental Informatics and can be treated as a branch of study. Environmental Informatics is a field of interdisciplinary practice, study and research. Environmental Informatics is the combination of two important subjects viz. Environmental Sciences and with other hand, Information Science or allied fields. it is the applications of Computing, Technologies, Informatics principles and tools in Environmental Management, Environmental Management, Sustainable Computing and Information Technology practice as well [10, 11, 33].

There are many subjects and professionals who can get the benefits from the Environmental Informatics viz. (but not limited to these) Earth Science, Marine Science, Geology, Climatology, Geography, Agriculture, Forest Management, can be the beneficiaries of Environmental Informatics and different tools and technologies can be added for more healthy output viz. Cloud Computing, Big Data, Geographic information system, Web and Usability Designing, Genetic algorithm, etc. [13, 18, 25].

Agriculture is actually part of the Environment; and thus Agricultural Informatics is also an important part or sub field of Environmental Informatics. There are different areas in which both the fields can work together or jointly.

3.4.2 Stakeholders of Agricultural Informatics

Agricultural Informatics is a broad field and can be considered as the combination of several components; further each stakeholder is important and valuable for healthy Agricultural Informatics practice. Figure 3.1 is depicted herewith the basic and mandatory components [15, 16, 45, 57].

3.4.2.1 Technology

Technology is the core and treated as most important component in Information Technology (IT) and among the basics components few important are Web Technology, Networking Technology, Database Technology, Multimedia Technology, etc. It is important to note that different kind of tools and are also valuable in technology development.

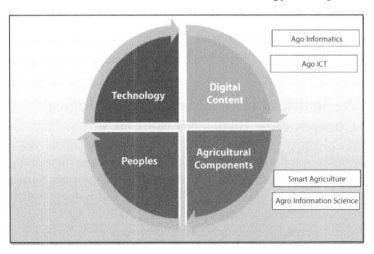

Figure 3.1 Stakeholders of Agro Informatics and allied Nomenclatures.

3.4.2.2   Digital Content

Content is vital for any kind of information systems designing and development. For building healthy Agricultural systems it is important and mandatory viz. Digital Agricultural Systems, E-Agriculture, E-Learning, ICT in Agriculture etc. Digital Content is most important and valuable in building of healthy Agro Informatics practice [17, 23, 36].

3.4.2.3   Agricultural Components

Agricultural Informatics as an interdisciplinary field is dedicated to the agricultural community due to its importance. In, Agricultural Informatics documents and allied components of the Agriculture including Horticulture, Fisheries, Animal Husbandry, and Forestry can also be treated as valuable and required.

3.4.2.4   Peoples

HumanResources can also be treated as a valuable stakeholder in designing as well as developing Digital Agricultural Systems. However people/HR can be categories into following regarding the aspects of Agricultural Informatics:

- Students/Learners/Trainees (with interest in Agricultural Informatics)
- Teachers/Faculties/Trainees (from the field or with interest in Agricultural Informatics)
- Administrators/Educational Authorities (from the Agricultural Informatics)
- Mediators (may be users as well).

3.5   Agricultural Informatics & Technological Components: Basics & Emergence

Initially the concept of Agricultural Documentation was there and gradually other areas have been emerged and included gradually viz. Agricultural Information Systems, Agricultural Information Technology, Agricultural Informatics/Information Science [20, 21, 43]. Within Agricultural Informatics the core and most important component of Technology can be treated as Information Technology; and within this field following can be considered as valuable:

- *Database Technology*—this is the technology responsible for data related activities including storing, retrieving of data and similar facet. As Agro Informatics is about Data Management so that Agricultural data can be stored logically and scientifically in Database and Database Management Systems (DBMS) play a good role in this regard.
- *Networking Technology*—this is important and required for better and healthy networking systems development of Agriculture. Connectivity among the devices involved in smart agriculture is purely done by the Networking technologies.
- *Web Technology*—this is the important component of Information Technology responsible for website, web portal and allied systems. As far as Agriculture is concerned web technology is important for development of web systems related to agricultural products and systems.
- *Software Technology*—this is dedicated to the designing, development and management of software and applications. This is treated as most important and vital component in IT. As far as agriculture is concerned, this technology is required for agro based apps and software development and implementation.
- *Multimedia Technology*—Multimedia is the combination of different kinds of media for better and healthy information presentation. As far as Agriculture is concerned, this technology can be useful for Agricultural Information Systems design and development different way [22, 24, 41].

3.6   IoT: Basics and Characteristics

Internet of Things in short called as IoT and it is an emerging technology with different types of objects. IoT is applicable in industrial machines to wearable devices in numerous areas. Entrepreneur Kevin Ashton in 1990s coined the term Internet of Things (IoT); he was also considered as founder, Auto-ID Center at MIT. Later on the improvement of Internet of Things (IoT) was considered [27, 30, 48].

As far as IoT is concerned, here various built-in sensors are responsible for communicating and collecting data; thus here connected network plays a leading role. In automatic adjustment with the attributes viz. heating and lighting etc the sensors are important and valuable. Practically the

IoT can be called as a future technology; responsible for making efficient and smarter life and digital society building. IoT devices are having the IP address for the collection, processing and transforming data having and thus gaining popularity in different sectors and areas viz. Business and Industries, Agricultural Systems including Horticulture, Education, Research and Training; Government, Management and Administration, Healthcare Systems, Transportation, Manufacturing systems, etc. [28, 29, 49].

This application is rising always and every moment; further here there are lots of areas where IoT-based systems can be applied. Wireless Internet, embedded sensors etc. lay on various technologies and thus are applicable in day to day personal and professional dealings as well as IoT architecture which also leans towards more complexities (refer Figures 3.2 & 3.3).

- Internet of Things (IoT) can be considered as an important area of Information Technology for smarter information solutions based on internet and allied technologies.

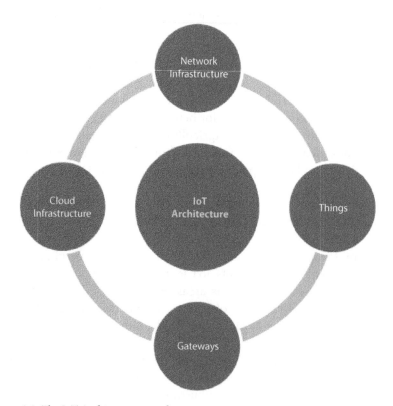

Figure 3.2 The IoT Architecture at a glance.

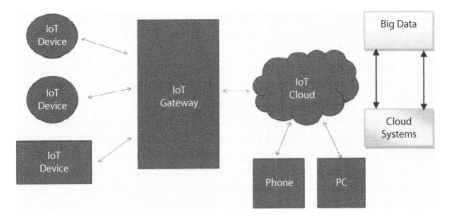

Figure 3.3 The gateway for IoT and its stakeholders.

- Different services can be considered as beneficiaries in Internet of Things (IoT) and here different allied technologies viz. Cloud Computing, Data Analytics can be considered as a valuable technology.
- Internet of Things (IoT) is sensor dependent and here Smart electric grids can be connected with renewable resources on smaller usage increments.
- In Internet of Things (IoT) the Machine monitoring sensors are responsible for intelligent machine and systems development.

3.7   IoT: The Applications & Agriculture Areas

Internet of Things (IoT) depends on internet systems, is digitally connected and is controlled anywhere. The IoT ultimately helps in increasing efficiency, safety, security, etc. with applications in wider zones viz. oil & gas, manufacturing, transportation, agriculture, retail sectors, etc.

Internet of Things (IoT) can be initially costly in implementation but later on organizational cost can be reduced radically [31, 32, 46]. Importantly, IoT devices can be used for the following broad areas (categories):

- Consumer (the users).
- Commercial.
- Industrial or organizational and
- Infrastructure spaces, etc.

In the areas viz. home automation & smart home development including the smart town and smart villages creation, etc. IoT can be considered as important and valuable [35, 37, 47].

For the development of *Smart Home*, the IoT devices can be considered important with the applications in air conditioning, lighting, heating, security systems, etc. The intelligent hub using control smart devices viz. iPhone or iOS native applications can be considered and useful in this regard. The concepts of *Smart Buildings* is also emerging which is responsible for reducing energy consumption, etc. [38, 40, 52].

The *old aged people* can get the benefits of IoT in the disabilities and elderly individuals. Here the technologies viz. assistive technology, voice control systems can be used in normal care and medical emergencies as well.

Smarter Healthcare is another name which one can get the benefits of IoT in health related activities viz. collection, analysis of data for healthy medical informatics building and development with proper medical resources.

Remote based health monitoring and emergency services and notification systems are the core part of IoT systems including the usages of pacemakers, smart beds, patient get up, nursing informatics practice, medical follow-up, etc. Furthermore introduction of 'm-health' is also valuable with the IoT [39, 43, 50].

In *Transportation* as well, IoT is important for different kinds of communication vehicles, Smart traffic control systems, Smart and electronic toll collection, the infrastructure management and even in Human Resource Management including driver, road safety, etc. The healthy transport system can be powered by IoT.

Internet of Things (IoT) based *Manufacturing* is another concern of IoT, which is responsible for identification, processing, communication of the

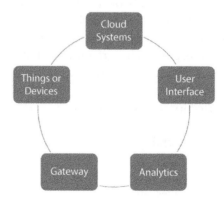

Figure 3.4 Major components of IoT.

affairs related to manufacturing of the industries also. It helps in Network control of manufacturing equipment, Healthy and rapid manufacturing, smarter supply chain systems and also Service information systems including the Smart Grid using Internet of Things (IoT). Thus the concept of Industrial Internet of Things or IIoT is gradually developing. Such and emerging services become only possible due to the increasing components in IoT, which may also be applicable in AIoT (refer Figure 3.4).

3.8   Agricultural Informatics & IoT: The Scenario

Internet of Things is applicable in increasing agricultural efficiency, reduction of cost of the agriculture, reduction of resources, automation including the traditional IT-based data driven processes. In agriculture IoT and Agro Informatics as a general one can bring with the following solutions and reduces different challenging problems, etc.

With the help of Agro IoT, the *Increased Efficiency* is important to note. Agro IoT allows in better monitoring of agro products as well as conditions in real-time. With this, farmers can get the insights fast, prediction become easy, decisions making and further process as well to prevent them. Due to AI & Expert Systems i.e. automation even few things are possible viz.:

- Demand-based irrigation,
- Agro fertilizing,
- Robot and automated harvesting,
- Weather Prediction, etc.

It is a fact that about 70% of the population of the world lives in town or urban areas and the use of IoT-based greenhouses may be able to end short food supply chain; this can raise the *Expansion* of Agro Informatics. Moreover, the Smart closed-cycle agricultural systems growing rapidly and it can be seen in everywhere and in all these areas Agro IoT can be applicable. IoT solutions are responsible for *Reducing Resources* by optimizing and increasing the use water, energy, land, etc. Such kind of Smart agriculture basically lies on the collected data from various sensors and this can ultimately led the accuracy in farming with limited resources [44, 54, 57].

In case of Cleaning and Purity IoT is very much useful and thus in case of managing pesticides and fertilizers as well IoT is important. IoT-based agricultural systems is helpful in following as well:

- It lead the precision farming by saving resources viz. water and energy.

- Agro Informatics as reduces and do with cleaning and green strategy so it produces greener farming and cultivation.
- Agro Informatics hence also helps in reducing less uses of pesticides and fertilizer.

Hence ultimately a cleaner, organic Agriculture is possible with the Agro Informatics practice than the conventional agricultural methods.

Quicker Agricultural Systems is also another important benefit of Agro IoT by the real-time monitoring AI and ES-based prediction systems, etc. As a result the cultivators and peoples associated with the agriculture can quickly do the needful in agriculture based on situation including the weather, humidity. Moreover due to this benefit, the health of each crop including soil may also good enough. The weather changes, etc. can be easily considerable with the introduction of this feature by the Agro Informatics and specially Agro IoT.

Hence the IoT-based Agriculture or Agro Informatics also helps in more and *Healthy & Quality Production*. The use aerial drone monitoring with crop sensors is helpful for farm mapping, better understanding of agro systems by the farmers. The conditions and the quality of the crops can be judged by the Agro IoT as well and as a result it helps in better quality products with nutritional value of the products.

Hence Agro Informatics is required in various affairs viz. farming, collection of the data on various aspects including temperature and weather viz. rainfall, humidity, the speed of wind, to find out and managing pest infestation, condition of soil, etc. Thus automated farming including the techniques and technology is possible with Agro Informatics. However based on categories following can be considered as important area where IoT applications are possible and rising.

3.8.1   Weather, Climate & Agro IoT

Weather and climates are important aspects of agriculture and farming; thus the information regarding climate results in quantity and quality of crop production and post-crop production activities. As real-time weather conditions are possible in IoT supported sensors so such are collect data from various means. So here the right crops and right weather, etc. can be benefited by the Agro IoT systems importantly to grow the particular climatic conditions. The detection of real-time weather viz. humidity, rainfall, temperature is possible with sensor enable IoT Eco Systems more accurately. Monitoring the condition of crops, field, and weather are to be noted with intelligent IoT systems then an alerting systems can be used and farmers take decision based on this. Hence there is no need of physical presence of the cultivators or peoples during the normal or bad climatic conditions; as a result Agro IoT improved agriculture benefits in weather by different means.

3.8.2   Precision Cultivation With Agro IoT

IoT is also applicable in Precision Agriculture and it leads the farming practice more efficient precise. Here IoT is applicable in livestock monitoring, field study and observation, inventory and budget monitoring, vehicle and transportation management. With IoT it is possible to get the analyzed data and such are normally generated via sensors; as a result the cultivation unit or organizations can take quick decisions; intelligent way. Further, with IoT-based precision farming it is also possible to get the soil conditions and allied aspects to reach healthy operational efficiency. Even such IoT enable systems helps in detect water and nutrient level which ultimately helpful in Smarter Precision Cultivation.

3.8.3   IoT in Making Green House Perfect

IoT makes smarter and intelligent weather stations which intelligently control the climate conditions as per the set of instructions. IoT in Greenhouses reduces the human intervention and the ready systems become cost-effective, more accuracy. Solar-power based IoT sensors help in modern and inexpensive greenhouses. Due to real time data collection and monitoring greenhouse can be in very precise manner in real-time situation. Even the water consumption can be monitored by the intelligent systems viz. emails or SMS alerts and as a result these sensors come with the information on the sun light levels, pressure, humidity, temperature. All these are possible by IoT-based Agriculture.

3.8.4   Data Analytics and Management by IoT in Agro Space

IoT sensors including the Cloud based data storage play a valuable role in developing smart agriculture system and traditional database systems become worthless or not suitable. Here sensors are responsible for the collecting data (primarily) on a large scale and thereafter these data can be analyzed and transformed using analytics tools which are important in better Agro Informatics practice. Ultimately Data Analytics and Big Data are responsible for the following solutions viz.:

- Weather and climate conditions

- Livestock and products conditions
- Crop conditions and management
- Better decisions systems and making into reality
- Real-time status of the crops, fields, etc.

Predictive analytics is important in making decisions and helpful in harvesting including knowing the upcoming weather conditions, crops etc. The complete Agriculture Industry may get the benefits of IoT in this respect including enhancement of the product volume and quality.

3.8.5 Drone, IoT and Agriculture

Technological advancements help in better agricultural operations and use of agricultural drones is important which covers the Ground and Aerial views to assess the crop health including the crop monitoring & spraying, and field work management and analysis, etc. drone technology provide us real time data and videos and ultimately these results in better agriculture industry output. Thermal or multispectral sensors can be with Drones and thus identify the areas and improvement in irrigation as well. After the corps develop and grow, the smart drones play a good deal and also reduced environmental impact. The massive reduction in chemical reaching the groundwater is also possible due to IoT based Agro powered by intelligent drones [44, 53, 57].

3.8.6 Livestock Management Using AIoT

Wireless IoT applications can be used perfectly by the agro industries to collect data on location, well-being, etc. Hence by this identification of the animals can be possible. Reduction of labor costs as well makes IoT-based systems worthy.

Here monitoring of different animals including Cows, sheep, pig, etc. are possible with IoT-based systems and in this regard a prime example is JMB North America that is responsible for cow monitoring solutions, including pregnancy identifications and those that are about to give birth [46, 55, 56].

3.8.7 Environmental Monitoring & IoT, Environmental Informatics

Energy management is required for various devices and electronic products viz. switches, power outlets, bulbs, televisions, etc. Metering infrastructure is applicable with the Internet and in this context Internet of Things

(IoT) is helpful in traditional IT components management in general Agro Informatics practice. As these issues are also related with environmental protection, it also helps in Environmental Informatics betterment and practice viz.:

- Environmental protection and benefits by the use of monitoring air or water quality.
- Movements of wildlife and their habitats.
- Earthquake or any disaster management related aspects and issues can also be an important point in which IoT can be used. There is a 31% increase rate on IoT year-over-year and it is will be 30 billion devices by end of 2020 as expected by the IoT and the value may reach $7.1 trillion by the end.

3.9   IoT in Agriculture: Requirement, Issues & Challenges

Agro Internet of Things (AIoT) is a wonderful weapon for modern Agriculture Management and Cultivation Systems; however there are many concerns, issues and challenges in respect to introducing these in practice.

- All kinds of electronic devices viz. sensors, cameras, robots, drones required as essential to put on farms for healthy and accurate monitoring and operation.
- Agro Internet of Things (AIoT) is based on different technologies and thus requires healthy and skillful HR/People or staff for various activities ranging from implementation, managing bots and insights of IoT, etc.
- It is worthy to note that most of the Agro Internet of Things (AIoT) devices are costly and mainly their initial implementation are fragile.
- Recurring maintenance budget on hardware and devices is also an important issue in Agro Internet of Things (AIoT) properly.
- It is worthy to note that in Agro Internet of Things (AIoT) computer imaging can be seen via sensor cameras with drones with manual operators; this is could be a vital issue.
- In many cases it is seen that in Agro Internet of Things (AIoT) no or unscientific supply chain management reduces the efficiency.

- It is worthy to note that Agro Internet of Things (AIoT) is so scalable and thus here individual data of a specific farm needs to be managed separately.
- Integration with already implemented devices with new one is quite challenging in Agro Internet of Things (AIoT).
- Continuous connectivity to the internet is an urgent and important issue in implementing sophisticated Agro Internet of Things (AIoT) Systems.

3.10   Development, Economy and Growth: Agricultural Informatics Context

Agriculture is the main concern of development in a country like India and it is even accounted for its value and employment generation throughout India. There are millions of farmers tilling on small and marginal holdings, who need best cultivation methods. There are different challenges, issues and concern on agriculture due to biotic and other impacts viz. drought, flood, disease, insect, pest infestations, heat, cold, weather and climate change, etc. Apart from these, a few other concerns are changes in food habits, nutritional requirements, global trade scenario and changes, technological development, ecological aspects, etc.

Strategic, scientific and methodological applications of ICT applications in Agricultural sector can lead the following in which indirect enhancement is possible and among the few important means are:

- Agricultural Input,
- Production and Output systems,
- Integrate and facilitate trade,
- Technology and food security,
- Through effective
- Value-chain and Supply-chain Models.

ICT, Computing & IT applications in Agriculture are rapidly gaining attention internationally & more importantly a huge demand is noticeable with Agricultural degree holders with proper ICTs skills and a combination of existing technologies for effective agricultural development and production. It is moreover a global enabler innovations and productivity in agriculture in nature, economic and social means. Further Agro Informatics is directly enabling agricultural development. According to a study it is noted that "agricultural graduates-ready" through agricultural informatics, are undertaking S&T-based agricultural development, and rejuvenating and ushering in agricultural dynamism in the country, by 2025 (Source: CAIeRS, Uttar Pradesh, India).

It is important and need of hour to introduce Agricultural Informatics programs for conceptual, theoretical and applied knowledge development in the field which include the IT & Computing, Management, Informatics, and Agriculture. This could be possible with the introduction of technologies and subjects related to the Information and Agriculture [2, 45].

Hence right skilling, knowledge including aptitude, communications, entrepreneurship including healthy leadership qualities are useful within qualified Agro Informatics practitioners for the promotion and development of complete agro solutions viz. agricultural production, supply-chain, extension services to the different stakeholders of agriculture including the following (not limited to):

- Farmers and cultivators
- Industry and organizations (with Agro or IT interest)
- Research and extension services (with Agro or IT interest)
- Scientific organizations (with Agro or IT interest)
- Educational Institutes (with Agro or IT interest).

Hence Agro Informatics or similar fields are responsible for the healthy and complete development in sustainable and modern Agro development that led to the complete development in many contexts.

3.11   Academic Availability and Potentiality of IoT in Agricultural Informatics: International Scenario & Indian Possibilities

Agricultural Informatics as an important interdisciplinary field is growing rapidly and it is the Science of agricultural Information management for promoting Agricultural Information Systems. There is a great need of Human Resources in respect of Agricultural Informatics and allied domains. In developing countries also this need is expected. As per the Report of DFI-2022 Committee, Indian Government it is expressed and expected that India needs about one lakh (100,000) skilled manpower in the field. This committee (of the Government of India) expressed about the need of introducing the Agricultural Informatics and about the Digitalization of Agricultural systems of India as well.

Farm management practices (by the farmer as well) basically generate lots of data and information. However it is important to note that mostly these data are not systematically captured. Hence the subsequent analysis, packing and interpretation may not be possible scientifically and in these circumstances in the field of Informatics can be a good tool for strengthening Agriculture and Environmental Value Chain Systems. Sustainable agricultural productivity is an emerging concern and at present this is the age of Agricultural Informatics practice to reach such goal which additionally helps in reaching Farmers Distress. Further the introduction of Agricultural systems can also be helpful for doing healthy financial aspects of the farmers and allied professional in a sustainable manner. India needs strategic use of IT and Computing in Farming System and therefore potential and impactful Agricultural Informatics discipline is the need of the hour in the Nation [5, 45, 57].

In a country like India, few institutes have started programs on this emerging fields and among these few important institutes are:

- Tamil Nadu Agricultural University, located in Coimbatore, Tamil Nadu
- Shobhit University, located in Meerut, Uttar Pradesh
- Rai University, Ahmedabad, Gujarat
- Anand Agricultural University, located in Gujarat
- Integral University, located in Lucknow, Uttar Pradesh.

Due to interdisciplinary nature, Agricultural Informatics is combined with the fields viz.

- Agricultural Science & Management
- Engineering Sciences
- Information Technology and Computing
- Social Science & Environment
- Basics of Management & Business, etc.

It is important to note that IT is a relatively new branch within the technology. But this field is more important in Agricultural Informatics practices in a healthy way. It is applicable in different sectors viz. Healthcare sector, education sector, Business sector, education and training, research and development, Core Industries, etc. Thus for promoting Digital Agriculture of Smart Agriculture, the field Agricultural Informatics plays a leading role.

Nationally and internationally many universities have started educational programs on the branch and among these few are listed (as per methodology) in Table 3.1.

Table 3.1 Depicted the available programs on Agro Informatics in few institutes.

Universities/Institutes	Programs
Tamil Nadu Agricultural University, Coimbatore, Tamil Nadu, India	BTech Agricultural Information Technology
Centre for Agricultural Informatics and E Governance Research Studies Shobhit University, Meerut, UP, India	MTech Agricultural Informatics
Faculty of Agriculture Egerton University, Nakuru, Kenya	MSc Agricultural Information & Communication Management
Dhirubhai Ambani Institute of Information and Communication Technology (A Deemed University), Gujarat, India	MSc-IT in Agriculture & Rural Development
Anand Agricultural University, Gujarat, India	MTech Agricultural Information Technology

Agricultural Informatics is helpful in enhancing and emerging the productivity and in agriculture in different sorts and means. Therefore, here the Agricultural Informatics is important and valuable field of study with the aim of following (but not limited to):

- To get a comprehensive understanding, needs and stakeholders of Agricultural Informatics.
- To find out the potential of sensor systems in the field especially to measure and monitor the agricultural environment.
- Agricultural Informatics is required for various affairs viz. managing, manipulating agri and allied environmental datasets.
- Formulate a conceptual understanding among the ecology, forestry, agriculture to reach a healthy ecosystem.
- Agricultural Informatics may be required in developing systematic skills, ability to interpret the agricultural data and also to obtain meaningful outcomes for smarter Agricultural systems.

Agricultural Informatics as a field of study is well noted in different universities. But as far as basic areas are concerned few important areas may be noted below which are taught in different short term programs and courses viz.:

- Introduction to Agricultural Systems
- Sensing and sensors and its applications in Agricultural Systems
- Spatial interactions of food production
- Basics of Information Management and Knowledge Economy
- Big data and Analytics
- Ecological Agriculture
- Decision making in Agro Informatics.

Agricultural Informatics helps in efficient designing of general agricultural systems and engineering viz. irrigation, storage. Growing populations also led the ideas to enhance the Agricultural Information Systems for enhancing way in production and further activities and as a result apart from the agricultural engineers Agricultural Informatics is also an important job centric field viz.:

- IT Facility Manager at Agro Space
- Weather Forecasting Expert
- Crop Forecasting Expert
- e-Learning Specialist in Agriculture
- Agro Knowledge Management Expert
- Commodity Trader in Agriculture
- Agricultural ERP Manager
- Agro Farm Manager
- Agro based e-Commerce Portal Manager
- Agro-Financial Analyst
- Agro-Supply Chain Manager
- Agro-BPO Center
- Crop and Agro Insurance Manager
- e-Governance Web Designer [2, 47].

Agriculture is the main driving force in managing healthy agricultural systems for its livelihood and here for its proper management ICT in Agriculture is an important tool. ICT is responsible for better agricultural data collection, selection, organization, processing, managing and disseminating to potential users and stakeholders. There are different program gradients in Agro Informatics and a sample of BTech Agricultural Information Technology, Tamil Nadu Agricultural University, located in Coimbatore, Tamil Nadu provided in Table 3.2.

Table 3.2 Sample Program components of Agro Informatics.

Universities & Programs	Papers/Courses

Program:
 	
BTech
(4 Years/8 Sem)
 	
Subject/Major:
Agricultural Information
  Technology
 	
University:
Tamil Nadu Agricultural
  University
 	
Territory:
Coimbatore, Tamil Nadu
	Core Taught Courses
	Fundamentals of Computers
	Programming in C
	Introduction to Web Scripting
	Introduction to Agriculture
	Economic Botany
	Bio-Mathematics
	Fundamentals of Physics
	English for Speaking and Writing Skills
	Data Structure Through C
	Discrete Mathematics
	Introduction to Multimedia
	Computer Organization and Architecture
	Environmental Science, Ecology and Forestry
	Field Crops (*Kharif & Rabi*)
	Commercial Horticulture
	Solid State Physics and Basic Electronics
	NCC/NSS/Physical Education-1
	OOP Using C++
	Relational Database Management System
	System Analysis and Design
	Website Development Using PHP
	Entrepreneurship Development
	Principles of Agricultural Economics
	Soil, Plant Nutrient and Water Management
	Agricultural Statistics-I
	NCC/NSS/Physical Education-2
	Software Engineering
	Introduction to .Net Framework and ASP .NET
	Information Security
	Management Information Systems
	Introduction to Biotechnology
	Agricultural Meteorology
	Fundamental of Agricultural Extension
	Agricultural Statistics–II Using SAS
	NCC/NSS/Physical Education-3
	Project-I
	Advance Asp.Net
	Java Technology
	Computer Networks

(*Continued*)

Table 3.2 Sample Program components of Agro Informatics.

Universities & Programs	Papers/Courses
	Gis and Remote Sensing Techniques Extension Methodologies for Transfer of Agril. Technology E-Content Development Using Multimedia Operating System With Unix/Linux Application Development in Mobile Technology Data Analysis With Matlab Educational Tour
	Seminar Courses Seminar-1 Seminar- 2 **Elective Courses** Total 6 Electives **Projects** Project 1 Mini Project Final Project

Most of these courses combined with both the areas from the Information Technology and Agriculture Sciences are suitable to get employed in both IT and agriculture-oriented jobs. The job opportunities are exists in both the Central and State Agriculture Departments including IT jobs viz. Database Management, Website Designing, Maintenance of the Systems, Software Engineering and Development etc. Interestingly due to interdisciplinary nature of the program the Agro Informatics or Agro IoT candidates would be eligible in both the areas as a teaching and research staff as well. Even in banking, finance, SMEs, private agriculture consultancy firms, marketing firms related to the Agriculture can be good place for jobs etc.

From Engineering sites, the programs with BE/BTech/ME/MTech can be useful in the following jobs as well:

- Equipment Manufacturing (with concentration on IoT Applications & Integrations)
- Food Manufacturing (with concentration on IoT Applications & Integrations)
- Food Processing (with concentration on IoT Applications & Integrations)

- Water Management (with concentration on IoT Applications & Integrations)
- Effluent Treatment (with concentration on IoT Applications & Integrations).

The skilled Agro IoT people or Agro Informatics skilled can be placed in suitable positions viz., reservoirs, canals, dams, cold storages, marketing of agro products, warehouses [5, 48]. The following are the core private and government jobs departments and sectors viz.:

- Agricultural Departments
- Irrigation Departments
- Dairy boards Departments
- Information Technology Departments.

As the field Agricultural Informatics is interdisciplinary in nature, there are potentialities to offer the programs in different levels. As far as the technology is concerned, the emerging IoT and allied areas can be a wonderful interdisciplinary program for the creation of suitable and healthy manpower in the field. Tables 3.3 to 3.6 show the perspective and possible proposed programs in Agriculture and Information Technology related streams as a major or specialized field of study.

Table 3.3 Depicted the proposed UG, PG & research programs on Agriculture with Agro IOT Concentration.

Under Graduate	Post Graduate & Research
BSc-Agriculture (Agricultural Informatics & IoT)	MSc-Agricultural Science (Agricultural Informatics & IoT)
BS-Agriculture (Digital Agriculture & IoT)	MS-Agricultural Science (Digital Agriculture & IoT)
BTech/BE-Agricultural Science & Engg. (Digital Agriculture & IoT)	MTech/ME-Agricultural Science (Digital Education/Education Technology, etc.)
BSc (Engg)-Agricultural Science & Engg. (Agro IoT)	MSc (Engg)-Agricultural Science (Digital Education/Education Technology, etc.)
	MS/MTech-Agricultural Science (by Research)-Agro IoT
	PhD (Science/Engg.)-Agricultural Science (Agro IoT/Agro Informatics with IoT, etc.)

Table 3.4 Depicted the proposed UG, PG & Research Programs on Computer Science with Agro IOT Concentration.

Under Graduate	Post Graduate & Research
BSc-Computer Science (Agro IoT/ Agro IT & IoT etc) BS-Computer Science (Agro IoT/ Agro IT & IoT, etc.) BTech/BE-Computer Science & Engg. (Agro IoT/Agro IT & IoT, etc.) BSc (Engg)-Computer Science & Engg. (Agro IoT/Agro IT & IoT, etc.)	MSc-Computer Science (Agro IoT/ Agro IT & IoT, etc.) MS-Computer Science (Agro IoT/ Agro IT & IoT etc) MTech/ME-(Agro IoT/Agro IT & IoT, etc.) MSc (Engg)-(Agro IoT/Agro IT & IoT, etc.) MS/MTech-CS/CSE (by Research)- (Agro IoT/Agro IT & IoT, etc.) PhD (Science/Engg.)-CS/CSE (Agro IoT/Agro IT & IoT, etc.)

Table 3.5 Depicted the proposed UG, PG & Research Programs on Computer Applications with Agro IOT Concentration.

Under Graduate	Post Graduate & Research
BCA (Agro IoT) BCA (Agro IT & IoT) BCA (Agro Informatics & IoT) BCA (Agro IoT & Analytics) BCA (Agro IT & IoT)	BCA (Agro IoT) BCA (Agro IT & IoT) BCA (Agro Informatics & IoT) BCA (Agro IoT & Analytics) BCA (Agro IT & IoT) BCA (by Research)-(Agro Informatics & IoT/Agro IoT/Agro Analytics & IoT, etc.) PhD-CA (Agro Informatics & IoT/ Agro IoT/Agro Analytics & IoT, etc.)

Agriculture is a growing field and most common programs are available with BSc/MSc/BTech/MTech/PhD in Agriculture and there are way in which Agro Informatics and IoT can be incorporated in these program with proper educational strategies that is depicted in Table 3.3. However, Agro Informatics is a combination of Agro field and IT & Computing field, so Table 3.4 depicted most common program on Computing area i.e. Computer Science with proposed IoT and Agro Informatics.

It is worthy to note that, Computer Science (CS) is mainly responsible for the designing and development of computer-based systems; in this

Table 3.6 Depicted the proposed UG, PG & Research Programs on Information Technology with Agro IOT Concentration.

Under Graduate	Post Graduate & Research
BSc-Information Technology (Agro IoT/Agro IT & IoT, etc.) BS-Information Technology (AIoT & Analytics, etc.) BTech/BE-Information Technology (Digital Agriculture & IoT, etc.) BSc (Engg)-Information Technology (Smart Agriculture & AIoT)	MSc-Information Technology (Agro IoT/Agro IT & IoT, etc.) MS-Information Technology (AIoT & Analytics, etc.) MTech/ME-Information Technology (Digital Agriculture & IoT, etc.) MSc (Engg)-Information Technology (Digital Agriculture & IoT, etc.) PhD (Science/Engg.)-IT/ICT (Digital Agriculture & IoT/Smart Agriculture etc.)

context with above mentioned programs are suitable to cater the manpower specially on designing and development on hardware.

In other hand, as Computer Application (CA) is software technology centric so that, the programs are suitable for direct Agro IoT manpower development who may be interested in Agriculture based software and applications designing and development. Table 3.5 in this context proposed few programs which can be offered with efforts of collaboration of existing Computer Applications Departments with Agriculture, etc. Among the Computing field, Information Technology is broad one, and treated as one of the largest field. Table 3.6 in this respect proposes few programs.

Information Technology is broader than CS and CA and additionally it incorporates the areas viz. Web Technology, Database Technology, Networking Technology, Multimedia Technology, Communication Technology and thus the candidates interested in developing Smart Agriculture or Agro Informatics can go with his/her interest accordingly. It is worthy to note that, Information Science (IS) is an interdisciplinary field of study and broader that these field and mainly applicable to other fields and areas and thus apart from these mentioned subjects Agro Informatics or Agro IT & IoT specialization can also possible and proposed to start IS and other areas viz.:

- Information Science/Informatics.
- Information Systems
- Information & Knowledge Management
- Knowledge Engineering, etc.

3.12   Suggestions

Implementing Agro Informatics in real sense is quite difficult but it has huge potentiality as well due to its numerous benefits as discussed in this research work. As far as suggestions are concerned, following should be important and to be noted:

- There should be proper and high initial investments in different devices and technologies viz. sensors, drones and bots and their setting up.
- Running the IoT-based Agriculture needs qualified and well trained staffs for designing and development to operating and further management.
- Connectivity is another important fact which required running well-operated Agro IoT systems including the concern on hardware maintenance costs.
- Development of the manpower is a challenging task as it is deals with many aspects and strategies. If starting full-fledged Agro IoT degrees are difficult to run then the specializations or major or concentration could be started with proper educational policies.
- Integration and collaboration are most important and vital these days, and in this context better industrial tie-ups are essential between the farm and technology organizations; on other hand, the educational institutes also need to think on proper collaboration with technology firm to create a healthy and solid man power.
- There are few technologies related with IoT and among these important are Cloud Computing, Big Data, Data Analytics, etc. And there should be proper connectivity among these technologies as well.

3.13   Conclusion

Smart Farming is the effective system for the healthy and sustainable agricultural systems. Agro IoT is the implementing the connected devices with emerging and innovative technologies in the field of agriculture and allied field. With the IoT-based agriculture there is no need of physical work by the cultivators and it is responsible for the productivity and efficiency in healthy manner. Internet of Things based Agriculture is comes with various benefits in other allied agro fields viz. water, optimization real-time manner, time saving and post cost effective. With the introduction of Agro IoT humidity, temperature, soil, etc. of the agriculture can be possible to find out. There are many challenges in Agriculture Informatics practice specially the IoT applications due to the specified aspects. However, regarding the manpower development there are many things need to care about viz. the proper planning, educational policies, collaboration process among the stakeholders, organizational aspects, etc. It should be noted that in case of full degree the specialization can be offered in IT and Computing field and in Agriculture domain. However, based on the healthy condition the Agro Informatics or Agro IoT based programs can be started as a full-fledged degree. Government, agricultural firms, companies, associations etc should be under one roof for real implementation of Agro based systems. In a country like India or other developing one are may face initial challenges but with proper overcoming of such issues it could be great deal.

References

1. Abbasi, A.Z., Islam, N., Shaikh, Z.A., A review of wireless sensors and networks' applications in agriculture. *Comput. Stand Inter.*, 36, 263, 2014.
2. Adão, T., Hruška, J., Pádua, L., Bessa, J., Peres, E., Morais, R., Sousa, J.J., Hyperspectral imaging: A review on UAV-based sensors, data processing and applications for agriculture and forestry. *Remote Sens.*, 9, 1110, 2017.
3. Adetunji, K.E. and Joseph, M.K., Development of a Cloud-based Monitoring System using 4duino: Applications in Agriculture, in: *2018 International Conference on Advances in Big Data, Computing and Data Communication Systems (icABCD)*, p. 4849, 2018.
4. Ahmad, T., Ahmad, S., Jamshed, M., A knowledge based Indian agriculture: With cloud ERP arrangement, in: *2015 International Conference on Green Computing and Internet of Things (ICGCIoT)*, IEEE, p. 333, 2015.
5. Ahmed, N., De, D., Hussain, I., Internet of Things (IoT) for smart precision agriculture and farming in rural areas. *IEEE Internet Things J.*, 5, 4890, 2018.
6. Anandhi, V., Belliraj, N., Ananthi, M., Pirabu, J.V., Cloud computing and climate-smart agriculture: An efficient transfer of technology mechanism. *Int. J. Farm Sci.*, 10, 59, 2020.
7. Atzberger, C., Advances in remote sensing of agriculture: Context description, existing operational monitoring systems and major information needs. *Remote Sens.*, 5, 949, 2013.
8. Aubert, B.A., Schroeder, A., Grimaudo, J., IT as enabler of sustainable farming: An empirical analysis of farmers' adoption decision of precision agriculture technology. *Decis. Support Syst.*, 54, 510, 2012.

9. Babu, S.M., Lakshmi, A.J., Rao, B.T., A study on cloud based Internet of Things: CloudIoT, in: *2015 Global Conference on Communication Technologies (GCCT)*, IEEE, p. 60, 2015.

10. Balamurugan, S., Divyabharathi, N., Jayashruthi, K., Bowiya, M., Shermy, R.P., Shanker, R., Internet of agriculture: Applying IoT to improve food and farming technology. *Int. Res. J. Eng. Technol. (IRJET)*, 3, 713, 2016.

11. Bauckhage, C. and Kersting, K., Data mining and pattern recognition in agriculture. *KI-Künstliche Intelligenz*, 27, 313, 2013.

12. Channe, H., Kothari, S., Kadam, D., Multidisciplinary model for smart agriculture using internet-of-things (IoT), sensors, cloud-computing, mobile-computing & big-data analysis. *Int. J. Comput. Technol. Appl.*, 6, 374, 2015.

13. Chandraul, K. and Singh, A., An agriculture application research on cloud computing. *Int. J. Curr. Eng. Technol.*, 3, 2084, 2013.

14. Choudhary, S.K., Jadoun, R.S., Mandoriya, H.L., Role of cloud computing technology in agriculture fields. *Computing*, 7, 1–7, 2016.

15. Elijah, O., Rahman, T.A., Orikumhi, I., Leow, C.Y., Hindia, M.N., An overview of Internet of Things (IoT) and data analytics in agriculture: Benefits and challenges. *IEEE Internet Things J.*, 5, 3758, 2018.

16. Ferrández-Pastor, F.J., García-Chamizo, J.M., Nieto-Hidalgo, M., Mora-Pascual, J., Mora-Martínez, J., Developing ubiquitous sensor network platform using internet of things: Application in precision agriculture. *Sensors*, 16, 1141, 2016.

17. Ghobakhloo, M., Hong, T.S., Sabouri, M.S., Zulkifli, N., Strategies for successful information technology adoption in small and medium-sized enterprises. *Information*, 3, 36, 2012.

18. Gill, S.S., Chana, I., Buyya, R., IoT based agriculture as a cloud and big data service: The beginning of digital India. *J. Organ. End User Comput. (JOEUC)*, 29, 1, 2017.

19. Gómez-Chabla, R., Real-Avilés, K., Morán, C., Grijalva, P., Recalde, T., IoT Applications in Agriculture: A Systematic Literature Review, in: *2nd International Conference on ICTs in Agronomy and Environment*, Springer, Cham, p. 68, 2019.

20. Goraya, M.S. and Kaur, H., Cloud computing in agriculture. *HCTL Open Int. J. Technol. Innov. Res. (IJTIR)*, 16, 2321, 2015.

21. Guardo, E., Di Stefano, A., La Corte, A., Sapienza, M., Scatà, M., A fog computing-based IoT framework for precision agriculture. *J. Internet Technol.*, 19, 1401, 2018.

22. Han, W., Yang, Z., Di, L., Mueller, R., CropScape: A Web service based application for exploring and disseminating US conterminous geospatial cropland data products for decision support. *Comput. Electron. Agric.*, 84, 111, 2012.

23. Honkavaara, E., Saari, H., Kaivosoja, J., Pölönen, I., Hakala, T., Litkey, P., Pesonen, L., Processing and assessment of spectrometric, stereoscopic

imagery collected using a lightweight UAV spectral camera for precision agriculture. *Remote Sens.*, 5, 5006, 2013.

24. Jaiganesh, S., Gunaseelan, K., Ellappan, V., IoT agriculture to improve food and farming technology, in: *2017 Conference on Emerging Devices and Smart Systems (ICEDSS)*, IEEE, p. 260, 2017.

25. Jinbo, C., Yu, Z., Lam, A., Research on monitoring platform of agricultural product circulation efficiency supported by cloud computing. *Wireless Pers. Commun.*, 102, 3573, 2018.

26. Kamble, S.S., Gunasekaran, A., Gawankar, S.A., Achieving sustainable performance in a data-driven agriculture supply chain: A review for research and applications. *Int. J. Prod. Econ.*, 219, 179, 2020.

27. Kajol, R. and Akshay, K.K., Automated Agricultural Field Analysis and Monitoring System Using IoT. *Int. J. Inform. Eng. Electron. Bus.*, 11, 17, 2018.

28. Khattab, A., Abdelgawad, A., Yelmarthi, K., Design and implementation of a cloud-based IoT scheme for precision agriculture, in: *2016 28th International Conference on Microelectronics (ICM)*, p. 201, 2016.

29. Liu, S., Guo, L., Webb, H., Ya, X., Chang, X., Internet of Things monitoring system of modern eco-agriculture based on cloud computing. *IEEE Access*, 7, 37050, 2019.

30. Manos, B., Polman, N., Viaggi, D., *Agricultural and environmental informatics, governance and management: Emerging research applications*, Z. Andreopoulou (Ed.), IGI Global, Hershey, Pennsylvania, 2011.

31. Muangprathub, J., Boonnam, N., Kajornkasirat, S., Lekbangpong, N., Wanichsombat, A., Nillaor, P., IoT and agriculture data analysis for smart farm. *Comput. Electron. Agric.*, 156, 467, 2011.

32. Na, A. and Isaac, W., Developing a human-centric agricultural model in the IoT environment, in: *2016 International Conference on Internet of Things and Applications (IOTA)*, IEEE, p. 292, 2016.

33. Nandyala, C.S. and Kim, H.K., Green IoT agriculture and healthcare application (GAHA). *Int. J. Smart Home*, 10, 289, 2016.

34. Nayyar, A. and Puri, V., Smart farming: IoT based smart sensors agriculture stick for live temperature and moisture monitoring using Arduino, cloud computing & solar technology, in: *Proc. of The International Conference on Communication and Computing Systems (ICCCS-2016)*, p. 94, 2016.

35. Ojha, T., Misra, S., Raghuwanshi, N.S., Wireless sensor networks for agriculture: The state-of-the-art in practice and future challenges. *Comput. Electron. Agric.*, 118, 66, 2015.

36. Othman, M.F. and Shazali, K., Wireless sensor network applications: A study in environment monitoring system. *Procedia Eng.*, 41, 1204, 2012.

37. Ozdogan, B., Gacar, A., Aktas, H., Digital agriculture practices in the context of agriculture 4.0. *J. Econ. Financ. Account.*, 4, 186–193, 2017.

38. Patel, R. and Patel, M., Application of cloud computing in agricultural development of rural India. *Int. J. Comput. Sci. Inf. Technol.*, 4, 922–926, 2013.

39. Patil, V.C., Al-Gaadi, K.A., Biradar, D.P., Rangaswamy, M., Internet of things (Iot) and cloud computing for agriculture: An overview. *Proceedings of Agro-Informatics and Precision Agriculture (AIPA 2012)*, India, p. 292, 2012.
40. Popović, T., Latinović, N., Pešić, A., Zečević, Ž., Krstajić, B., Djukanović, S., Architecting an IoT-enabled platform for precision agriculture and ecological monitoring: A case study. *Comput. Electron. Agric.*, 140, 255, 2017.
41. Paul, P.K., Ghosh, M., Chaterjee., D., Information Systems & Networks (ISN): Emphasizing Agricultural Information Networks with a case Study of AGRIS. *Scholars J. Agric. Vet. Sci.*, 1, 122, 2014.
42. Paul, P.K., Information and Knowledge Requirement for Farming and Agriculture Domain. *Int. J. Soft Comput. Bio Inf.*, 4, 80–84, 2013.
43. Paul, P.K. *et al.*, Agricultural Problems in India requiring solution through Agricultural Information Systems: Problems and Prospects in Developing Countries. *Int. J. Inf. Sci. Comput.*, 2, 33, 2015.
44. Paul, P.K. *et al.*, Cloud Computing and Virtualization in Agricultural Space: A Knowledge Survey. *Palgo J. Agric.*, 4, 202, 2016.
45. Paul, P.K. *et al.*, Information and Communication Technology and Information: Their role in Tea Cultivation and Marketing in the context of Developing Countries—A Theoretical Approach. *Curr. Trends Biotechnol. Chem. Res.*, 5, 155, 2015.
46. Prasad, R., Kumar, V., Prasad, K.S., Nanotechnology in sustainable agriculture: Present concerns and future aspects. *Afr. J. Biotechnol.*, 13, 705, 2014.
47. Rajeswari, S., Suthendran, K., Rajakumar, K., A smart agricultural model by integrating IoT, mobile and cloud-based big data analytics, in: *2017 International Conference on Intelligent Computing and Control (I2C2)*, IEEE, p. 1, 2017.
48. Rezník, T., Charvát, K., Lukas, V., Charvát Jr., K., Horáková, Š., Kepka, M., Open data model for (precision) agriculture applications and agricultural pollution monitoring, in: *EnviroInfo and ICT for Sustainability 2015*, Amsterdam, Netharland, Atlantis Press, 2015.
49. Singh, S., Chana, I., Buyya, R., Agri-info: Cloud based autonomic system for delivering agriculture as a service. *Internet Things*, 9, 100, 2020.
50. Somov, A., Shadrin, D., Fastovets, I., Nikitin, A., Matveev, S., Hrinchuk, O., Pervasive agriculture: IoT-enabled greenhouse for plant growth control. *IEEE Pervasive Comput.*, 17, 65, 2018.
51. Szilágyi, R., Lengyel, P., Herdon, M., Portal for knowledge of agricultural informatics, in: *Agricultural Informatics*, Sideridis, A.B., Herdon, M., Várallyai, L. (Eds.), p. 37, 2010.
52. Tan, L., Cloud-based decision support and automation for precision agriculture in orchards. *IFAC-PapersOnLine*, 49, 330, 2016.
53. TongKe, F., Smart agriculture based on cloud computing and IoT. *J. Converg. Inf. Technol.*, 8, 166, 2013.
54. Tsekouropoulos, G., Andreopoulou, Z., Koliouska, C., Koutroumanidis, T., Batzios, C., Internet functions in marketing: Multicriteria ranking of

agricultural SMEs websites in Greece. *AGRÁRINFORMATIKA/J. Agric. Inf.*, 4, 22, 2013.

55. Vejan, P., Abdullah, R., Khadiran, T., Ismail, S., Nasrulhaq Boyce, A., Role of plant growth promoting rhizobacteria in agricultural sustainability—A review. *Molecules*, 21, 573, 2016.

56. Wilson, A.D., Diverse applications of electronic-nose technologies in agriculture and forestry. *Sensors*, 13, 2295, 2013.

57. Zamora-Izquierdo, M.A., Santa, J., Martínez, J.A., Martínez, V., Skarmeta, A.F., Smart farming IoT platform based on edge and cloud computing. *Biosyst. Eng.*, 177, 417, 2019.

4

Application of Agricultural Drones and IoT to Understand Food Supply Chain During Post COVID-19

Pushan Kumar Dutta[1]* and Susanta Mitra[2]

[1]*Amity University Kolkata, Kolkata, India*
[2]*The Neotia University, Sarisha, India*

Abstract

The role of smart farming by gathering information on productive crop management has been addressed. Current advances in data management for smart farming acquired using sensors based data driven architecture has been found to increase efficiency in generating both qualitative and quantitative approaches along a range of challenges that will shake the existing agriculture methodologies. The study highlights the potential of wireless sensors and IoT in agriculture and similar techniques which are feasible for surveillance and monitoring from sowing and harvesting and similar packaging operations. In this study, we highlight the technologies in IoT by highlighting the design of a novel drone concept with 3D mapping and addressing post COVID19 issues in agriculture and proposed monitoring in comparative analysis. The role of emerging technology in particular the participation of the IoT, is very critical in achieving this aim. Our study reviews that artificial intelligence based decision making system will create supplementary benefits of precision agriculture. Machine learning also gives a critical role in farming in terms of nutrients management. It is further found that automation in agriculture through IoT is a proven technology even for small farms that can work for Indian context.

Keywords: Smart farming, precision agriculture, sensors, internet, soil nutrition management, smart packaging and reliability, data sequence, value chain analysis

Corresponding author: pkdutta@kol.amity.edu

Amitava Choudhury, Arindam Biswas, Manish Prateek and Amlan Chakrabarti (eds.)
Agricultural Informatics: Automation Using the IoT and Machine Learning, (67–88) © 2021
Scrivener Publishing LLC

4.1   Introduction

The COVID-19 pandemic has forced human daily existence through chaos pushing or deciding to abstain from doing other routines and restricting their activity to a minimum, food supply issue. On the contrary, most have secured personal supplies of essential food items known as panic-buying, given the psychological pressure of the situation. The effect can be seen in terms of food supply shortages, demand for semi-perishable food products particularly during lock-down, food inflation, rural labor reverse migration, etc. The food supply chain is a dynamic network including farmers, customers, supplies from agriculture and fisheries, manufacturing and storage, transportation and distribution, and so on. Fluctuations are marginal because food production has been sufficient and prices have been steady to date. Global cereal supplies are at manageable levels, and the 2020 outlook is favorable for wheat and other main staple crops. While less food production of high-value goods (i.e. fruit and vegetables) is already likely, they are not yet visible due to lockdowns and disruptions in the value chain. The use of a Smartphone is growing as specific Internet communication systems are being used. With the global situation of the Corona Pandemic, shifting into modern innovation appears probable for transition in various farming sectors. By 2050 the world's population is forecast to reach 9.6 billion—this poses a major problem for the agricultural industry. Despite fighting challenges such as heat waves, rapidly increasing global warming, and the environmental consequences of farming, demand for more food has to be met. Farming has to turn to new technologies to ensure these growing requirements. New IoT-based smart farming implementations will enable the farming manufacturers to understand waste and increase productivity from enhancing fertilizer use to enhancing the efficiency of farm vehicle tracks. Smart farming is a capital-intensive [1–7], high-tech system of cleanly and sustainably growing food for the populace. It is the result of new ICT (Information and Communication Technologies) in agriculture. Entrepreneurship has received a tremendous progress in agriculture and sustainable growth for automated irrigation and monitoring and solving many pre-dominant problems associated with linking and clearing wastes is that the symbol of business tenacity and achievement. Entrepreneurial innovation in the field of agriculture and environmental sustainability has allowed India to take its first steps, in a sector which is soaring globally & demonstrating a model to save the planet. With our agricultural biodiversity & the opportunity to benefit, our farmers & talented workforce, India can be a lynchpin of growth for the global sector [8–12]. Covid-19 has underscored that we can no longer take our planet for granted shining example of market demand for a more healthy, sustainable just food system. There are many pockets in India where villages and involvement of smart agriculture plays an important role for development of country. In our country, agriculture depends on the monsoons which has insufficient source of water whereby irrigation is employed in agriculture field. In irrigation system, it's identified upon the soil type and water retention provided whereby vital information about the fertility of soil and second to soak up and infuse moisture content in soil. Nowadays, there are various irrigation techniques available that reduce the reliance on weather. And much of the system is powered by electrical power and on/off cycles. During this procedure, the water level indicator mounted in the water reservoir and the soil moisture sensors are situated in the root zone of the plant and near to the module and the gateway device manages the sensor information and transmits the data to the processor [13–16]. The revolution of young entrepreneurs should be supported by new and novel agricultural practices which are essential for the improvement of the current agricultural markets. Significant emphasis should be paid to value-added items and limited manufacturing and the same. Proper cold storage facilities will minimize the loss of crops and food and it is advised that the cold storage facility be built *in-situ* near the farm/production location. This can be achieved as a joint initiative between farmers' collectives and central self-government bodies. It would provide farmers with the potential to monitor the value of their goods and to make more profits [17].

4.2   Related Work

With the advent of IoT, Robotics, Data Science, AI, these technologies would demonstrate to be useful tools for small and marginal farmers to enrich their livelihoods and provide varied opportunities for rural India. Information and communication technology can link farmers to information, networks, and institutions to boost opportunities for productivity and jobs. For example, it can provide access to information about extension facilities, fertilizer supply, weather predictions, markets, etc. Drones are Unmanned Ariel Vehicles (UAVs) carrying a number of useful devices such as cameras, GPS, specialized software and hardware for processing, and spray-able resources (see Figure 4.1). Drones have successfully been employed in a wide variety of applications such as, law enforcement, fisheries, surveillance, water management, various military applications and others. It is a matter of concern that the total agriculture land that has been made available for food production has experienced a sharp fall in terms of both surplus and demand [18–21]. Since 1991, the total agriculture area for food production was 19.5 million square miles (39.47% of the world's land area), and there has been a total land loss of 2.3% over the entire globe in 2013. It has been also extensively difficult to monitor crops in different growing seasons due to the changing patterns of water requirement and vegetation growth in the land tilling area. In our country where rural resources are more the benefit of the poor will depend on developing a wide diversified model of public resources, crop resistance, social capital. Further the combined effect of climate change [22] and a fast growing population in rural India means that Indians will need to find a way to produce more sustainable habitat for food without causing harm to the environment. In contrast, given the long-standing experience of some farmers assembled but after many years of field work, technology [23] may provide a systemic tool to

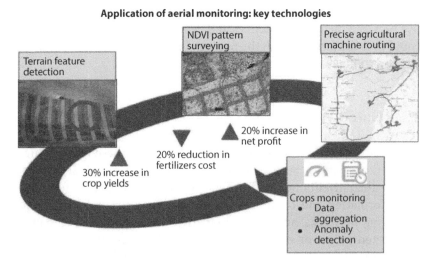

Figure 4.1 Applying drone technology to precision agriculture.

detect unforeseen problems which are hard to notice by visual inspection on regular reviews. And you'll need supporting agronomic data—such as soil, water and weather—for calibration of crop models to make informed decisions. Today, helicopters and light aircraft are being used to collect aerial photographs around the fields.

Through using technology that is used in precision farming using Drones, Satellite, Wireless Sensor Network, IoT, and so on, we recognize growing crop yield or production while reducing crop production costs. In precision calculation of a seed, there may be several variables to test. Generational transformation in the context of rural development goes beyond the reduction of the mean lifespan of farmers; it is also about empowering a new generation of highly qualified young farmers to make full use of technology in order to support sustainable farming practices, as indicated in the paper of Vision 2020 [24] and Vision 2030 [25] documents of ICAR for strategizing a global information system for farming knowledge sharing and best practices in sustainable development. The system will collect copious volumes of historically annotatable datasets and would employ Big Data Analytics [26–28] over the Cloud computing environment [29–31] and extensive software systems so that small and medium size farmers can benefit from integrated farm and crop management processes. This design and implementation methodology forms part of the larger Agricultural Internet of Everything (also known as Internet of Things (IoT)) [32–34] in that all farm related monitoring can now be brought from the field to the farmer-at-home. Drones equipped with advanced camera systems are actually available to capture photographic imagery ranging from standard to ultraviolet and hyper spectral imaging. Some of those cameras are also able to film footage. Additionally, the image quality used by the drones is continuously increasing and will allow farmers to get reliable field data [13]. Drones for the benefit of agricultural and entomological safety. The technology treats drones as independent and coordinating entities so that they can operate on a cooperative basis. Further, a comprehensive 3D Digital Elevation Model (DEM) [35] will be studied for the field at large—i.e., in the case of small farmers this implies that the farms surrounding them will also be modeled so that they can get extensive view of their agricultural necessities and understand the limitations within which they can operate. Big Data over a cloud computing environment would be used to perform necessary analytics in order to provide a comprehensive decision support system [36–38].

4.3   Smart Production With the Introduction of Drones and IoT

The usage cases we've seen in the fight against COVID-19 show we've always had the technology to continue the war against the epidemic at least. Use cases that were put into practice on the front line in the test, proof of concept, or production phases, showing that the ideas were already available— we only needed the right trigger. Providers were able to understand, after some initial confusion, how to use IoT technology as solution. Companies can use IoT in conjunction with other technologies to deal with infectious diseases, but they are divided and will need more infrastructure to link the data collection [39–42], processing, analysis and storage components. A comprehensive outbreak response plan encompasses all programs in the same way, including hospitals, surveillance, disease monitoring and others. Despite of the negative factors such as the low land availability, low per capita water availability, land slope and climate changes in the recent years: our society has shown positive approach towards farming and agricultural sector in general [42–44]. The increase in the number of entries by young educated people into agripreneurship is really promising. The IoT alters web functioning and usage. Web 1.0 denotes one-way communication, i.e. sending some information to consumers in order to render it 'readable' via browser. Web 2.0 meant that Web 1.0 was updated to two-way communication with the aid of modern technologies (blogs, social network sites, video sharing). Content creators for Web 1.0 and Web 2.0 were person, while the introduction of IoT brought a modern data generation. This qualitative shift in the function of data generation, and in particular the quantitative increase in data amount, offers the foundation for the development of the current paradigm of using the World Wide Web in reference. According to the IoT technology explanation (without any of the structured, strict Approach) in which, if no more but at least the fundamental pillars (technologies) are complex 'structures' (of the IoT), then a strict definition of the Internet of Things can be attempted. Focused on the above short overview, it can be argued that the IoT architecture encompasses a broad variety of financial, operational, network and info communication (ICT—Information and Communications Technologies) components that must function in synch to maintain basic facilities, and it is nearly unreasonable to assume that a particular interpretation is appropriate to all parties. The revolution by young entrepreneurs should be supported with new and novel agricultural practices which is essential for the advancement in this section by the current agricultural markets.

Special attention to be given to value added products and minimal processing and the same should be promoted among the farmers as well as food processing firms. Proper cold storage facility can reduce the wastage of vegetables and foods and it is recommended to install *in-situ* the cold storage facility near the farm/production catchment. This can be done as a joined venture by farmer collectives and local self-governing bodies. This will provide the further the capability to control the pricing of their products and earn better profits. If we compare rural and urban, major proportion of the population living in rural is unable to creep the imbalances, to achieve balanced economic development, to develop rural India. it becomes inevitable to promote Agripreneurship. To take the leverage of the rich rural resources, to find the potential in rural India the best strategy is to promote Agripreneurship. In India's agriculture tech startups with funding of S24S million in the first half of 2019 over three-fold compared to an investment of $73 million in 2012. Interestingly the Agri tech startups may be one of the only startups that can be truly be a Make in India' model with more than 25 Indian Agrotech companies having global presence. More than half of estimated 450 agrotech startups in India offer supply chain solutions like better access to inputs for farmers or market linkage with the ecosystem tilted towards B2B models. World Economic Forum and Asian Development Bank have also invested in Indian Agritech startups. Thus the Indian Agritech ecosystem is maturing quickly amid emerging business opportunities in market linkage, digitalization in agriculture, offering better access to inputs, farm services and finance. The reason the sector has so many opportunities can be attributed to the number of broken links in supply chain which have led to Sl3 billion losses in post-harvest. The inspiration for trying to introduce the IoT is classifiable from the object aspect, i.e. Medium which implements the solution given (Figure 4.2).

4.3.1   Real-Time Surveyed Data Collection and Storage Utilizing an IoT System

4.3.1.1   Efficient Control of Distributed Networks of Services (Using the Integrated Networks Sensors Provided)

Processing and processing data from IoTs housed in libraries or data centers in the information core of the enterprise, the cloud, the local repository (gateway to be built in the segment below) or the node itself to which the sensors are connected (see below for more details).

- Active tracking and its analysis techniques in real-time as essential
- Documents form the foundation for effective management decisions and sound business judgments guarantee the efficient productivity that leads to the organization's sustainable development;
- Conducting monitoring of the operation of the equipment, monitoring the development and status of the plants, as well as animal movement relevant to the production and operation of the organization, ensures a reduction in the cost of business;

4.3.1.2   Human Participation in Surveillance and Monitoring can be Identified to Take the Following Roles

a. Surveillance of essential activities in humans
b. Observing the characteristics of the disorders of patients remotely with the prospect of taking the appropriate steps, if any
c. Tracking real-time vehicle availability in urban transport and carpooling
d. Reduction and control of heat and electric power consumption

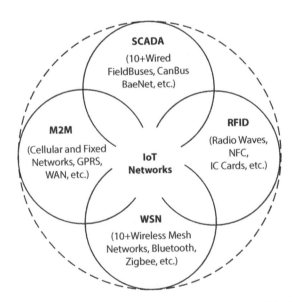

Figure 4.2 Four technologies of the IoT technology management used in the process.

e. Private Property monitoring and security, etc.
f. Smart city deployment (monitoring and regulation by electricity delivery, water, communication sources, emergency services, etc.)
g. Realization and integration of self-guided cars into the smart city, Think about it. Social property monitoring and security etc.

4.4   Agricultural Drones

Some of the better functionalities of agriculture IoT will allow the farmers to monitor the storage facilities real time [45–48] for cost saving using different machinery, cameras, gates and wide variety of equipment in a two way messaging service. This will allow management of critical water resources in farmlands using on demand function of pumps. Agriculture IoT can use sensors to collect agricultural production process, product logistics and related information for connecting to the transmission network. The deep integration of information and agricultural industry will produce a new force by changing the agricultural landscape. There is no one correct route "to conduct the incubation of agribusiness." Rather, the work of incubation of agribusiness depends on the state of development of the agribusiness ecosystem and changes over time as the ecosystem matures and develops. It was in its early phases. Incubators demonstrate the viability of new business models and seek to create and capture additional value from primary agricultural products. In underdeveloped agricultural ecosystems, incubators help to reinforce and promote relations between businesses and new commercial opportunities. They create fresh platforms on innovations that are suitable for agribusiness enterprises and allow agricultural enterprises to find innovative and even more profitable forms of doing business. During the subsequent stages of growth, incubators serve as network facilitators: they connect specific service providers to agribusinesses and link different agribusinesses to one another. The incubation cycle for agribusiness focuses on cultivating creative early-stage agro-businesses with strong growth potential to become profitable enterprises. Agribusiness incubators also allow creative value-added agribusiness start-ups and development. Over the past two decades, several development organizations such as the World Bank have been testing alternative approaches to transforming comparative advantage in commodity markets into competitive advantages in differentiated product markets. The Food and Agriculture Organization, and the International Finance Corporation. Agribusiness Incubators [49], which facilitate enterprise formation in the agricultural sector must think and work differently than other types of incubators because the functions that agribusiness incubators execute are more complex and the risks. Finally, in a more mature stage of market growth, incubators serve as platforms for product sharing. Products, inputs and methods of management work across national borders. The incubation process for agribusiness focuses on nurturing innovative early-stage agribusinesses with high growth potential to become competitive enterprises. Over the past two decades, several development organizations such as the World Bank, the Food and Agriculture Organization and the International Finance Corporation have tested alternative approaches for the transfer of comparative advantages in commodity markets to competitive advantages in differentiated product markets. Surface nutrient seeds raise the expense of planting and surface and field study and planting of soil nutrient feed crops. Surface nutrient seeds raising the expense of planting and surface and field study and planting of soil nutrient feed crops. Crop spraying will inspect the soil and spray the appropriate volume of fluid modulating space [50–55]. Crop tracking, hyperspectral, multispectral or thermal irrigation and crop scanning can provide a health evaluation utilizing both visible and near-infrared pictures. Precise applications of fertilizers, pesticides or herbicides that be applied to specifically defined and established problems within a specified region. Before the crop cycle begins, drone engineering may be used to determine soil quality and therefore future yields. The main tool in the estimation of the soil quality is the actual 3D mapping of the soil with a detailed soil color coverage. Drone technologies may be applicable to a broad variety of applications in agricultural development, from the potential to be successful for planning purposes, field and plant evaluation to precise crop spraying. But, just like all the other tools, the right strategy and setup are needed to actually leverage the technology available. One of the main distinctions between conventional and contemporary cultivation, apart from the degree of mechanization, are the data obtained directly from the crops. In conventional farms, where farmers determine by visual appraisal, judgments are conditional and arbitrary. Agricultural development provides an evaluation of the quantitative results generated by sound decisions. Drone technology will give the agricultural production industry a high-tech facelift with strategy and tactics predicated on real-time data collection and handling. Recently, advancements in image recognition and optical signal processing have improved WSN's ability to reliably assess crop quality and health [56–58]. These drones execute monitoring and observations in-flight. The farmers enter the field details to be surveyed and select an altitude or ground negotiated settlement. We may draw insights from drone data on plant growth indices, crop tracking and yield forecasting, germination percentage measurement, canopy cover tracking, field water pond mapping, scouting reports, inventory measurement, wheat chlorophyll measurement, drainage mapping, weed pressure mapping, and so on. Throughout the flight, the drone captures multispectral, kinetic, and graphical imagery, and then land at the same place it took off. Drought is a big concern that reduces the efficiency of crop yields. Many areas across the globe face this problem with differing degrees of impact to the weak and vulnerable population. In order to address this problem, particularly in rural and marginalized areas, remote sensing is used to obtain frequent soil moisture data that help to understand agricultural drought in remote regions. Agribusiness Incubators that enhance the creation of ventures in the farming industry will perceive and work differently than other types of incubators, as the functions undertaken by agribusiness incubators are more specific and the threats they handle are much more severe than those experienced by other industries. The goal of business incubation lies in the agriculture industry [59–62]. Moreover, the leverage points are both greater in amount and more dynamic in their implementation, and the risk tolerance of investors in the business is typically stronger than in other industries. Subsistence or close subsistence farmers may be assumed to be extremely risk-adverse.

4.5   IoT Acts as a Backbone in Addressing COVID-19 Problems in Agriculture

IoT is already used for the management and other aspects of COVID-19, and it helps us combat the epidemic. Here, we'll discuss Drone as a use cases IoT in the COVID-19 pandemic in agriculture. Modern agriculture needs continuous monitoring of the seeds, animals and machines as to achieve optimal efficiency. In the current age of agricultural robotization, it is important to create an effective automated data collection program, specifically for plant and animal status, which will deliver the requisite data within a limited period of time. There are usually two alternatives for this purpose: an IoT (Internet of Things) computer network, and drones (predominantly for plants) with specific, mostly audio, visual equipment, ensures cost-reduction. IoT solutions form the backbone of technology that can support all these systems.

4.5.1   Implementation in Agriculture—Drones

The specific objectives of this study are to detect almost all elements contain a significant degree of novelty, include the following:

- Designing a multi-device small-scale drone using Commercial Off-The Shelf (COTS) products and software in addition to using a commercial COTS drone (so that one can perform comparisons of various nature),
- Develop a suite of near-Infrared image processing software for crop growth modeling and create crop-specific database,
- Develop a suite of near-Infrared image processing software for dynamic disease profiling (including their life-cycle analyses) and create crop-specific database
- Develop a suite of near-Infrared image processing software for seasonal entomological modeling and create crop-specific database,
- Develop a software system that can identify entomological corridors of activities and create crop-specific database,
- Identify 3D vectors of spread for diseases and insects.
- Induct post-disaster management and monitoring processes,
- Develop 3-Dimensional Digital Elevation (DEM) model of the land in order to understand water and nutrient usage, and,
- Develop of a cost–benefit model for the application of a satellite based precision agriculture.

Modern agricultural drones employ flying-by-wire technology and are fully autonomous and programmed to follow a given trajectory or corridor. These are fitted with devices such as accelerometers, gyroscopes, compasses and equipment to clear obstacles. The autopilot controls a route, calculating everything from the take-off and the trip to the landing, looking for full field coverage, thus collecting all the required data. "Users are never needed to manually create or map mission paths or construct flight plans on the basis of weather conditions." These devices meet the needs of four major functional areas [63], namely, Photogrammetric, Protection, Communication & Coordination and Navigational. These devices are mounted on a single stable platform under the drone. One of the drones will carry a hyper spectral camera, as it has been shown in the literature that hyper spectral images can give a better understanding of the crops and disease profile; however, comprehensive work in this area is still not in the public domain. All drones will carry high resolution visual camera, near-Infrared camera and a Depth-Sensing Camera (DSC) Works in Bright Light and Darkness. It has been shown that the DSC can work well through smoke, smog and fog-ridden conditions also. Dust and sand protection will also be available in all drones, besides a GPS and gyroscopic unit. We intend to deploy COTS-based drones such as [64], but where it is prohibitively expensive, a local variation will be attempted.

4.5.2 Communication and Networking Mechanisms

Typical drones employ the ZigBee Pro/IEEE 802.15.4 communications protocol [65], whose typical characteristics. The ZigBee standard supports three device types: ZigBee Coordinator, ZigBee Router and ZigBee End Device, with each device type implementing several types of functions, thereby impacting overall cost of the device. ZigBee Pro/IEEE 802.15.4 Packet Communication Format/s is well-documented and relevant software systems are also available. The overall architecture of the proposal, as a drone based agricultural IoE System, wherein farmer at the home (or cooperative) can find out about the nature of the soil, plant growth and control nutrient and flows and many other parameters. Further, this set up will be enhanced through cameras placed at strategic places. It is noted that the farmer can communicate with each node via a smart phone and, in addition, appropriate APPS will be developed so that on-line engagement with their farms can be effected from anywhere, anytime.

Typical drones employ the ZigBee Pro/IEEE 802.15.4 communications protocol, whose typical characteristics are provided in Table 4.1 and its typical communications packet is shown in Figure 4.3. The ZigBee standard supports three device types: ZigBee Coordinator, ZigBee Router and Zidee End Device, with each device type implementing several types of functions, thereby impacting overall cost of the device. ZigBee Pro/IEEE 802.15.4 Packet Communication Format/s is well-documented and relevant software systems are also available. As noted, the ZigBee communication supports point-to-point, point-to-multipoint and peer-to-peer

Table 4.1 Nature of devices in a drone.

Photogrammetric Devices
• High resolution visual camera
• Near-Infrared camera
• (Hyperspectral camera)
• Depth-Sensing Camera Works in Bright Light and
Protection Devices
• Dust & Sand protection units
Communication & Coordination Devices
• Agent-based communication devices
Navigation Devices
• GPS unit Gyroscope unit

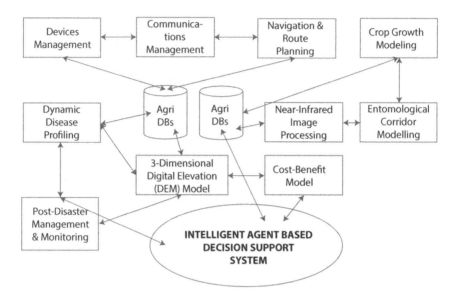

Figure 4.3 Overall architecture of the precision agriculture environment.

topologies. In addition, self-routing, self-healing and fault-tolerant features are also available in this network. Many countries in South East Asia including India are agrarian economies and depend on marshy water reservoirs for cleaning and farming. It is very easy to find small water bodies across the Indian subcontinent which are filled with green duckweed and molasses and it will be easy to farm lotus and other aquatic based food items which can be of good use. We design using our automation tools a suitable environment whereby we develop a robot capable of performing operations like automatic cleaning of the duckweed, irrigation, use fertilizers using drones. There will be two robotic designs one which will float on the surface of water to clear duckweed, identify the ph level of water and other relevant data.

The other technology which we will be using is the aerial drone which will in turn move in the direction of dense duckweed and spray fertilizers. The robots are small, lightweight, floating, energy efficient, environmentally compatible and are able to navigate autonomously and in coordination with each other, in a variety of scenarios, such as coastal waters, artificial and natural lakes, lagoons, rivers. As a part of our design, we will monitor the density of the duckweed using sensors and make the data available to the drone for spray killing dense duckweed.

- The system will provide post-disaster management (e.g., flood, cyclone, wind, tornado, etc.), and follow-up monitoring processes; this sub-system will spawn the latest disaster management datasets—post disaster [66].

- The system will provide 3-Dimensional Digital Elevation (DEM) [67] model of the land in order to understand water and nutrient usage.

4.5.3 Managing Agricultural Data Safety and Security of Individual Farmers

Data security and their safety aspects are key issues in the digital world and they are so in the Agricultural digital world also. Drone usage using e-agriculture policies will lead to better opportunities and regulation and practices in the commercial market of surveying and land use planning. It is also noted that the collated statistical information of the collective farmers would be useful to all farmers and hence the cumulative or composite results would be made available in a statistically independent manner. Many countries in Asia including India are agrarian economies and most of their rural populations depend on agriculture to earn their livelihood. Aimed at increasing the productivity and reducing the labor involved, we have designed a surface water cleaning and fertilizer spraying robot and IoT-based agribot that can spray on top of deep duckweeds and clean them for further use. This robot is designed to execute the basic functions required to be carried out in farms. Our aim is to provide a controlled automotive spraying mechanism with atmospheric conditions in surface water cleaning system and monitoring design. This limitation is overcome in the existing system. Based on the trials done the system is capable of performing the seeding operation.

4.6 Conclusion

Using IoT (Internet of Things) in agriculture has the potential to change the environment for the better and make factories more efficient; all the elements of IoT solutions are smarter cities and smart vehicles. However, the use of technology such as IoT in agriculture has a significant impact. So, in order to fulfill the population's appetite, the farming sector has to take the IoT power. And in every scenario the need for more food requirement has to be met against all the challenges. People can't die from food and starvation! Sustainable agriculture relies on IoT innovation allowing farmers and growers reduce waste and improve efficiency varying from the quantity of fertilizer used to the amount of trips taken by farmers' automobiles.

In IoT-based smart farming, an agricultural field screening tool is rendered using sensors to optimize the farming method. The farmers in all places will monitor the state of the agricultural sector. IoT-powered smart farming is especially effective as contrasted with conventional method. The usage of IoT-based smart cultivation not only emphasizes on conventional, large-scale farming practices but also enhances other specific patterns and increasing farming opportunities, such as organic farming, as well as enhancing highly conductive agriculture. When it comes to climate change issues, IoT-based agricultural trends can deliver huge benefits such as efficient water use, optimizing the inputs and treatment required, and so on. In this situation, it's all about the massive implementations of IoT-based smart agriculture, which has been a reinvented field. Technological innovation has improved over time as well as the drones used in agriculture are an excellent illustration for this. Agricultural production is one of the big corporations that use drones in post COVID-19 situations. In agriculture drones are being used to boost different agricultural practices. The processes in agriculture that surface-based and air-based drones take charge of are irrigation, crop health evaluation, seed harvesting, seed inspection, planting, and field or soil examination. Many of the benefits of choosing drones include crop quality monitoring, ease of usage, automated GIS analysis, yields-enhancing capacity and time-saving. The drone system provides a high-tech makeover to the farming environment, with preparation and policy focused on current data collection and analysis. Using the data we gather from drones, it provides us visibility into plant growth measures, field estimation, plant monitoring, canopy cover tracking, germination percentage calculation, field water tracking, stock calculation, scouting reports, grain nitrogen measurement, chlorophyll measurement, irrigation mapping, plant pressure visualization, and much more.

So, in this pandemic situations drone performs [68–70]

- Delivery of supplies
- Monitoring and ensuring compliance with lockdown
- Spraying disinfecting chemicals.

References

1. Moskvitch, K., Agricultural drones: The new farmers' market. URL, Retrieved 21 August 2015 from: http://eandt.theiet.org/magazine/2015/07/farming-drones.cfm.

2. Wadke, R., *Insurers now employing drones to check claims by farmers*, The Hindu-Business Line, 14 March 2020, [online] http://www.the-hindubusinessline.com/economy/agribusiness/insurers-now-using-deploy-drones-to-check-claims-by-farmers/article9583909.ece.
3. Team, D., *Data Science in Agriculture—Advancing Together and Benefiting Farmers*, DataFlair, 27-Sep-2019, [Online]. Available: urlhttps://dataflair. training/blogs/data-science-in-agriculture/.
4. Jiménez-Donaire, V. *et al.*, Optimising calibration of on-line visible (vis) and near infrared (NIR) sensor for measurement of key soil properties in vegetable crop fields, *EGUGA*, 927, 2014.
5. *Indian Council of Agricultural Research, Vision 2020*, ICAR, URL, (20th Aug 2015): http://www.icar.org.in/en/node/9638.
6. *Indian Council of Agricultural Research, Vision 2030*, ICAR, URL, (20th Aug 2015): http://www.icar.org.in/en/node/9638.
7. Schimmelpfennig, D., *Farm profits and adoption of precision agriculture*, ERR-217. U.S. Department of Agriculture, Economic Research Service, No. 1477-2016-121190, 2016.
8. Reardon, T., Echeverria, R., Berdegué, J., Minten, B., Liverpool-Tasie, S., Tschirley, D., Zilberman, D., Rapid transformation of food systems in developing regions: Highlighting the role of agricultural research & innovations. *Agric. Syst.*, 172, 47–59, 2019.
9. Saiz-Rubio, V. and Rovira-Más, F., From smart farming towards agriculture 5.0: A review on crop data management. *Agronomy*, 10, 2, 207, 2020.
10. Díez, C., Haciaunaagriculturainteligente. *Cuaderno de Campo*, 60, 4–11, 2017.
11. Accenture Digital, Digital Agriculture: Improving Profitability. Available online: https://www.accenture.com/_acnmedia/accenture/conversionassets/dotcom/ documents/global/pdf/digital_3/accenture-digital-agriculture-point-of-view. pdf (accessed on 29 December 2019).
12. CEMA, Digital Farming: What Does It Really Mean? Available online: http:// www.cema-agri.org/publication/digital-farming-what-does-it-really-mean (accessed on 17 September 2019).
13. Nierenberg, D., Agriculture Needs to Attract More Young People. Available online: http://www.gainhealth.org/knowledge-centre/worlds-farmers-age-new-blood-needed (accessed on 18 September 2019).
14. European Commission, *Generational Renewal in EU Agriculture: Statistical Background*, pp. 1–10, DG Agriculture & Rural Development: Economic analysis of EU agriculture unit, Brussels, Belgium, 2012.
15. Paneva, V., Generational Renewal. Available online: https://enrd.ec.europa. eu/enrd-thematic-work/generational-renewal_en (accessed on 28 December 2019).
16. Brown, Alpha, What is IoT in Agriculture? Farmers Aren't Quite Sure Despite $4bn US Opportunity—Report. Available online: https://agfundernews.

com/iot-agriculture-farmers-arent-quite-sure-despite-4bn-usopportunity. html (accessed on 28 December 2019).

17. Gralla, P., Precision Agriculture Yields Higher Profits, Lower Risks. Available online: https://www.hpe.com/us/en/insights/articles/precision-agriculture-yields-higher-profits-lower-risks-1806.html (accessed on29 December 2019).

18. Manyica, J., Chui, M., Brown, B., Bughin, J., Dobbs, R., Roxburgh, C., Hung Byers, A., Big data: The next frontier for innovation, competition, and productivity. McKinsey Global Institute 2011, 1–137, May 2011.

19. Cloud Computing. URL (26th Aug 2015): https://en.wikipedia.org/wiki/Cloud_computing.

20. Internet of Things. URL (26th Aug 2015): https://en.wikipedia.org/wiki/Internet_of_Things.

21. Perera, C., Liu, H., Jayawardena, S., The Emerging Internet of Things Marketplace From an Industrial Perspective: A Survey. *Emerg. Top. Comput. IEEE Trans.*, 3, 4, 585–598, February 2015.

22. Earon, Founder of PrecisionHawk, URL (26th Aug 2015): http://dronelife.com/2015/04/06/qa-weith-precisionhawk-founder-dr-ernest-earon/.

23. Sarni, W., Mariani, J., Kaji, J., From Dirt to Data: The Second Green Revolution and IoT, Deloitte insights. Available online: https://www2.deloitte.com/insights/us/en/deloitte-review/issue-18/second-greenrevolution-and-internet-of-things.html#endnote-sup-9 (accessed on 18 September 2019).

24. Mykleby, M., Doherty, P., Makower, J., *The New Grand Strategy: Restoring America's Prosperity, Security, and Sustainability in the 21st Century*, St. Martin's Press, 2016.

25. Manyica, J., Chui, M., Brown, B., Bughin, J., Dobbs, R., Roxburgh, C., Hung Byers, A., *Big Data: The Next Frontier for Innovation, Competition, and Productivity*, McKinsey, Available online: https://www.mckinsey.com/business-functions/mckinsey-digital/our-insights/big-data-the-next-frontier-for-innovation (accessed on 21 November 2019).

26. Zambon, I., Cecchini, M., Egidi, G., Saporito, M.G., Colantoni, A., Revolution 4.0: Industry vs. Agriculture in a Future Development for SMEs. *Processes*, 7, 36, 2019.

27. Walch, K., How AI Is Transforming Agriculture. Available online: https://www.forbes.com/sites/cognitiveworld/2019/07/05/how-ai-is-transforming-agriculture/ (accessed on 1 January 2020).

28. Bechar, A. and Vigneault, C., Agricultural robots for field operations: Concepts and components. *Biosyst. Eng.*, 149, 94–111, 2016.

29. Husni, M.I., Hussein, M.K., Bin Zainal, M.S., Hamzah, A., Md Nor, D., Poad, H., Soil Moisture Monitoring Using Field Programmable Gate Array. *Indones. J. Electr. Eng. Comput. Sci.*, 11, 1, 169–174, July 2018.

30. Tzounis, A., Katsoulas, N., Bartzanas, T., Kittas, C., Internet of things in agriculture, recent advances and future challenges. *Biosyst. Eng.*, 164, 31–48, Dec 2017.

31. *E-agriculture in Action: Drones for Agriculture*, Book published, March, 2018, Available at, http://www.fao.org/in-action/e-agriculture-strategy-guide/documents/detail/en/c/1114182/ Accessed: Apr. 25, 2019. [Online]. https://steveblank.com/2014/02/19/how-to-be-smarter-than-your-investors-continuous-customer-discovery/.

32. Bechar, A. and Vigneault, C., Agricultural robots for field operations, Part 2: Operations and systems. *Biosyst. Eng.*, 153, 110–128, 2017.

33. Bergerman, M., Billingsley, J., Reid, J., van Henten, E., Robotics in agriculture and forestry, in: *Springer Handbook of Robotics*, pp. 1463–1492, Springer, Cham, 2016.

34. Shamshiri, R.R., Weltzien, C., Hameed, I.A., Yule, I.J., Grift, T.E., Balasundram, S.K., Pitonakova, L., Ahmad, D., Chowdhary, G., Research and development in agricultural robotics: A perspective of digitalfarming. *Int. J. Agric. Biol. Eng.*, 11, 1–14, 2018.

35. Barnes, G., Volkmann, W., Sherko, R., Kelm, K., Drones for peace: Part 1 of 2 design and testing of a UAV-based cadastral surveying and mapping methodology in Albania, in: *Proceedings of the Annual World Bank Conference on Land and Poverty*, Washington, DC, USA, 2014, March, pp. 24–27.

36. da Silva, F.B., Scott, S.D., Cummings, M.L., *Design Methodology for Unmanned Aerial Vehicle (UAV) Team Coordination, MIT Technical Report*, URL (26th Aug 2015): http://web.mit.edu/aeroastro/labs/halab/papers/HAL2007-05.pdf.

37. *Top 5 Drones For Commercial And Consumer Applications*, URL (26th Aug 2015): http://www.bidnessetc.com/business/top-5-drones-for-commercial-and-consumer-applications/.

38. Keshtgari, M. and Deljoo, A., A wireless sensor network solution for precision agriculture based on Zigbee technology. 4, 25–30, 2012.

39. Lu, G., Krishnamachari, B., Raghavendra, C.S., Adaptive energy-efficient and low-latency MAC for data gathering in sensor networks. *Proc. WMAN, Institute fur MedienInformatik*, Ulm, pp. 2440–2443, 2004.

40. Busetta, P., Rönnquist, R., Hodgson, A., Lucas, A., Jack intelligent agents—Components for intelligent agents in Java, in: *AgentLink News Letter*, vol. 2, no. 1, pp. 2–5, 1999.

41. Graham, J.R. and Decker, K.S., Towards a distributed, environment-centered agent framework, in: *International Workshop on Agent Theories, Architectures, and Languages*, Springer, Berlin, Heidelberg, pp. 290–304, 1999.

42. Agent Oriented Software Pty Ltd., *JACK Intelligent Agents User Guide*, 2012, URL (26th Aug 2015):http://www.aosgrp.com/documentation/jack/Agent_Manual.pdf.

43. Cooperative Engagement Capability, 1995. (of US DoD), URL (26th Aug 2015): http://www.jhuapl.edu/ techdigest/td/td1604/APLteam.pdf.

44. Peterson, J.L., *Petri Nets for Modelling of Systems—Theory and Practice*, Prentice-Hall, 1982, ArcView Geospatial Information System, URL (26th Aug 2015):https://en.wikipedia.org/wiki/ArcView.

45. Reddy, N., Reddy, A., Kumar, J., A critical review on agricultural robots. *Int. J. Mech. Eng. Technol. (IJMET)*, 7, 6, 2016.
46. Taskin, D., Taskin, C., Yazar, S., Developing a bluetooth low energy sensor node for greenhouse in precision agriculture as internet of things application. *Adv. Sci. Technol. Res. J.*, 12, 4, 88–96, 2018.
47. Lamborelle, A. and FernándezÁlvarez, L., Farming 4.0: The Future of Agriculture? Available online: https://www.euractiv.com/section/agriculture-food/infographic/farming-4-0-the-future-of-agriculture/ (accessed on 21 November 2019).
48. Elijah, O., Rahman, T.A., Orikumhi, I., Leow, C.Y., Hindia, M.N., An Overview of Internet of Things (IoT) and Data Analytics in Agriculture: Benefits and Challenges. *IEEE Internet Things J.*, 5, 5, 3758–3773, Oct. 2018.
49. Murugesan, R., Sudarsanam, S.K., Malathi, G., Vijayakumar, V., Neelanarayanan, V., Venugopal, R., Rekha, D., Summit, S., Rahul, B., Atishi, M. *et al.*, Artificial Intelligence and Agriculture 5. 0. *Int. J. Recent Technol. Eng. (IJRTE)*, 8, 8, 2019.
50. Zhang, Q., *Precision Agriculture Technology for Crop Farming*, 1st ed, CRC Press and Taylor & Francis Group, Boca Raton, FL, USA, 2015.
51. Rovira-Más, F., (Coordinator), VineScout European Project. Available online: www.vinescout.eu (accessed on 21 November 2019).
52. Tobe, F., What's Slowing the Use of Robots in the Ag Industry? Available online: https://www.therobotreport.com/whats-slowing-the-use-of-robots-in-the-ag-industry/ (accessed on 21 November 2019).
53. Diago, M.P., Rovira-Más, F., Saiz-Rubio, V., Faenzi, E., Evain, S., Ben Ghozlen, N., Labails, S., Stoll, M., Scheidweiler, M., Millot, C. *et al.*, The "eyes" of the VineRobot: Non-destructive and autonomous vineyard monitoring on-the-go, in: *Proceedings of the 62nd German Winegrowers' Congress*, Sttutgart, Germany, 27–30 November 2016.
54. Dikaiakos, M.D., Katsaros, D., Mehra, P., Pallis, G., Vakali, A., Cloud computing: Distributed internet computing for IT and scientific research. *IEEE Internet Comput.*, 13, 5, 10–13, 2009.
55. Suradhaniwar, S., Kar, S., Nandan, R., Raj, R., Jagarlapudi, A., Geo-ICDTs: Principles and Applications in Agriculture, in: *Geospatial Technologies in Land Resources Mapping, Monitoring and Management, Geotechnologies and the Environment*, vol. 21, G. Reddy, and S. Singh, (Eds.), Springer, Cham, 2018.
56. Steidle Neto, A.J., Zolnier, S., de Carvalho Lopes, D., Development and evaluation of an automated system for fertigation control in soilless tomato production. *Comput. Electron. Agric.*, 103, 17–25, 2014.
57. Venkatesan, R., Kathrine, G., Jaspher, W., Ramalakshmi, K., Internet of Things Based Pest Management Using Natural Pesticides for Small Scale Organic Gardens. *J. Comput. Theor. Nanosci.*, 15, 9-10, Sep. 2018.

58. Lavanya, G., Rani, C., Ganeshkumar, P., An automated low cost IoT based Fertilizer Intimation System for smart agriculture. *Sustainable Comput.: Inf. Syst.*, 2019.

59. Saiz-Rubio, V., Diago, M., Rovira-Más, F., Cuenca, A., Gutiérrez, S., Tardáguila, J., Physical requirements for vineyard monitoring robots, in: *Proceedings of the XIX World Congress of CIGR*, Antalya, Turkey, 22–25 April 2018, pp. 1–4.

60. Naïo Technologies, Features & Benefits OZWeeding Robot. Available online: https://www.naio-technologies.com/en/agricultural-equipment/weeding-robot-oz/ (accessed on 21 November 2019).

61. Thomson, G., The global unmanned spray system (GUSS). *Resource*, 26, 9–10, 2019.

62. K. Cavender-Bares and J.B. Lofgren, Robotic Platform and Method for Performing Multiple Functions in Agricultural Systems, U.S. Patent US9265187B2, 23 February 2016.

63. Hameed, I.A., A Coverage Planner for Multi-Robot Systems in Agriculture, in: *Proceedings of the IEEE International Conference on Real-time Computing and Robotics (RCAR)*, Kandima, Maldives, 1–5 August 2018, pp. 698–704.

64. Ball, D., Ross, P., English, A., Patten, T., Upcroft, B., Fitch, R., Robotics for Sustainable Broad-Acre Agriculture. Available online: https://www.research-gate.net/publication/283722961_Robotics_for_Sustainable_Broad-Acre_Agriculture (accessed on 21 November 2019).

65. Tobe, F., The Ultimate Guide to Agricultural Robotics, Available online: https://www.roboticsbusinessreview.com/agriculture/the_ultimate_guide_to_agricultural_robotics/ccessed on 21 November 2019).

66. Mouazen, A.M., Alhwaimel, S.A., Kuang, B., Waine, T.W., Fusion of data from multiple soil sensors for the delineation of water holding capacity zones. *Precis. Agric.*, 13, 745–751.

67. Vågen, T.-G., Winowiecki, L.A., Tondoh, J.E., Desta, L.T., Gumbricht, T. *et al.*, Mapping of soil properties and land degradation risk in Africa using MODIS reflectance. *Geoderma*, 263, 216–225, 2016.

68. Waine, T.W., Simms, D.M., Taylor, J.C., Juniper, G.R., Towards improving the accuracy of opium yield estimates with remote sensing. *Int. J. Remote Sens.*, 35, 16, 6292–6309.

69. Mondal, T. and Madhur, M., Keep An Eye On Covid-19 Drone Use Cases For Future Business Opportunities, https://www.hfsresearch.com/pointsofview/Keep-an-eye-on-COVID-19-drone-use-cases-for-future-business-opportunities Accessed May 13, 2020.

70. Santhi, P.V., Kapileswar, N., Chenchela, V.K.R., Prasad, C.H.V.S., Sensor and vision based autonomous AGRIBOT for sowing seeds. *International Conf. on Energy, Communication, Data Analytics and Soft Computing*, Chennai, 2017.

5

IoT and Machine Learning-Based Approaches for Real Time Environment Parameters Monitoring in Agriculture: An Empirical Review

Parijata Majumdar[1] and Sanjoy Mitra[2*]

[1]*Department of Computer Science and Engineering, National Institute of Technology, Agartala, India*
[2]*Department of Computer Science and Engineering, Tripura Institute of Technology, Agartala, India*

Abstract

Agriculture monitoring is a promising domain for the economy as it is the primary contributor of job market and food production. Farmers are facing challenges in reducing water consumption and formulating the best irrigation schedules due to discontinuous monsoon, changing weather conditions for improvising crops yield and soil fertility. IoT-based decision making gives real time insight of weather parameters based on cost-effective sensor data acquisition and intelligent processing that reduces manual labor and saves time in Agriculture. Here in this chapter, we present an empirical review on real time visualization and on demand access of weather parameters even from remote locations and intelligent processing using IoT-based solutions like Machine Learning (ML). The ever-augmenting technologies like Machine Learning paved the way for identifying and adapting changes of crop design and irrigation patterns taking into account multi-dimensional large variety of weather data to accurately predict climate conditions suitable for crop irrigation. Hence, this chapter offers a detailed review of IoT-based Machine Learning solutions for precision Agriculture depending on weather and irrigation schedules. This chapter also highlights security solution based on Machine learning capable of handling illegal data access by intruders during cloud data storage.

Corresponding author: mail.smitra@gmail.com

Amitava Choudhury, Arindam Biswas, Manish Prateek and Amlan Chakrabarti (eds.)
Agricultural Informatics: Automation Using the IoT and Machine Learning, (89–116) © 2021
Scrivener Publishing LLC

Keywords: IoT, wireless sensors, machine learning, smart agriculture, weather, irrigation

5.1 Introduction

India is primarily an agricultural economy. Farmers need to control irrigation, as intermittent monsoon droughts and flooding lead either to low or excessive irrigation, which decreases soil fertility and interferes with crop yield. Due to unequal water supply, lixidation, denitrification and rolling out of mud the amount of fertilizer is also wasted. Traditional irrigation methods such as furrows, water sprinklers cannot predict the exact water needed and water supply duration. Emerging concepts of Internet of Things (IoT) and wireless sensor networks allow smart agricultural monitoring, processing and storage of real-time weather data. The wireless sensors used for weather data analysis help us to understand climate change's influence on crop growth and reduce the problem of instability and parameter variability due to distant location in real time. Such a study of soil moisture and weather restrictions may also be rendered in order to control irrigation schedules minimizing loss of water. Unlike conventional methods, the weather data implanted in small microcontrollers are exchanged in real time by using appropriate communication protocols from near or remote areas which lead to precise, economic time-saving monitoring of agriculture.

IoT can solve in real time the problem of soil conditions, the content of soil moisture, temperature and humidity levels, use of fertilizers, cultivation of crops to optimize water usage, which is unaddressed by conventional farming techniques for sustainable agriculture growth.

5.2 Machine Learning (ML)-Based IoT Solution

IoT-centered ML solutions include the autonomous framework for local farmers based on the sensor data, which is highly scalable, simple to use, reliable and offers flexibility. Machine learning can provide a range of suggestions and insights into the decisions of farmers by analyzing statistically and recognizing links between these sensor-generated Big data. Machine learning helps farmers by determining the most suitable type of crop to be grown based on location, weather and soil type etc. all over the world.

Figure 5.1 shows IoT-based solution for smart farming based on irrigation and weather parameters.

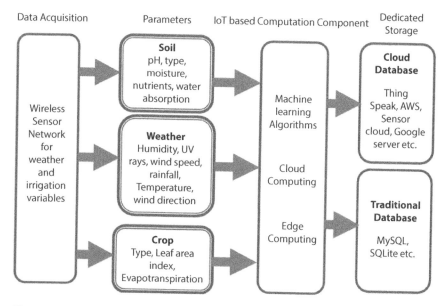

Figure 5.1 IoT-based intelligent agriculture monitoring.

5.3   Motivation of the Work

Solutions focused on IoT provide versatile, easy to use, robust and adaptable autonomous system for local farmers based on sensor generated data. For effective decision making in light of the problem of management of irrigation schedules reducing water and fertilizer wastage by environmental parameter acquisition in real time, several IoT based approaches are used in irrigation and weather monitoring perspective as these two factors are pivotal for precision Agriculture management.

5.4   Literature Review of IoT-Based Weather and Irrigation Monitoring for Precision Agriculture

In order to guarantee a high degree of agricultural precision, IoT brings automation through the irrigation methods such as furrow, soil, dripping, capillary and sprinklers by allowing sensor communication according to different weather parameters such as temperature, humidity, wind speed, wind direction, pressure, gases, UV radiation, etc. On processing sensor data, actuator is enabled to take irrigation controlling measures, even in remote locations. Via accurate prediction of weather parameters using cost effective sensors and reduced manual work by farmers, IoT enables intelligent decision-making to increase crop yield.

Table 5.1 gives an overview of IoT-based irrigation methods with claimed advantages and shortcomings. Pivotal environment parameters, unmonitored parameters and mode of the work are also shown.

Table 5.2 gives an overview of Communication protocols used to communicate sensor data to the cloud with Security attack perception in IoT layered architecture used by different methods of IoT-based irrigation monitoring.

Table 5.3 details about the Sensors with measuring range, microcontrollers with communication interfaces and data storage used by different methods of IoT-based irrigation monitoring.

Table 5.4 gives an overview of IoT-based weather parameter methods with claimed advantages and shortcomings. Pivotal environment parameters, unmonitored parameters and mode of the work are also shown.

Table 5.5 gives an overview of Communication protocols used to communicate sensor data to the cloud with security attack perception in IoT-layered architecture used by different methods of IoT-based weather parameter monitoring.

Table 5.6 details about the sensors with measuring range, microcontrollers with communication interfaces and data storage used by different methods of IoT-based weather parameter monitoring.

5.5 Literature Review of Machine Learning-Based Weather and Irrigation Monitoring for Precision Agriculture

The IoT solution based on machine learning is a close loop intelligent irrigation control system, which makes decisions and gathers knowledge from sensor-generated weather parameters. A broad variety of weather data is used to adjust irrigation schedules according to changing weather conditions by applying artificial neural networks, classification and regression algorithms. For mathematical modeling fuzzy logic is also used where accuracy of user dependent fuzzy logic must be measured by long data surveillance periods of unpredictable weather parameters. The ideal weather parameters is set as a threshold value to be compared with changing weather parameters for agriculture precision to improvise crop yield based on current climate conditions in order to continuously update irrigation schedules. The nomenclature of various ML algorithms used in

Table 5.1 Review of different methods on IoT-based smart irrigation monitoring.

Method	Claimed advantages	Shortcoming	Mode of work	Monitored parameters	Unmonitored parameters
[1]	Automated inexpensive irrigation system.	More parameters are required for precision in monitoring.	Hardware field.	Soil moisture, gas, light intensity.	Temperature, humidity, wind speed, direction, rain and solar energy, pH.
[2]	Consistent monitoring of current crop condition.	Low cost sensors have to be used for cost effective irrigation.	Hardware field.	Temperature, wind speed, humidity, wind direction, solar radiation, rain.	Soil moisture, soil pH, wind speed.
[3]	Weather parameters are compared with past data to increase adaptability.	Sensors data accuracy is needed to be analyzed.	Hardware prototype.	Soil moisture, Temperature, humidity, air pollutants.	Soil pH, wind speed and direction, rain, solar energy.
[4]	Soil condition is monitored for regulating water supply using Travelling Salesman.	Sensors data accuracy and power consumption has to be analyzed.	Hardware field.	Soil pH, soil moisture.	Temperature, humidity, wind speed and direction, rain, solar energy.
[5]	Crop transpiration is also used with water balance to decide irrigation schedules.	Accuracy of sensor data, power issues are not unaddressed.	Hardware field.	Soil moisture, temperature, humidity.	Wind speed and direction, rain, solar energy.

Table 5.2 Details of communication protocols used with security vulnerabilities.

Method	Protocol & N/W	Frequency	Data rate	Range	IoT layer with security attack
[1]	WiFi–LAN.	92.4–5 GHz	54–600 Mb/s, 6.75 Gb/s	100 m	Network access and physical layer-DoS, jamming, man in the middle, spoofing, routing attacks.
[2]	Zigbee–LAN, GSM–LAN.	868–915 MHz, 2.4 GHz	850–1,900 MHz, 250 kb/s, 80–384 Kb/s	10–50 m, 5–30 km	MAC layer-DoS, jamming, eaves dropping, User Tracking. Network access and physical layer-DoS, jamming, man in the middle, spoofing, routing attacks.
[3]	WiFi–LAN, GSM–LAN.	2.4–5 GHz, 850–1,900 MHz	54–600 Mb/s,6.75 Gb/s, 80–384 Kb/s	100 m, 5–30 km	Network access and physical layer-DoS, jamming, man in the middle, spoofing, routing attacks.
[4]	Zigbee—LAN.	868–915 MHz	250 kb/s	10–50 m	MAC layer-DoS, jamming, man in the middle, spoofing, routing attacks.
[5]	GPRS—LAN.	850–1,900 MHz	80–384 Kb/s	5–30 km	Network access and physical layer-DoS, jamming, man in the middle, spoofing, routing attacks.

Table 5.3 Details of sensors, micro-controllers and data storage used by different methods.

Method	Sensor & measuring range	Micro-controller & communication interface	Data storage
[1]	Undefined Soil moisture, CO_2, SO_2, light intensity sensor.	Raspberry Pi 3 with Serial Interface, Display Serial Interface.	Undefined database.
[2]	SHT 15-1,800 w/m², Solar Pyranometer, wind speed sensor measuring wind speed from 3 to 125 mph.	PIC18F2620 with Serial Interface, GSM Modem or Zigbee module, RS 232 Interface.	Undefined database.
[3]	DHT11-55–150 °C, 20–90%, MQ2-200–10,000 ppm, MQ135-10–300 ppb, MQ131-100 ppb/50 ppb, MQ9-500–10,000 ppm.	Undefined microcontroller.	Undefined server.
[4]	Unnamed Soil moisture, temperature, humidity, sunshine, radiation, wind speed, rain fall sensor	Unnamed central controller.	Cloud database.
[5]	–	MCU ARM M3 kernel STM32F103 with I²C, SPI, UART.	Weather database.

Agriculture monitoring are Support vector machines (SVM), Artificial neural network (ANN), Support vector regression (SVR), Linear discriminant analysis (LDA), Radial basis function (RBF), Decision tree classifier (DTC), Genetic algorithm (GA), Fuzzy logic (FL), Random forest (RF), Reinforcement learning (RL), etc.

Table 5.7 gives an overview of irrigation algorithms with claimed advantages, shortcomings, Pivotal environment parameters and overlooked parameters. Mode of the work is also shown.

Table 5.4 Review of different IoT-based smart weather parameters monitoring.

Method	Claimed advantages	Shortcomings	Mode of the work	Monitored parameters	Unmonitored parameters
[6]	Economic and low power monitoring.	More parameters have to be compared for precision in monitoring.	Hardware field.	Temperature humidity, wind direction	Wind speed, direction, pressure, gas, soil moisture, UV radiation.
[7]	Cost effective and adaptable monitoring.	Accuracy of the sensor data and power consumption has to be taken care off.	Laboratory Proto type.	Temperature, humidity, wind, UV radiation, rain.	Wind speed, direction, pressure, sunset, moon phase, UV radiation.
[8]	Cost effective, flexible monitoring.	System without net connectivity using renewable energy sources for rural area.	Laboratory Proto type.	Wind speed, wind direction and rainfall	Temperature, atmospheric pressure, humidity, UV radiation.
[9]	Cost effective monitoring.	Accuracy of sensor data is needed& high power consumption.	Laboratory Proto type.	Temperature, humidity, pressure, rainfall, light intensity.	Wind speed, wind direction and rainfall, UV radiation.

(Continued)

Table 5.4 Review of different IoT-based smart weather parameters monitoring. (*Continued*)

Method	Claimed advantages	Shortcomings	Mode of the work	Monitored parameters	Unmonitored parameters
[10]	Cost effective monitoring.	Long-time weather forecasting for coverage of larger area has to be done.	Simulation based.	Temperature pressure, humidity, wind speed.	Wind direction and rainfall, UV radiation.
[11]	Flexible cost effective data acquisition in real time.	Low power consumption and range of sensors has to be increased.	Laboratory Proto type.	Temperature, humidity, pressure, altitude.	Wind speed, wind direction and rainfall.
[12]	Real-time cost-effective monitoring.	Data analysis from multiple sensors has to be done while minimizing power usage.	Hardware field.	Temperature, relative humidity, soil pH.	Wind speed, wind direction, atmospheric pressure.

Table 5.5 Details of communication protocols used with security vulnerabilities.

Method	Protocol and Network	Frequency	Data rate	Range	IoT layer with security attack
[6]	Xbee-LAN WiFi-LAN.	868–915 MHz, 2.4 GHz, 2.4–5 GHz.	250 kb/s, 54–600 Mb/s, 6.75 Gb/s	10–50 m, up to 100 m	MAC Layer-DoS, jamming, eaves dropping, user tracking. Network access and physical layer-DoS, jamming, man in the middle, spoofing, routing attacks.
[7]	nRF24l01+ -WAN	2.4 GHz	250 kbps–2 Mbps	100 m.	Perception Layer-DoS, jamming, eaves dropping, User Tracking.
[8]	Wi-Fi-LAN, GSM-LAN	2.4–5 GHz, 850–1,900 MHz	54–600 Mb/s, 6.75 Gb/s, 80–384 Kb/s	Up to 100 m, 5–30 km	Network access and physical layer-DoS, jamming, man in the middle, spoofing, routing attacks.
[9]	WiFi-LAN	2.4–5 GHz	54–600 Mb/s, 6.75 Gb/s	Up to 100 m	Network access and physical layer-DoS, jamming, man in the middle, spoofing, routing attacks.

(Continued)

Table 5.5 Details of communication protocols used with security vulnerabilities. (*Continued*)

Method	Protocol and Network	Frequency	Data rate	Range	IoT layer with security attack
[10]	Zigbee-LAN	868–915 MHz 2.4 GHz	250 kb/s	10–50 m	MAC Layer-DoS, jamming, eaves dropping, user tracking.
[11]	WiFi-LAN	2.4–5 GHz	54–600 Mb/s, 6.75 Gb/s	Up to 100 m	Transport Layer-DoS, jamming, man in the middle, spoofing, routing attacks. Network access and physical layer-DoS, jamming, man in the middle, spoofing, routing attacks.
[12]	GPRS -LAN	850–1900 MHz	80–384 Kb/s	5–30 km	Network access and physical layer-DoS, jamming, man in the middle attacks, spoofing, routing attacks.

Table 5.6 Details of sensors, micro-controllers and data storage.

Method	Sensor and measuring range	Micro-controller and communication interface	Data storage
[6]	Unnamed temperature, moisture, humidity, light, wind speed sensors.	Raspberry Pi 2 model B.	Cloud-MySQL database
[7]	FC-37 −0 to 1,024, ML8511-280–390 nm, H21A1—ON and OFF, DHT-11-55–150 °C, 20–95%.	Arduino UNO ATmega8L with I²C, SPI, UART.	–
[8]	DHT22-10–40 °C, 0–99.9% RH, BMP180-300–1,100 hPa.	Raspberry Pi with I²C, SPI, SERIAL, Arduino withI²C, SPI,UART.	MySQL database
[9]	–	ESP8266-EX with I²C.	Thing speak cloud
[10]	BMP085-30 to 110 kPa , SHT21-0–100% RH.	ArduinoUno with I²C, SPI, UART.	–
[11]	DHT11-55–150 °C, 20–95%, BMP180-300–1,100 hPa.	Raspberry Pi B+ with I²C, SPI, SERIAL.	–
[12]	Unnamed Temperature, Relative Humidity, Soil pH Sensors.	Raspberry-Pi 3.	AWS

Table 5.8 gives an overview of communication protocols used to communicate sensor data to the cloud with security attack perception in IoT layered architecture used by different methods of machine learning based irrigation monitoring.

Table 5.7 Review of different machine learning-based smart irrigation monitoring.

Method	Claimed advantages	Shortcomings	Mode of work	Monitored parameter	Unmonitored parameters
SVR and RF [13]	Interconnected Sensor nodes used for economic monitoring.	System needs to be trained on big data and has to be protected from climate adversities.	Hardware field.	Soil moisture, humidity, temperature.	Wind speed, wind direction, pressure, gas, soil pH, UV radiation.
SVR and K-MEANS clustering [14]	High precision with low error prediction of soil moisture.	Soil moisture difference has to be compared for longer duration to improve accuracy.	Hardware field.	Soil moisture, humidity, solar radiation, temperature	Wind speed, wind direction, pressure, gas, soil pH.
FL [15]	Decentralized database with Block chain security.	Accurate prediction of likelihood of a specific disease by measuring more parameters.	Hardware field.	Soil moisture, light intensity, humidity, air temperature.	Wind speed, wind direction, pressure, gas, soil pH.
FL [16]	Monitoring based on renewable energy.	Flexible system is needed to suit each farm size.	Hardware field.	Soil moisture, humidity, temperature, water level.	Wind speed, wind direction, pressure, gas, soil pH, UV rays.

(Continued)

Table 5.7 Review of different machine learning-based smart irrigation monitoring. (*Continued*)

Method	Claimed advantages	Shortcomings	Mode of work	Monitored parameter	Unmonitored parameters
RBF and FL [17]	Real-time monitoring with minimum error.	Inaccurate classification and precision is user dependent.	Hardware field.	Soil moisture, temperature, humidity, CO_2 and UV intensity	Wind speed, wind direction, pressure, soil pH.
LDA and SVM [18]	Precision, economic, low powered implementation.	Big data to be handled saving memory and with more parameters.	Hardware field.	Soil type, temperature, moisture, humidity, gas, UV intensity.	Wind speed, wind direction.
Regression [19]	Easily accessible, reliable parameter implementation.	Overfitting of unconstrained parameters to remember the training data.	Hardware field.	Soil moisture, rain and temperature.	Wind speed, wind direction, gas, solar radiation.
Feed Forward Network [20]	Consistent monitoring using structural similarity index.	No explanations are provided for parameters monitored.	Hardware field.	Soil moisture, temperature, humidity, gas, solar radiation.	Wind speed, wind direction, gas, soil pH.

(*Continued*)

Table 5.7 Review of different machine learning-based smart irrigation monitoring. (*Continued*)

Method	Claimed advantages	Shortcomings	Mode of work	Monitored parameter	Unmonitored parameters
DTC [21]	Precise monitoring done to predict fertilizer quantity and water requirement.	Security and integrity of sensor data has to be ensured for accurate analysis.	Hardware field.	Soil moisture, Temperature, Humidity.	Wind speed, wind direction, gas, soil pH.
GA [22]	Consistent monitoring to optimize power and water supply.	Exact location of water supply has to be determined regardless of the wind.	Hardware field.	Soil moisture.	Temperature, Humidity, Wind speed, wind direction, gas, soil pH.

Table 5.8 Details of communication protocols used with security vulnerabilities.

Method	Protocol and Network	Frequency	Data rate	Range	IoT layer with security attack
SVR and RF [13]	WiFi-LAN, GSM-LAN, Bluetooth- PAN	2.4–5 GHz, 850–1,900 MHz, 2.4 GHz.	54–600 Mb/s, 6.75 Gb/s, 80–384 Kb/s, 25 Mb/s.	100 m, 5–30 km, Less than 10 m	Network access and physical layer-DoS, jamming, man in the middle, spoofing, routing attacks.
SVR and K-MEANS clustering [14]	ZigBee-LAN	868–915 MHz 2.4 GHz	250 kb/s.	10–50 m	MAC layer-DoS, jamming, man in the middle, spoofing, routing attacks.
FL [15]	Wi-Fi Module ESP 8266–01-LAN	2.4–5 GHz	54–600 Mb/s, 6.75 Gb/s.	100 m	Network access and physical layer-DoS, jamming, man in the middle, spoofing, routing attacks.
FL [16]	WiFi-LAN	2.4–5 GHz	54–600 Mb/s, 6.75 Gb/s.	100 m	Network access and physical layer-DoS, jamming, man in the middle, spoofing, routing attacks.
RBF and FL [17]	Zigbee-LAN, WiFi-LAN	868–915 MHz, 2.4 GHz, 2.4–5 GHz	250 kb/s, 54–600 Mb/s, 6.75 Gb/s.	10–50 m, 100 m	MAC layer-DoS, jamming, man in the middle, spoofing, routing attacks, network access and physical layer-DoS, jamming, man in the middle, spoofing, routing attacks.

(Continued)

Table 5.8 Details of communication protocols used with security vulnerabilities. *(Continued)*

Method	Protocol and Network	Frequency and data rate	Range	Power use	IoT layer with security attack
LDA and SVM [18]	Zigbee-LAN	868–915 MHz, 2.4 GHz, 250 kb/s	10–50 m	Low	MAC layer-DoS, jamming, man in the middle, spoofing, routing attacks.
Regression [19]	WiFi-LAN	2.4–5 GHz, 54–600 Mb/s, 6.75 Gb/s	100 m	Low–high	Network access and physical layer-DoS, jamming, man in the middle, spoofing, routing attacks.
Feed Forward [20]	Zigbee-LAN WiFi-LAN	868–915 MHz, 2.4–5 GHz, 250 kb/s, 54–600 Mb/s, 6.75 Gb/s	10–50 m, 100 m	Low, Low–high	MAC Layer-DoS, jamming, man in the middle, spoofing, routing attacks. Network access and physical layer-DoS, jamming, man in the middle, spoofing, routing attacks.
DTC [21]	Wi-Fi-LAN	2.4–5 GHz, 54–600 Mb/s, 6.75 Gb/s	100 m	Low–high	Network access and physical layer-DoS, jamming, man in the middle, spoofing, routing attacks.
GA [22]	WiFi-LAN, GSM-LAN	2.4–5 GHz, 850–1,900 MHz, 54–600 Mb/s, 6.75 Gb/s, 80–384 Kb/s	100 m, 5–30 km	Low–high, High	Network access and physical layer-DoS, jamming, man in the middle, spoofing, routing attacks.

Table 5.9 details about the sensors with measuring range, micro-controllers with communication interfaces and data storage used by different methods of machine learning-based irrigation monitoring.

Table 5.10 gives an overview of weather parameter monitoring methods with claimed advantages, shortcomings. Pivotal environment parameters and overlooked parameters. Mode of the work is also shown.

Table 5.11 gives an overview of communication protocols used to communicate sensor data to the cloud with security attack perception in IoT layered architechture used by different methods of machine learning-based weather parameter monitoring.

Table 5.12 details about the sensors with measuring range, micro-controllers with communication interfaces and data storage used by different methods of machine learning-based weather parameter monitoring.

Figure 5.2 below shows the mode of work in IoT-based weather and irrigation monitoring. Figure 5.3 below shows the mode of work in ML-based weather and irrigation monitoring. Figure 5.4 below shows data storage used in IoT-based weather and irrigation monitoring. Figure 5.5 below shows data storage used in ML-based weather and irrigation monitoring.

From Figure 5.2 it is quite evident that most of the work in IoT solution based weather and irrigation monitoring mainly relies on hardware field implementation in real time. Whereas, very least work is done in software simulation.

From Figure 5.3 it is quite evident that most of the work in ML-based IoT solution based weather and irrigation monitoring mainly relies on Hardware field implementation in real time. Whereas, very least work is done in Software Simulation.

From Figure 5.4 we can see that in most of the methods, database names are not defined. In rest of the methods, data has been stored in Cloud platforms like ThingSpeak, AWS, Sensor Cloud etc. Very few methods relies on traditional database like SQLite, MySQL etc.

From Figure 5.5 we can see that data has been widely stored in Cloud platforms like ThingSpeak, AWS, Sensor Cloud etc rather than traditional database like SQLite, MySQL etc. In few methods, database name are not defined.

Cloud Storage is very economic compared to traditional Databases. Cloud is capable of storing data in a single data repository and chances of losing data are also minimized. Cloud storage though offers high flexibility in data storage, it is very much vulnerable to security attack when sensor generated data is communicated by means of IoT protocols in IoT layered architechture to the Cloud.

Table 5.9 Details of sensors, micro-controllers and data storage.

Method	Sensor & measuring range	Micro-controller & communication interface	Data storage
SVR and RF [13]	DHT11—20–90%, 55–150 °C, MQ2—200–10,000 ppm.	Arduino Uno Mega 2560 Rev3 with I^2C, SPI, UART, Raspberry Pi 3 B+ with I^2C, SPI, SERIAL.	Server/Database Cloud
SVR, K-MEANS clustering [14]	VH-400-0-3v, DHT22—10–40 °C, 0–99.9% RH	Raspberry Pi with I^2C, SPI, SERIAL, Arduino Uno with I^2C, SPI, UART.	SQLite database, MySQL database
FL [15]	DHT-11—20–90%, 55–150 °C, YL-69-0-1023.	Arduino UNO R3 with I2C, SPI, UART.	Plant database.
FL [16]	Unnamed Soil moisture & Humidity/Temperature sensor, flow sensor with 0.5 power.	ARM Processor with UART.	SQL database
RBF and FL [17]	Unnamed Soil moisture Humidity/Temperature, CO_2 sensor.	Raspberry Pi with I^2C, SPI, SERIAL	Wireless Gateway with embedded web server.

(Continued)

Table 5.9 Details of sensors, micro-controllers and data storage. (*Continued*)

Method	Sensor and measuring range	Micro-controller and communication interface	Data storage
LDA and SVM [18]	DHT11-20–90%, 55–150 °C, VH400-0-3v.	Raspberry Pi with I²C, SPI, SERIAL.	ThingSpeak
Regression [19]	Unnamed moisture, temperature, rain, current sensor.	Raspberry Pi with I²C, SPI, SERIAL.	Sensor Cloud
Feed Forward [20]	Unnamed Soil moisture, temperature/humidity Sensor, CO_2 sensor.	ATMEGA328 with I²C, SPI, SERIAL, Raspberry Pi 2 with I²C, SPI, SERIAL.	MySQL database
DTC [21]	DHT-11-20–90%, 55–150 °C, YL-69-0-1023.	Arduino with I²C, SPI, UART.	ThingSpeak
GA [22]	Unnamed Soil moisture sensor.	Arduino UNO with I²C, SPI, UART.	Sensor cloud

Table 5.10 Review of different machine learning-based smart weather monitoring.

Method	Claimed advantages	Shortcoming	Mode of work	Monitored parameters	Unmonitored parameters
ANN and RBF [23]	Energy and power independent monitoring.	Faster computation of data is needed.	Laboratory Prototype.	Humidity, temperature and solar radiation.	Wind speed, direction, pressure, gas, soil moisture, temperature, UV radiation.
NN [24]	Inexpensive real-time monitoring.	Data storage in a dedicated place is needed.	Laboratory Prototype.	Temperature, wind speed, wind direction.	Air humidity, temperature, soil moisture and solar radiation.
Multiple linear regression [25]	Inexpensive higher precision monitoring.	Security, integrity of sensor data has to be ensured.	Simulation based.	Temperature, pollutants, humidity, pressure, rainfall, dust particles and light etc.	Wind speed, direction, pressure, gas, soil moisture, temperature, UV radiation.

Table 5.11 Details of communication protocols used with security vulnerabilities.

Method	Protocol and Network	Frequency	Data rate	Range	IoT layer with security attack
[23]	Xbee-LAN	2.4 GHz	250 KB/s	10–100 m	Physical layer-DoS, jamming, man in the middle, spoofing, eaves dropping, routing attacks.
[25]	Wi-Fi-LAN	2.4–5 GHz	54–600 Mb/s, 6.75 Gb/s	100 m	Network access and physical layer-DoS, jamming, man in the middle, eaves dropping, spoofing, routing attacks.

Table 5.12 Details of sensors, micro-controllers and data storage.

Method	Sensor & measuring range	Micro-controller and communication interface	Data storage
[23]	SP-110-0–400 mV, SHT75-0–100%.	Raspberry PI version B with I²C, SPI, SERIAL interface.	SQLite database
[24]	CNY70-0.8–4.8 V, MCP9700-(−40 °C to + 125 °C).	MC9S 12DG256.	–
[25]	MQ135-10–1,000 ppm, MQ7-20–2,000 ppm, DHT11-20–90%, 0–50 °C BMP180-300 to 1,100 hPa.	Arduino Mega ATmega2560 with I²C, SPI, UART interface.	ThingSpeak

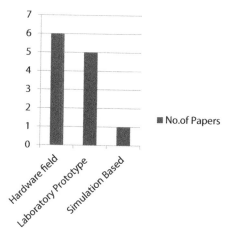

Figure 5.2 Mode of work in IoT-based weather and irrigation monitoring.

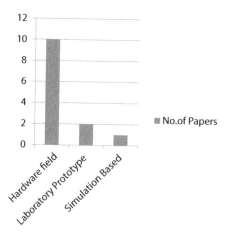

Figure 5.3 Mode of work in ML-based weather and irrigation monitoring.

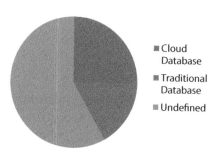

Figure 5.4 Data storage in IoT-based weather and irrigation monitoring.

Figure 5.5 Data storage in ML-based weather and irrigation monitoring.

Table 5.13 ML algorithms to handle security threats in IoT layered architecture.

ML methods	IoT layers	Security attack solution
ANN, RL [26]	Physical/Perception Layer	DoS, jamming, man in the middle, spoofing, routing attacks.
SVM,K means [26]	Network Layer	DoS, jamming, man in the middle, spoofing, routing attacks.
DT,RF,K means [26]	Application Layer	DoS, repudiation, eaves dropping, Blue snarfing and Bluejacking.

Machine Learning (ML)-based IoT solution can handle unwanted tampering and illegal access of these sensor data during transmission to cloud. Machine Learning (ML) has the capability to provide security handling attacks like DoS, jamming, man in the middle, spoofing, routing attacks, repudiation, eaves dropping, Blue snarfing and Bluejacking [26].

Table 5.13 below shows different Machine Learning (ML) algorithms capable of handling different types of security threats.

5.6   Challenges

- A keen analysis of the literature reveals that weather- and irrigation automation requires particular attention towards unmonitored parameters. More number of parameters monitored more is the accuracy in optimizing irrigation schedules for improvising crop yield.

- Cost analysis of different IoT-based solutions relying on sensors and embedded micro controllers has to be done to device an economic IoT-based smart farming approach as farmers have a very low income.
- IoT layers in which various IoT communication protocols function are subjected to serious threats like altering data processing, illegal access by intruders, etc. Security mechanisms must therefore be incorporated to prevent infringement of sensor generated data during processing and storage.
- In ML-based IoT security measures, correct identification of any attack is a burning issue since if any impostor identifies the type of attack than the training data set used for implementing ML solutions can easily be modified. Hence, the attackers can change their mode of attack and its consequences on the cloud network.

5.7 Conclusion and Future Work

This paper presents a thorough analysis of weather and irrigation parameters pivotal in the IoT-based solutions for smart farming. Frequently used communication protocols working in IoT layered architecture along with security attack perception is discussed. The susceptibility of IoT security threats is also shown. Most monitored weather parameters that are critical for optimizing irrigation schedules are also established. Cheaper sensors used to predict irrigation schedules accurately help farmers to minimize manual work unlike traditional methods while obtaining high-precision data. Costly sensors would have to be replaced with economical sensors in future to derive maximum benefit by the farmers using automated IoT solutions in commercial markets. Security mechanisms like machine learning algorithms shown above and keeping data at the edge of the network may be used to trigger an intervention using actuating devices upon threat identification using Big data for training purposes for connecting things using a secure network. Cost analysis of things (sensors) has to be done to implement smart inexpensive IoT-based solution for precision in agriculture monitoring.

References

1. Dhineesh, T., Rajvi Mohammed, K., Arunprasath, S., Haribaskar, M., Madhusudanan, G., Analysis of IoT based Wireless Sensors for Environmental Monitoring in Agriculture. *Int. Res. J. Eng. Technol.*, 6, 610–614, 2019.
2. Fourati, M.A., Chebbi, W., Kamoun, A., Development of a web-based weather station for irrigation scheduling. *Third IEEE International Colloquium in Information Science and Technology (CIST)*, pp. 37–42, 2014.
3. Choudhury, S. and Chattopadhyay, S.P., Smart irrigation: IoT-based irrigation monitoring system. *Proceedings of the International Ethical Hacking Conference*, Springer, Singapore, 2018.
4. Karunanithy, K. and Velusamy, B., Energy efficient Cluster and Travelling Salesman Problem based Data Collection using WSNs for Intelligent Water Irrigation and Fertigation. *Measurement*, 161, 107835, 2020.
5. Zhang, S., Wang, M., Shi, W., Zheng, W., Construction of intelligent water saving irrigation control system based on water balance. *Proceedings of the International Federation of Automatic Control*, pp. 466–471, 2018.
6. Tenzin, S., Siyang, S., Pobkrut, T., Kerdcharoen, T., Low cost weather station for climate-smart agriculture. *Proceedings of the 9th international conference on knowledge and smart technology*, pp. 172–177, 2017.
7. Solano, G., Lama, F., Terrazos, J., Tarrillo, J., Weather station for educational purposes based on Atmega8L. *Proceedings of the 24th International Conference on Electronics, Electrical Engineering and Computing*, pp. 1–4, 2017.
8. Brito, R.C. and Favarim, F., Development of low cost weather station using free hardware and software. *Proceedings of the Latin American Robotics Symposium (LARS) and 2017 Brazilian Symposium on Robotics*, pp. 1–10, 2017.
9. Kodali, R.K. and Sahu, A., An IOT based weather information prototype using WeMos. *Proceedings of the 2nd International conference on Contemporary Computing and Informatics*, pp. 612–616, 2016.
10. Saini, H. and Thakur, A., Arduino based automatic wireless weather station with remote graphical application and alerts. *Proceedings of the International Conference on Signal Processing and Integrated Networks (SPIN)*, pp. 605–609, 2016.
11. Savic, T. and Radonjic, M., One approach to weather station design based on Raspberry Pi platform. *Proceedings of the 23rd Telecommunication Forum*, pp. 623–626, 2015.
12. Carlos, A.D.J., Rojas Estrada, L., Cardenas-Ruiz, C.A., Ariza-Colpas, P.P., Piñeres-Melo, M.A., Ramayo González, R.E., Morales-Ortega, R.C., Ovallos-Gazabon, D.A., Collazos-Morales, C.A., Monitoring system of environmental variables for a strawberry crop using IoT tools. *Procedia Comput. Sci.*, 170, 1083–1089, 2020.
13. Vij, A., Vijendra, S., Jain, A., Bajaj, S., Bassi, A., Sharma, A., IoT and Machine Learning Approaches for Automation of Farm Irrigation System. *Procedia Comput. Sci.*, 167, 1250–1257, 2020.

14. Goap, A., Sharma, D., Shukla, A.K., Krishna, C.R., An IoT based smart irrigation management system using Machine learning and open source technologies. *Comput. Electron. Agric.*, 155, 41–49, 2018.

15. Munir, M.S., Bajwa, I.S., Cheema, S.M., An intelligent and secure smart watering system using fuzzy logic and blockchain. *J. Comput. Electr. Eng.*, 77, 109–119, 2019.

16. Al-Ali, A.R., Al Nabulsi, A., Mukhopadhyay, S., Awal, M.S., Fernandes, S., Ailabouni, K., IoT-solar energy powered smart farm irrigation system. *J. Electron. Sci. Technol.*, 17, 100017, 2020.

17. Mohapatra, A.G., Lenka, S.K., Keswani, B., Neural network and fuzzy logic based smart DSS model for irrigation notification and control in precision agriculture. *Proc. Natl. Acad. Sci. India Sect. A: Phys. Sci.*, 89, 67–76, 2019.

18. Kabilan, N. and Selvi, M.S., Surveillance and steering of irrigation system in cloud using Wireless Sensor Network and Wi-Fi module. *Proceedings of the International Conference on Recent Trends in Information Technology (ICRTIT)*, pp. 1–5, 2016.

19. Kumar, A., Surendra, A., Mohan, H., Valliappan, K.M., Kirthika, N., Internet of things based smart irrigation using regression algorithm. *International Conference on Intelligent Computing Instrumentation and Control Technologies (ICICICT)*, pp. 1652–1657, 2017.

20. Keswani, B., Mohapatra, A.G., Keswani, P., Khanna, A., Gupta, D., Rodrigues, J.J., Improving weather dependent zone specific irrigation control scheme in IoT and big data enabled self driven precision agriculture mechanism. *Enterp. Inf. Syst.*, 1–22, 2020.

21. Goldstein, A., Fink, L., Meitin, A., Bohadana, S., Lutenberg, O., Ravid, G., Applying machine learning on sensor data for irrigation recommendations: Revealing the agronomist's tacit knowledge. *Precis. Agric.*, 19, 421–444, 2018.

22. Roy, S.K. and De, D., Genetic Algorithm based Internet of Precision Agricultural Things (IopaT) for Agriculture 4.0. *Internet Things*, 100201, 2020.

23. Ruano, A.E. and Mestre, G., A neural-network based intelligent weather station. *Proceedings of the IEEE 9th international symposium on intelligent signal processing (WISP)*, pp. 1–6, 2015.

24. Shaout, A., Li, Y., Zhou, M., Awad, S., Low cost embedded weather station with intelligent system. *Proceedings of the 10th International Computer Engineering Conference*, pp. 100–106, 2014.

25. Parashar, A., IoT Based Automated Weather Report Generation and Prediction Using Machine Learning. *Proceedings of the 2nd International Conference on Intelligent Communication and Computational Techniques (ICCT)*, pp. 339–344, 2019.

26. Tahsien, S.M., Karimipour, H., Spachos, P., Machine learning based solutions for security of Internet of Things (IoT): A survey. *J. Netw. Comput. Appl.*, 161, 102630, 2020.

6

Deep Neural Network-Based Multi-Class Image Classification for Plant Diseases

Alok Negi[1], Krishan Kumar[1]* and Prachi Chauhan[2]

[1]Department of Computer Science and Engineering, National Institute of Technology, Srinagar, India
[2]College of Technology, G.B. Pant University of Agriculture and Technology, Pantnagar, India

Abstract

Recognition of plant disease is significantly a difficult challenge in agriculture farming field. Faster and more accurate prediction of leaf diseases in plants will help to improve crop production and market value in an effective management strategy while dramatically reducing environmental damage. Disease detection in plant needs a lot hard work, knowledge of all plant diseases with more processing time. Hence, plant disease recognition is the majority promising approach in agriculture, which is attracting significant attention in both the farming and computer communities. Therefore, in this paper we describe Deep Convolutional Neural Network (CNN) model to care for farming by identifying leaf disease that help in growing up the healthy plants. We apply CNN techniques on large agricultural plant dataset for accurate detection of plant leaves diseases.

Keywords: CNN, dropout, normalization, plant disease

6.1 Introduction

Agriculture sector plays a crucial role in establishing young crop seedlings to be raised or handled until they become ready for much more mandatory and durable seeding. According to the IPCC [1], possible impact of climate

---

*Corresponding author: kkberwal@nituk.ac.in

Amitava Choudhury, Arindam Biswas, Manish Prateek and Amlan Chakrabarti (eds.)
Agricultural Informatics: Automation Using the IoT and Machine Learning, (117–130) © 2021
Scrivener Publishing LLC

change includes reduced yields on agriculture due to heat stress in warmer regions, crop destruction, soil loss and soil insufficiency due to heavy precipitation events, and soil degradation resulting from increased drought. In these perspectives agricultural crop infection present an utmost hazard to food security, but fast recognition in several parts of the world remains challenging because of its lack of infrastructure needed and these global circulation scenarios [2] indicate that the downturn in agricultural production will be more serious in temperate areas where food production is still lacking. And this is where organic farming commences. Organic farming seems to have the ability to improve each of those issues and this farming's main practice depends on soil selection, treatment of seeds, irrigation process and so on; soil should be fertile, rich in organic matter with excellent medium for better seed germination and seedling growth.

A plant disease in order to respond to just a continuous inflammation via an infectious causative factor, also known as a pathogen, is defined as a plant deficiency. A plant disease may cause several signs and symptoms which can affect the ability of the plant to yield, replicate or properly grow. A healthy plant is the very first best protection toward plant diseases which is really the primary objective of an incredibly talented gardener. Just before plant selection begins to avoid and control plant disease. Agritechnology and precision farming, also known as digital farming, have emerged as modern scientific disciplines that employ data-intensive methods to improve agricultural production while reducing its environmental impact. Data generated in intensive farming practices are supported by a variety of different sensors which really allow a greater understanding of the regulatory environment (an interface between complex crop, soil and climate conditions) and the procedures itself (machine data), likely to result in more accurate and rapid decision-making. The challenge with appropriate plant disease protection is tightly linked to the concerns of sustainable agriculture and changes in the environment. Detection of crop [3, 4] diseases by looking with a naked human eye at the impact on plant leaves consolidates increasing complexity. Because of such a challenge and the vast number of agricultural crops and their current phyto-pathological concerns, even trained agricultural experts including plant pathologists may often fail to effectively diagnose infectious diseases; and furthermore, erroneous conclusions are made and fear remedies.

Traditionally, full examination has relies heavily on the detection of plant diseases through human annotation. Everywhere now, the identification [5, 6] of the different diseases is mixed or replaced with various technologies such as artificial neural networks (CNN, RNN, GAN). Besides that, latest research advances and significant efficiency improvements in the area of technology image acquisition. Consequently, enhanced in artificial intelligence, image recognition [7, 8] improves and enhances practitioners of accurate and consistent plant protection as well as growth [9]. Deep network is trained by estimating the parameters of the neural network [10] in such a way as to improve mapping [11] during training. This procedure is computationally demanding and has been improved significantly in recent times by an amount of mathematical and computer science breakthroughs [12]. For the specific reason of plant diseases diagnosis, we required a bigger, reviewed number of healthy images and infected plants to develop accurate image classifiers. Till very recently, such a raw data simply didn't exist, and sometimes even relatively small datasets were also not freely accessible.

6.2   Related Work

Azlah *et al.* [12] introduced the plant systematics could be labeled and recognized according to their reproductive organs and morphology of leaves. Neural networks are among most powerful algorithm for leaf images classification. The pretty widely utilize neutral networks are artificial neural networks, probabilistic neural networks, CNN, k-nearest neighbors, and supporting vector machines, perhaps other studies have used paired technology to enhance precision. The use of certain different preprocessing strategies and characteristic gathered feature extraction parameters seemed to change the classification functionality of plant leaves. An image recognition approach that can fully ignore the context of the image speeds up its process of identification and seems to be suitable for extremely complex observations of plant leaves. A device that completely ignores distortion greatly improves recognition capabilities and also makes it much more realistic to identify aquatic fauna, because aquatic plants or algae would not have a standardized type. The latest technique of image processing should also be stable under the different lighting intensities. This novel technique can be established by modifying the detection methodology which can progress to accurate disease detection. The benefit can also be extended for recognition of herbal plants to protect adulteration for decent quality control, particularly for effectiveness and safety of the products. This paper aimed at reviewing and analyzing the effectiveness and performance of the different plant classification methodologies.

Mohanty *et al.* [13] discussed that the combination of rising global pervasion of smartphones and newly machine vision developments made necessary by deep learning that has been prepared the path for mobile phone-assisted disease diagnosis. Train a deep convolutional neural network to classify 14 crop species and 26 diseases (or their absence) using a publicly available dataset of 54,306 images of infected and stable plant leaves captured under controlled circumstances. The trained approach outperforms a 99.35% accuracy on a stand-out test range, highlighting this approach's feasibility. All in all, the training methodology of deep learning algorithms onto increasingly large image datasets, available to the public provides a straightforward path forward massive global diagnosis of smartphone-assisted crop disease. The method discussed was not really intended to substitute, but instead to complement, existing strategies for diagnosing the disease. At the end of the day, laboratory experiments are much more accurate than diagnoses determined by visual symptoms individually, and sometimes early stage assessment is difficult even by visual examination. All in all, the method described works fairly well with several different crop species including diseases, although with further training data, it's also needed to enhance considerably.

Zhong et al. [14] aimed to build a deep, time series classification system for remote sensing, based on learning. The analysis was performed in Yolo County, California, which now has overtaken productive crops by a highly complex irrigated farming method. Two categories of deep learning architectures were developed for the difficult task in order to classify summer crops employing Landsat Enhanced Vegetation Index time series: one dependent on Long Short-Term Memory (LSTM), while the other focused on one dimensional convolutional layers. The Conv1D dependent model's behavior was checked by analyzing the activation on various layers. The method incorporates EVI time series in a hierarchical way by examining shapes at different scales. Conv1D layers including its optimization results capture sequential variations across small scale, whereas upper layers concentrate on general seasonal variations. Conv1D layers were used during the classification model as an integrated multi-level function extractor that systematically extracts features from time series content during training. The feature's automated extraction reduces reliance on manual system engineering and standardized crop growing phase equations. This research reveals that in hyper spectral classification challenges, deep learning based on Conv1D system offers an accurate and effective activity of representing the time series.

Toda et al. [15] reviewed miscellaneous neuronal and layer experience computer vision techniques employed with CNN model, trained with such a publicly accessible dataset of plant disease image and demonstrates that neural networks have been able to capture textures and colors of the respective disease specific abnormalities upon diagnostic test that accurately represent human decision making. Although some methods of visualization have been used since decades, others now have to be modified to target a particular layer that encompasses the features entirely to produce consequential performance. Collaboratively, CNN's visual representation reveals the likelihood of opening the deep learning data recorder. The findings suggest that even though the visualization approaches yield meaningful conclusions, humans always play the main important role throughout interpreting the visualization outcomes, for instance, linking the computer-generated findings with professional expertise in plant research. This research, which introduces the functionality of visualization approaches for diagnosing disease, represents a new road to creating a workflow of plant scientific research, where machines and plant researchers work together to interpret plant biology across deep learning methods.

Waldchen *et al.* [16] reviewed the technological status of computer vision based techniques for plant diseases identification illustrates the major research obstacles to be addressed in the provision of appropriate resources. Authors envisage identification systems which allow users to obtain field photographs of specimens with the built-in camera system of a mobile device, that many are then handled by an automated taxon classification program or, at least, by receiving a number of selected taxa. This method is easy, as identifying involves no user work except to take an image and browse by the best species to match. In addition, minimal expertise is needed, which is particularly important despite the ongoing shortage of credentialed botanists. An exact automated recognition program also makes it possible for no experts despite limited botanical knowledge and experience to participate to the world's biodiversity survey. Approaching developments and innovations, such as virtual reality, digital glasses and 3D scanning, offers these projects a long term outlook for study and development. Then again, vast-character datasets can indeed be generated automatically (e.g. while taking measurements from dozens of specimens in one taxon). Authors only get more realistic representation of the species and their usual behaviour expressions but also investigate the probability distributions of each character along with variation and skew.

6.3   Proposed Work

Crop diseases prove to be a significant threat to world food supply. The objectives of this work are:

- To prove the technological viability of a Deep learning approach to enable automatic diagnosis of disease.

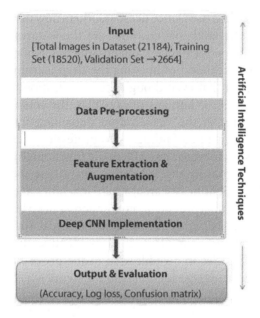

Figure 6.1 Proposed work flow chart.

- To develop a CNN model to classify the disease present on a plant leaf among 10 classes.

Figure 6.1 shows the flowchart of proposed work.

6.3.1 Dataset Description

A dataset that includes images of around 21,184 belonging to 10 classes at several significant growth stages has been used. Dataset consist training and validation set with 18,520 and 2,664 images respectively. The 10 classes of different healthy and diseased plant leaves are: Apple Black rot, Corn Cercospora leaf spot (Gray leaf spot), Grape Black rot, Orange Haunglongbing (Citrus greening), Peach Bacterial spot, Pepper-bell Bacterial spot, Potato Early blight, Strawberry Leaf scorch, Tomato Bacterial spot and Tomato Target Spot as shown in Figure 6.2.

6.3.2 Data Pre-Processing and Augmentation

Images are transformed from BGR to RGB because python expects (R, G, B) using the pre-process input function by default, and images are resized to 224 × 224 × 3 to prevent data leakage issues because most images look

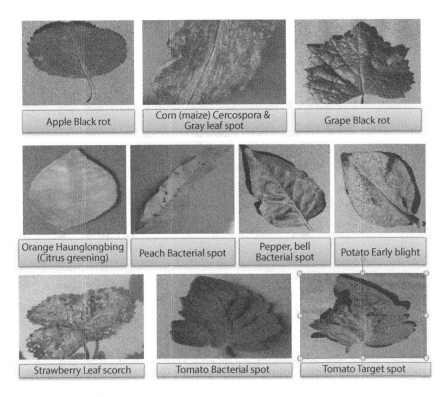

Apple Black rot	Corn (maize) Cercospora & Gray leaf spot	Grape Black rot
Orange Haunglongbing (Citrus greening)	Peach Bacterial spot	Pepper, bell Bacterial spot	Potato Early blight
Strawberry Leaf scorch	Tomato Bacterial spot	Tomato Target spot

Figure 6.2 Sample images.

identical. Data augmentation is a technique that allows the data diversity available for training models to be substantially expanded, without actively collecting new data. For Data Augmentation, proposed work uses the concept of Keras Image Data Generator (rescale, zoom range, horizontal flip and rotation range).

6.3.3 CNN Architecture

In terms of image recognition CNN are commonly used by the different network architectures used in deep learning. A CNN is a type of deep neural networks, widely used for visual image processing [17] and built to learn feature hierarchies from small to high visibility patterns, automatically and adaptively. CNN is a structure typically consisting of three key components layers: convolution, pooling, and layers that are fully connected as shown in Figure 6.3.

Convolutional layers are indeed the layers which apply filters to the actual image, or with other feature maps in a CNN architecture [18].

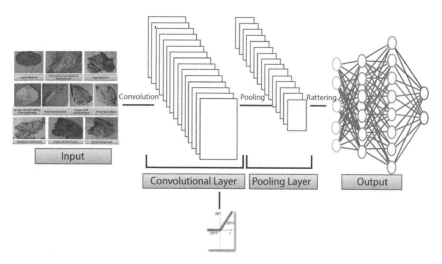

Figure 6.3   CNN architecture.

This is where the majority of user-defined parameters are in the network. The much more essential factors are kernel size and kernel count. Pooling layers are closely related to convolutional layers, but perform a specific function such as max pooling that requires the maximum value up in a particular filter region or average pooling that uses the mean value on a filter region. Usually these are used to start reducing the network's dimensionality. Fully connected layers have been placed even before outcome of a CNN classification [19] and used prior to actually classification to flatten these same results. This is analogous to an MLP's output layer. A survey of the architecture of a CNN, as well as training required. A CNN consists of just a positioning of many basic components blocks: convolution layers, pooling layers (max pooling layer) and layers that are completely linked layers (also known as fully connected). The output of a model underlying different kernels and biases is determined with a loss function via forward propagation on a testing set, and learnable parameters, i.e. kernels as well as weights, are modified and as per the loss value through backpropagation with gradient descent optimization technique.

6.4   Results and Evaluation

The proposed work is implemented in ANACONDA 3.0 with TensorFlow as a backend. A single PC equipped with a 2.30 GHz Intel(R) Core(TM) i5 3567CPU, 64-bit operating system, 8 GB RAM and 2 GB of AMD Radeon

R5 M330 graphics engine running on the Windows 10 operating system was used for the entire training and testing phase of the model that was significantly defined in this research. As the activation function, Softmax and ReLU are used and Adam (Adaptive Moment Estimation) is the optimizer.

Accuracy curve, loss curve, and confusion matrix based analysis are performed on the training and validation set of deep CNN model. The measured model's efficiency is calculated using accuracy as shown in Equation (6.1).

$$Accuracy = (TP + TN) / (TP + TN + FP + FN) \qquad (6.1)$$

The logarithmic loss of multiple classes is also widely recognized as the categorical cross entropy is used as a metric and can be calculated using Equation (6.2). The log loss of 0 gets a perfect classifier.

$$logloss = 1/N \sum_{i}^{N} \sum_{j}^{M} y_{ij} \log(p_{ij}) \qquad (6.2)$$

The proposed work recorded 96.91% training accuracy with logarithm loss 0.03 and the validation accuracy 96.02% with logarithm loss 0.01 in just 32 epochs. Figures 6.4, 6.5, 6.6 and 6.7 show the accuracy, log loss curve and confusion matrix (with and without normalization) for the proposed work.

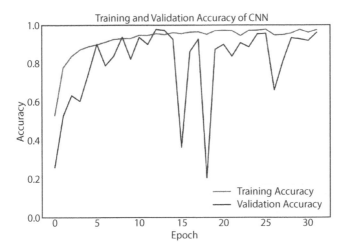

Figure 6.4 Training and validation accuracy of CNN.

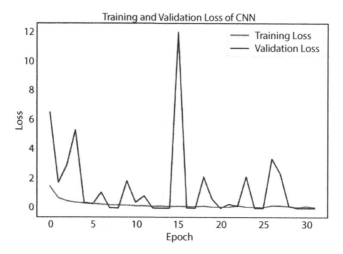

Figure 6.5   Training and validation loss of CNN.

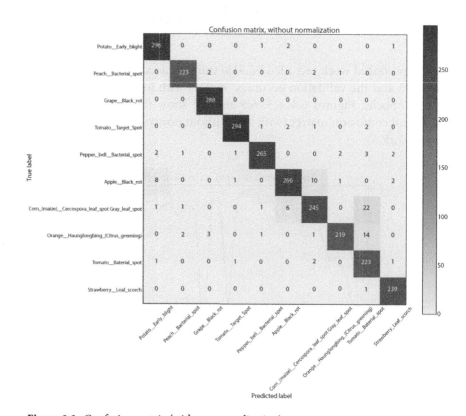

Figure 6.6   Confusion matrix (without normalization).

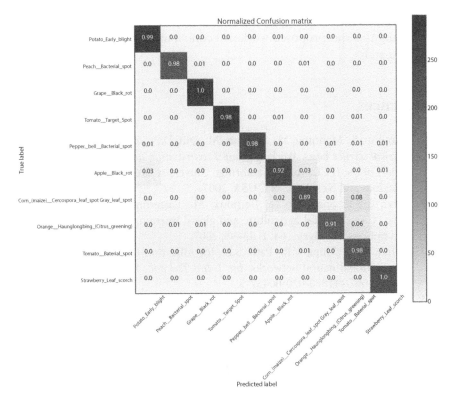

Figure 6.7 Confusion matrix (with normalization).

6.5 Conclusion

For site-specific weed management information is relevant as to which weed species are present within agricultural fields. It is supposed to improve efficiency and help to understand better of the relationship between environmental and health factors cultivates, reduces labour costs for farmers and raises velocity and precision of action. Deep learning is modern research techniques for image analysis and pattern recognition, and it can effectively solve the problems of recognizing plant leaf diseases. The number of epochs for training, batch size and dropout affected the respective outcomes further. This chapter presented a method which uses a deep CNN model to recognize plant species in color images. Experimental findings show that the CNN-based method is substantially successful with an accuracy of approximately 96.02% with logarithm loss 0.01 in just 32 epochs on 10 plant classes. While our proposed work does have better results, it is possible to increase the number of epochs for better results. We are hoping that our proposed work will contribute significantly to agricultural research.

References

1. Solomon, S., Manning, M., Marquis, M., Qin, D., *Climate change 2007—The physical science basis: Working group I contribution to the Fourth Assessment Report of the IPCC*, vol. 4, Cambridge University Press, Cambridge, United Kingdom and New York, NY, USA, 2007.
2. Cerri, C.E.P., Sparovek, G., Bernoux, M., Easterling, W.E., Melillo, J.M., Cerri, C.C., Tropical agriculture and global warming: Impacts and mitigation options. *Sci. Agric.*, 64, 1, 83–99, 2007.
3. Jadhav, S.B., Udupi, V.R., Patil, S.B., Identification of plant diseases using convolutional neural networks. *Int. J. Inf. Technol.*, 1–10, 2020, https://doi.org/10.1007/s41870-020-00437-5.
4. Karthik, R., Hariharan, M., Anand, S., Mathikshara, P., Johnson, A., Menaka, R., Attention embedded residual CNN for disease detection in tomato leaves. *Appl. Soft Comput.*, 86, 105933, 2020.
5. Boulent, J., Foucher, S., Théau, J., St-Charles, P.-L., Convolutional neural networks for the automatic identification of plant diseases. *Front. Plant Sci.*, 10, 941, 2019.
6. Ngugi, L.C., Abelwahab, M., Abo-Zahhad, M., Recent Advances in Image Processing Techniques for Automated Leaf Pest and Disease Recognition—A Review. *Inf. Process. Agric.*, 2020, https://doi.org/10.1016/j.inpa.2020.04.004.
7. Barbedo, J.G., Factors influencing the use of deep learning for plant disease recognition. *Biosyst. Eng.*, 172, 84–91, 2018.
8. Barbedo, J.G.A., Impact of dataset size and variety on the effectiveness of deep learning and transfer learning for plant disease classification. *Comput. Electron. Agric.*, 153, 46–53, 2018.
9. Bharate, A.A. and Shirdhonkar, M.S., A review on plant disease detection using image processing, in: *2017 International Conference on Intelligent Sustainable Systems (ICISS)*, IEEE, pp. 103–109, December 2017.
10. Alom, M.Z., Taha, T.M., Yakopcic, C., Westberg, S., Sidike, P., Nasrin, M.S., Asari, V.K., The history began from alexnet: A comprehensive survey on deep learning approaches, arXiv preprint arXiv:1803.01164, 2018, http://arxiv.org/abs/1803.01164.
11. Chalapathy, R. and Chawla, S., Deep learning for anomaly detection: A survey. arXiv preprint arXiv:1901.03407, 2019.
12. Azlah, M.A.F., Chua, L.S., Rahmad, F.R., Abdullah, F.I., Wan Alwi, S.R., Review on Techniques for Plant Leaf Classification and Recognition. *Computers*, 8, 4, 77, 2019, https://arxiv.org/abs/1906.02694.

13. Mohanty, S.P., Hughes, D.P., Salathé, M., Using deep learning for image-based plant disease detection. *Front. Plant Sci.*, 7, 1419, 2016.
14. Zhong, L., Hu, L., Zhou, H., Deep learning based multi-temporal crop classification. *Remote Sens. Environ.*, 221, 430–443, 2019.
15. Toda, Y. and Okura, F., How convolutional neural networks diagnose plant disease. *Plant Phenomics*, 2019, 9237136, 2019.
16. Wäldchen, J., Rzanny, M., Seeland, M., Mäder, P., Automated plant species identification—Trends and future directions. *PLoS Comput. Biol.*, 14, 4, e1005993, 2018.
17. Brahimi, M., Arsenovic, M., Laraba, S., Sladojevic, S., Boukhalfa, K., Moussaoui, A., Deep learning for plant diseases: Detection and saliency map visualisation, in: *Human and machine learning*, pp. 93–117, Springer, Cham, 2018.
18. Schmidhuber, J., Deep learning in neural networks: An overview. *Neural Netw.*, 61, 85–117, 2015.
19. O'Shea, K. and Nash, R., An introduction to convolutional neural networks, arXiv preprint arXiv:1511.08458, 2015, https://arxiv.org/abs/1511.08458.

7

Deep Residual Neural Network for Plant Seedling Image Classification

Prachi Chauhan[1]*, Hardwari Lal Mandoria[1] and Alok Negi[2]

[1]*College of Technology, G.B. Pant University of Agriculture and Technology, Pantnagar, India*
[2]*Department of Computer Science and Engineering, National Institute of Technology, Srinagar, India*

Abstract
Efficient plant cultivation depends in large measure on weed control effectiveness. Weed conservation within the first six to eight weeks since planting is critical, because during this time weeds are competing aggressively with the crop for nutrients and water. In general, yield losses will range from 10 to 100% depending on the degree of weed control practiced. Yield losses are caused by weed interfering with growth and production of the crop. This explains why successful weed control is imperative. The first vital prerequisite to do successful control is accurate identification and classification of weeds. In this research we conduct a detailed experimental study on the ResNet to tackle the problem of yield losses. We used Plant Seedling dataset to train and test the system. Using ResNet (advanced convolution neural network) we classify the images with a high accuracy rate, that can ultimately change how weeds affect the current state of agriculture.

Keywords: Augmentation, CNN, dropout, plant seedling, ResNet

7.1 Introduction

The production of best featured quality seedlings is important if yields are to be improved and quality achieved. Plant seedling production is

---

Corresponding author: prachi3apr@gmail.com

Amitava Choudhury, Arindam Biswas, Manish Prateek and Amlan Chakrabarti (eds.)
Agricultural Informatics: Automation Using the IoT and Machine Learning, (131–146) © 2021
Scrivener Publishing LLC

conducted in most developed countries that tackle by specialized companies for exclusive operation. In India, the plant seedling production methodology is moderately growing from susceptible field [1] to production in protected seedling trays or raised beds. In some intensive growing areas, advanced seedling manufacturing industries also take off. Recently, yields per unit area are normally at lowest point. Most of the seeds on the retail market are not certified and have inferiority low production quality. The prominent moment [2] of germination of seeds always necessitates extra care and attention. Automatic plant image recognition is the major promising approach for bridging the taxonomic gap in agriculture, which is attracting significant attention in both the farming and computer communities. Therefore, in this chapter we describe how to care for seedlings by classifying using deep learning plant technique that helps in growing up the healthy plants. Deep learning inclusively is referred as one of the machine learning comprehensive techniques which usually involves the hierarchical features of learning. In several forms of computer vision activities, these techniques have been appearing to be effective, including image classification and their detection [3]. Learning is an agile area of research in field of agriculture and its practices to science of plant even now in early stages. Previous research has essentially shown the benefit of profound learning for the same task in complex images plant tasks over conventional engineering under computer vision activities. These activities involve counting of leaves, estimating the age of plants, mutant classification, identification of plant diseases [4], fruit and other seedling classification [5]. The small part of the existing research on the deep learning in plant image classification [6] explores assurance for future work in this area. The weed classification model is then checked for images of seedling and evaluation done using precision, selectivity and loss. The findings of the study examined would be a magnificent offering to the ongoing development growth of crop germinating management care and to providing the newest technique for promoting and encouraging agricultural practices. Convolutional Neural Networks are nowadays considered narrowly the dominant method just for object classification. The Deep Convolutional Neural Network (CNN) is trained by tuning the parameters of the network to enhance linking during the training process and performs conscientiously in plant seedling classification [7]. In computer vision concept, CNNs were known to the strong visual models which produce feature hierarchies that allow for accurate and remarkable segmentation and also execute predictions comparatively faster than other more algorithms, and simultaneously retaining competitive performance.

7.1.1   Architecture of CNN

In bygone models of image classification, there is a use of actual raw pixels to classify or identify the images. Images can be categorized by color histogram and edge detection. These approaches have been exclusively successful but before more complex variants are encountered. That is where the classical image recognition keeps failing, because some other features are not taken into consideration by the model and thus the consideration of convolutional neural network (ConvNet). CNN is a type of model of the neural network that helps to extract feature or higher image representations [8]. CNN takes the raw pixel data from the image, trains the model, and then automatically extracts features [9] such as margins, highlighted patterns from the image for better classification. CNN began in 2012 with AlexNet, and has grown exponentially [10, 11]. Researchers have advanced from AlexNet with 8 layers to ResNet 152 layers [12]. CNN is blowing competition in concept of accuracy. Recommending system programs, natural language processing and much more are also successfully implemented. CNN's one biggest benefit compared with its predecessors is that it identifies the essential features automatically without any human oversight interaction.

7.1.1.1   Principles of ConvNet

Convolution: On the image, a convolution is applied then calculates its input data and the pixel values of the filter dot product using a convolution filter to generate the appropriate feature chart. The convolved features will also adjust in order to minimize loss of prediction that depends onto the filter values impacted by some gradient descent.

Max Pooling: ConvNet requires max pooling for substitute output to max analysis, reducing data size as well as time for processing. This approach is useful in defining or removing highly impacting features which limits the chance of overfitting. This layers learn each feature map independently and reducing the height and width without depth intact. Activation Function: Apply activation function after every convolutional and max pooling operation such rectified linear unit (ReLU), sigmoid and softmax. This approach is effective in solving the diminishing gradients.

Figure 7.1 shows the cumulative CNN architecture comprises of two primary parts: Extractor feature functionality and Classifier. The layer throughout the network expects to receive certain output from the immediate prior feature map layer as in its input throughout the feature

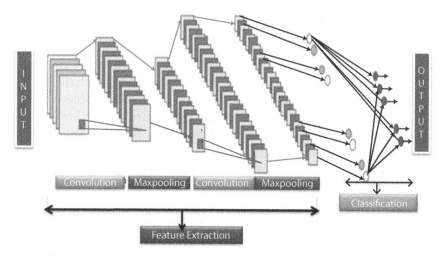

Figure 7.1 CNN architecture.

extraction stages, and transfers its output as its input towards the subsequent layer. The architecture of the CNN [13] comes in the form of a mixture of three-layered types: convolution, max pooling, and identification. Throughout the middle and lower stages of the network there have been two categories of layers: deep convolutional layers and max-pooling layers. There is an even equally spaced layers are designed for convolutions, as well as the odd marked layers are there for max-pooling. The convolution network output and also the max-pooling layers are grouped together into the 2D plane designated feature mapping. Typically, each plane across layers is generated from the composition of one or many prior layer planes. Plane nodes are directly linked to a slight region of every one of the preceding layers integrated planes. That node throughout the convolution layer extracting features mostly on input layer from its input images through convolution operations.

7.1.2   Residual Network (ResNet)

ResNet is a strong backbone model which is very widely used in multiple computer vision tasks and developed by research team from Microsoft. Model design is focused on the principle of residual blocks that enable use of shortcut connections. Throughout the network architecture, these are basically connections where all the input is kept as it is (not weighted) and conveyed to a deeper layer. It implemented revolutionary to prove a new approach for deep neural networks to a huge problem. By using

Identification shortcut link or skipping connections that miss one or several layers, ResNet addresses the problem of gradient vanishing. ResNets have varying sizes depends on how broad any of the model layers are and how many layers it has, such that ResNet-18, ResNet-34, ResNet-50, ResNet-101, ResNet-110, ResNet-152, ResNet-164, ResNet-1202. Deep residual networks (ResNets) consist of several stacked "Residual Units".

In a simplified form, each unit can be represented by Equations (7.1) and (7.2):

$$y_i = h(x_i) + F(x_i W_i) \qquad (7.1)$$

$$x_{i+1} = f(y_i) \qquad (7.2)$$

where x_i and x_{i+1} are input and output of the ith unit, and F is a residual function with $h(x_i) = x_i$ is an identity mapping [14] and f is a ReLU function.

Figure 7.2 shows the mapping between regular and residual block. The ideal mapping of regular block that obtain by learning is: f(x) and Ideal mapping of residual block is:

$$x + f(x)$$

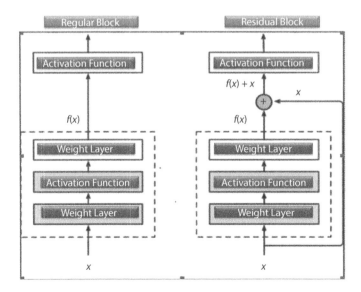

Figure 7.2 Left: regular block and Right: residual block.

7.2   Related Work

The key premises of the automated system for classifying plants are shown in Figure 7.3. The plant images will originally be acquired through real camera, scanner, as well as some other equipment. Then, those images have been pre-processed to complete remove of noise and enhance efficiency. Noise appears as image pixels value during image processing and does not reflect the actual intensities of an image.

Image enhancement is indeed a practice often used highlight each image's feature information [14]. Deleting the image noises is indeed a required step to emphasize or highlight the important image features. Accordingly, the region of interest (ROI) was segregated mainly from images, assisted by feature extraction. Finally, the characteristics extracted are transferred to a method of classification or identification.

Very recently Jiang *et al.* [13] reviewed CNN-based processing plant phenotyping approaches that have been extensively examined to have advantages and drawbacks of just using them with different particular plant phenotyping activities. Effective learning is yet another attempt to reduce the risk of labeling results. Associated with normative data augmentation, learning environment seeks to identify and mark samples which really optimize the output of a model. So, most samples should not be validated to just save time as well as labor costs. Data collection is indeed a productive way to annotate data which needs lesser labor productivity expenditure. Some experiments have shown how quantitative research can be used to rapidly mark massive image repositories for automated learning algorithms. There are several commercial data annotation applications, in particular, including as amazon robotic Turk as well as Crowd flower. Through all those services, data annotation can indeed be ensured with a satisfactory standard and throughput. CNN-based approaches stated their tremendous potential through all these studies to solve the most difficult problems faced in different plants phenotyping application scenarios. Other forms of end-to-end CNN structure in general and especially have greatly simplified the mechanism of order to extract phenotypic traits through images. This would allow data processing when being improved, and eventually plant phenotyping techniques.

Figure 7.3 General approach for automated classification of plant block.

Smith *et al.* [15] concentrated on annotation period, as time criteria for annotation instead of the amount of images readily accessible to become more important to the needs of their majority bulk of plant data analysis groups wanting to use profound learning towards image analysis. The results, especially for appropriate remedial training, affirm first hypothesis besides demonstrating that any deep learning prototype could be trained with high accuracy with less of around two hours for annotation also for three corresponding datasets of contrasting target items, context and image reliability and illustrate the feasibility through training a specific model utilizing short-term annotations questioning arguments that scores to around thousands of data image or significant marking data required for using CNNs. In reality, authors are often anticipating longer cycles of annotation to offer more change. The R2 to ward corrective development had a strong association with length of annotation suggesting whether it would help to enhance efficiency by investing more time annotating. There was the tendency to accept recognize increasing percentage of perceived images without any further annotation probably later in mostly in the preventive training suggesting less of that images needed corrections because as performance throughout the model started improving. This aligns again with decrease to growth rate in the total quantity of corrections showing continued progress throughout the accuracy within the model across time during their corrective training. Although preventive annotation appeared to produce better accurate than dense models, their lack of such a statistically substantial difference prohibits a more concrete conclusion about its benefits for corrective against dense annotation.

Tan *et al.* [16] stated that automated fully plant species recognition system may aid speedy species of plant identification by botanists and laymen. Advanced learning is comprehensive in extracting features, since it becomes superior in producing deeper image knowledge. A novel CNN-based approach called D-Leaf has been introduced in this study. The leaves images became pre-trained as well as the features have been extracted employing three separate CNN concepts, namely pre-processing AlexNet, AlexNet as well as D-Leaf, which were finely tuned. The researchers concluded that CNN is best than conventional morphological approaches towards the extracting features of plant species. In comparison with the CNN, more quite pre-processing work needs to be accomplished when utilizing conventional strategies. In addition, in this research, CNN would be found be a preferable method of extraction of features, instead of a method of classification. Compared to various classifiers, the ANN classifier along with its CNN feature extractor recorded a very optimal result. In fact, best result of this research would be to achieve better precision testing since using a D-Leaf besides extraction of the feature as well as the ANN as a classifier. In addition, D-Leaf achievement is validated using CV methods, and also some MalayaKew, Flavia and Swedish datasets. The success of the validation showed that the D-Leaf system could be used for automatic classification of plant species.

Alimboyong *et al.* [17] concluded a new approach for early growth process categorization of plant species was researched using advantage of deep learning neural convolutional networks. This methodology includes a CNN during training and do augmentation of data to classify 12 species of plant using a range of image transformations: equalization of the dimensions, rotation, shift, levelling, resizing and histogram and became a relevant contribution fairly towards ongoing development suggested in the field of environmental research as well as to universal objective of increase in global agricultural output yield. The classification model of plant is then checked for seedling different images and evaluated successfully using precision, sensitivity and specificity and the findings of this research has an outstanding supplement to the ongoing growth of crop management and to offering a newest technique for promoting and encouraging farming different practices.

Rashad *et al.* [9] introduced a plant classification strategy that is focused on characterizing the properties of the textures. Author used the combined classifiers learning vector quantization, and randomly took out 30 blocks of every texture as a training sample and then some 30 blocks as a test sample. The study identified that integrated classification method offers high performance which is preferable to another test method. The experimental findings demonstrated the applicability of the algorithm and its average correct recognition rate was good. The proposed system has an advantage in its capabilities to recognize and classify the crop from the small proportion of every leaf without depending on whether the texture of a leaf and its color characteristics, although the system essentially depends mostly on textural characteristics. The system is therefore useful to botany researchers when they want to recognize a damaged plant, as this can only be done depending on a small part of the rotted and damaged plant.

Nkemelu *et al.* [18] addressed an efficient deep learning model for seedlings classification that helped farmers for optimize crop yields and significantly reduce losses. In this paper, author proposed a deep, convolutional neural network approach for classification of plant seedlings. A dataset has been used which contains images of about 960 unique plants belonging to 12 species at several growth stages. In the wild the model detected and distinguished a weed from other plants. A baseline version of the proposed system obtained a precision. The system proposed could be expanded to operate with robotic arms to conduct actual weeding operations in large farmlands. The findings have shown that, when used in farming automation, CNN-driven seedling classification applications have the potential to optimize crop yield and improve productivity and efficiency when appropriately designed.

7.3   Proposed Work

The aim of the weed cultivation activity is to provide the best crop opportunity to develop and grow vigorously up to maturity time. The key goals of weed control are to improve the soil conditions by reducing soil surface convection. It encourages the growth of the desirable plant species and prevents the establishment of weeds in a cultivated crop, pasture, or farmland. Encouraged by this presumption, weed cultivation applications are seeking to better classify input data into the underlying seedling group. Plant Seedling Dataset has been used from an evolutionary experimental viewpoint and includes the following twelve types of plant crop groups for plant classification: BlackGrass, Charlock, Cleavers, Common Chickweed, Common wheat, Fat Hen, Loose silky bent, Maize, Scentless Mayweed, Shepherd Purse, Small flowered Cranesbill and Sugar beet category. The objective is to train an Advance CNN model (Resnet50) efficient of classifying the plant crop into these twelve categories and this makes it a challenge in respect of deep learning classification.

7.3.1   Data Collection

Dataset includes representations of several different crop species, with many categories. Some of the commercial crops such as Black Grass, Charlock, Cleavers, Common Chickweed, Common wheat, Fat Hen, Loose Silky-bent, Maize, Scentless Mayweed, Shepherd Purse, Small-flowered Cranesbill and Sugar beet are included in this framework. Good and healthy leaves were all obtained from sources such as image download from the Internet by directly downloading the plant seedling data collection for those above crop categories. Figures 7.4 and 7.5 show the distribution of classes between training and validation.

7.3.2   Data Pre-Processing

As per ResNet's need for transfer learning implementation, images are pre-processed as performed in the architecture of the origin. Additionally,

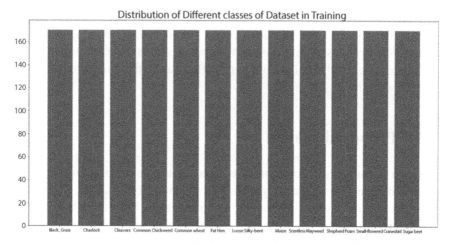

Figure 7.4 Distribution of classes during training.

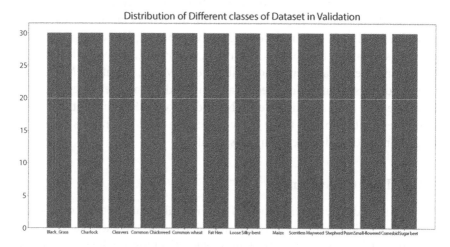

Figure 7.5 Distribution of classes during validation.

their processing system required input in (B, G, R) order while by standard python prefers (R, G, B), so the images have to be transformed from BGR to RGB. Therefore, in data pre-processing, we implemented color space transformation and image enhancement to unique images of plants pertinence with 12 species of plants in separate seedling stages development and conversion of color space to evaluate chromaticity and luminosity layers in order to improve visual analysis. If images vary then resize them from 54 × 54 to as much as M × N image sizes. The RGB images of that same crops are modified into the L × a × b color space by empirically adjusting the existing color channel for creating a new color channel appropriate for classification within almost every species of plants.

$$r1 = R/(G + e) \tag{7.3}$$

$$r2 = B/(G + e) \tag{7.4}$$

By comparison Equations (7.3) and (7.4) represent each pixel's nonconformity.

R and G and B denoted the pixel represented values for red and green and blue channels, while e is used to prevent zero divisions. To allow the very same image dimensions for training and validation using the machine learning model, and the image sizes should be of M × M size, in which M = 256. All images of whole datasets are resized to a color space of 256 × 256 RGB. Following resize of image presents a newest different image with the set of rows and also columns defined by a 1D array of two elements with the representation of [256, 256].

7.3.3 Data Annotation and Augmentation

Image annotation, the process in which images are categorized according to features extracted. This approach functions as an individual class through semantic concept and applies each concept as a single classifier. For image retrieval networks this method is often used to classify and accurately locate specific images from a database automatically. However, in this proposed methodology we manually annotate the locations of each image which contain the leaves with the help of bounding box. Depending on its clearness status certain leaves can look identical. Figure 7.6 shows the annotated image.

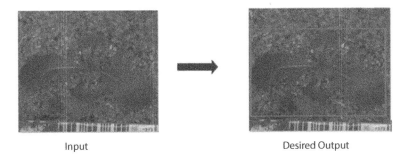

Input   Desired Output

Figure 7.6 Annotated image.

Annotation procedure can be capable of labeling the class and position in the image of the leaf areas. The results of the this stage are the dimensions including its bounding boxes of varying sizes with their respective crop class, which will then be assessed as the intersection over union (IoU) with the expected results during the testing.

7.3.4   Training and Fine-Tuning

Architecture to random weights is initialized and trained for a number of epochs. The model recognizes attributes from data with each epoch. The training was using the stochastic momentum gradient descent (SGDM) optimizer, with an initial learning rate of 0.001, a mini batch size of 8 and 65 epochs overall. Then complete full connected layers of ResNet-50 are accurately replaced with dense layer which has new segments such as batch normalization and dropout to learn various features that specific to the seedling of plant. For each batch, batch normalization normalizes previous layer activations as it helps train networks faster and also normalizes each layer's inputs to address the internal covariate, change problem. Dropout is a strategy used during the training to prevent a model from overfitting by dropping the parts of hidden units into one layer. The performance of evaluated model is assessing using accuracy as shown in Equation (7.5).

$$Accuracy = (TP + TN) \, / \, (TP + TN + FP + FN) \qquad (7.5)$$

7.4   Result and Evaluation

In ANACONDA 3.0 the method was put into practice. A standard PC fitted with 2.30 GHz Intel(R) Core(TM) i5-3567 CPU, 64-bit operating system, 8 GB RAM and 2 GB AMD Radeon R5 M330 graphics engine run on Windows 10 operating system has been configured throughout the entire training and testing phase of the model mentioned significantly in this chapter. First, the description is given for the dataset used in this analysis and our dataset was accurately divided into 85% training set and 15% validation set to conduct the experiments. Evaluation is carried out on the Validation set after the testing is completed on the training set.

7.4.1   Metrics

Logarithmic loss of multiple classes also widely recognized as the categorical cross entropy is used as a metric for this work and calculated using Equation (7.6). A perfect classifier gets the log loss of 0.

$$logloss = 1/N \sum_{i}^{N} \sum_{j}^{M} y_{ij} \log(p_{ij}) \qquad (7.6)$$

7.4.2 Result Analysis

7.4.2.1 Experiment I

The first experiment on the plant seedling dataset performed with batch normalization. The training accuracy was (95%) with logarithm loss (0.0634) and the validation accuracy was (85%) with logarithm loss (0.567). Figures 7.7 and 7.8 show the accuracy and loss curve for the experiment 1.

7.4.2.2 Experiment II

The second experiment performed without batch normalization. The training accuracy was (93%) with logarithm loss (0.2578) and the validation

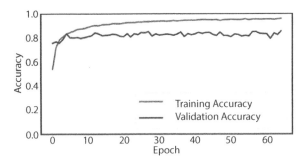

Figure 7.7 Training and validation accuracy of ResNet-50 using batch normalization.

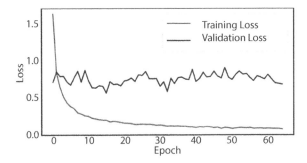

Figure 7.8 Training and validation loss of ResNet-50 using batch normalization.

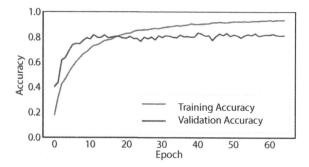

Figure 7.9 Training and validation accuracy of ResNet-50 without batch normalization.

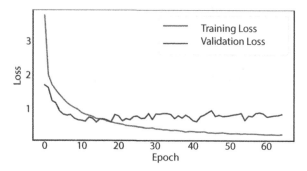

Figure 7.10 Training and validation loss of ResNet-50 without batch normalization.

accuracy was (83%) with logarithm loss (0.8382). Figures 7.9 and 7.10 show the accuracy and loss curve for the experiment 2.

7.5   Conclusion

Protection of crops is not really a trivial matter in organic farming. It depends on a detailed knowledge of that same harvested crops and their probable weeds. In our system we developed comprehensive deep learning models for the classification of plant species by means of leaf images of healthy plants, predicated on advanced convolutional neural networks framework. A dataset has been used that includes images of around 2,400 distinct plants actually belonging to twelve species at several significant growth stages. Our experimental findings showed how our deep-learning model is capable of successfully categorizing various types of plants. We hope that our proposed program will make a significant contribution to the research in agriculture.

References

1. Kołodziejek, J., Effect of seed position and soil nutrients on seed mass, germination and seedling growth in *Peucedanum oreoselinum* (Apiaceae). *Sci. Rep.*, 7, 1, 1–11, 2017.
2. Yuan, X. and Wen, B., Seed germination response to high temperature and water stress in three invasive Asteraceae weeds from Xishuangbanna, SW China. *PLoS One*, 13, 1, e0191710, 2018.
3. He, K., Zhang, X., Ren, S., Sun, J., Deep residual learning for image recognition, in: *Proceedings of the IEEE Conference on Computer Vision and Pattern Recognition*, pp. 770–778, 2016.
4. Ubbens, J., Cieslak, M., Prusinkiewicz, P., Stavness, I., The use of plant models in deep learning: An application to leaf counting in rosette plants. *Plant Methods*, 14, 1, 6, 2018.
5. Akila, M. and Deepan, P., Detection and classification of Plant Leaf diseases by using Deep Learning Algorithm. *Int. J. Eng. Res. Technol.*, 6, 2–7, 2018.
6. Mohanty, S.P., Hughes, D.P., Salathé, M., Using deep learning for image-based plant disease detection. *Front. Plant Sci.*, 7, 1419, 2016.
7. Malinao, R.M.L. and Hernandez, A.A., Artocarpus Trees Classification using Convolutional Neural Network, in: *2018 IEEE 10th International Conference on Humanoid, Nanotechnology, Information Technology, Communication and Control, Environment and Management (HNICEM)*, IEEE, pp. 1–6, 2018.
8. Srivastava, N., Hinton, G., Krizhevsky, A., Sutskever, I., Salakhutdinov, R., Dropout: A simple way to prevent neural networks from overfitting. *J. Mach. Learn. Res.*, 15, 1, 1929–1958, 2014.
9. Rashad, M.Z., El-Desouky, B.S., Khawasik, M.S., Plants images classification based on textural features using combined classifier. *Int. J. Comput. Sci. Inf. Technol.*, 3, 4, 93–100, 2011.
10. Gu, J., Wang, Z., Kuen, J., Ma, L., Shahroudy, A., Shuai, B., Chen, T., Recent advances in convolutional neural networks. *Pattern Recognit.*, 77, 354–377, 2018.
11. O'Shea, K. and Nash, R., An introduction to convolutional neural networks, arXiv preprint arXiv:1511.08458, 2015. https://white.stanford.edu/teach/index.php/An_Introduction_to_Convolutional_Neural_Networks
12. Khan, R.U., Zhang, X., Kumar, R., Aboagye, E.O., Evaluating the performance of ResNet model based on image recognition, in: *Proceedings of the 2018 International Conference on Computing and Artificial Intelligence*, 2018, March, pp. 86–90.
13. Jiang, Y. and Li, C., Convolutional Neural Networks for Image-Based High-Throughput Plant Phenotyping: A Review. *Plant Phenomics*, 4152816, 1–22, 2020.
14. Labach, A., Salehinejad, H., Valaee, S., Survey of dropout methods for deep neural networks, arXiv preprint arXiv:1904.13310, 2019. https://arxiv.org/abs/1904.13310

15. Smith, A.G., Han, E., Petersen, J., Olsen, N.A.F., Giese, C., Athmann, M., Dresbøll, D.B., Thorup-Kristensen, K., Rootpainter: Deep learning segmentation of biological images with corrective annotation. *BioRxiv*, 2020. https://www.biorxiv.org/content/10.1101/2020.04.16.044461v2

16. Tan, J.W., Chang, S.W., Kareem, S.B.A., Yap, H.J., Yong, K.T., Deep learning for plant species classification using leaf vein morphometric. *IEEE/ACM Trans. Comput. Biol. Bioinf.*, 17, 1, 82–90, 2018.

17. Alimboyong, C.R., Hernandez, A.A., Medina, R.P., Classification of plant seedling images using deep learning, in: *TENCON 2018-2018 IEEE Region 10 Conference*, 2018, October, IEEE, pp. 1839–1844.

18. Nkemelu, D.K., Omeiza, D., Lubalo, N., Deep convolutional neural network for plant seedlings classification, arXiv preprint arXiv:1811.08404, 2018. http://arxiv.org/abs/1811.08404

8

Development of IoT-Based Smart Security and Monitoring Devices for Agriculture

Himadri Nath Saha[1]*, Reek Roy[2], Monojit Chakraborty[3] and Chiranmay Sarkar[3]

[1]Department of Computer Science, Surendranath Evening College, Calcutta University, Kolkata, India
[2]Department of Computer Science, Belda College, Vidyasagar University, Paschim Medinipur, India
[3]Department of Information Technology, RCC Institute of Information Technology, Kolkata, India

Abstract

Smart farming technologies have empowered farmers which help them to compete with significant problems they face through much better remedies. The growth pattern and environmental parameters of crop growth provide scientific guidance and optimum countermeasures for agricultural production. The proposed system uses a Raspberry Pi board and an array of sensors—PIR sensor, pH sensor, and capacitance dielectric soil moisture sensor, and is robust and more accurate than existing systems in tracking the soil contents and the security of the crops. If soil nutrient, pH, or moisture of the soil is not at par with the requirements for a given crop the user will be notified to take action using an alarm sent through buzzer and LED. A monitoring system (Unmanned Aerial Vehicle (UAV) equipped with RGB-D sensor) is deployed to regularly check the status of the crops such that in case of pest attacks or when the crop health looks degraded it can be efficiently noted and necessary steps can be taken. The various data generated is stored in the cloud are sent to the website and phone application and will be used for further study to enhance the agricultural process.

Keywords: Raspberry Pi, pH sensor, soil parameter, RGB-D sensor, PIR sensor, smart farming, unmanned aerial vehicle (UAV), wireless sensor networks (WSNs)

Corresponding author: contactathimadri@gmail.com

Amitava Choudhury, Arindam Biswas, Manish Prateek and Amlan Chakrabarti (eds.)
Agricultural Informatics: Automation Using the IoT and Machine Learning, (147–170) © 2021
Scrivener Publishing LLC

8.1   Introduction

Internet of Things (IoT) has become the most progressive idea in the cutting edge time of the present times, offering help to all the aspects of the world, for example, home, industry, and numerous different applications. Agriculture is one of such fields which utilize IoT to improve smart cultivating. To cope up with climate changes and also to understand the growth of crops in customized small-scale environments, a wide range of research and study of the behavior of crop is needed. The term itself says that the IoT paradigm will give us a mechanical universe, where ordinary instruments, machines are upgraded using computing power. These instruments will have a system and network abilities, sensors. To put it plainly, physical objects which can be delegated as "Things" will be able to function as single units or as a fusion of coordinated efforts of heterogeneous gadgets [1].

The present and coming innovations of the Internet of Things (IoT) have an incredible probability of interfacing machine-to-machine, human-to-human through smart technologies like mobile processing, remote sensor systems, and so forth and making it an overall smart correspondence. IoT is serving over all the world smart conditions in regular daily existence areas, for example, the healthcare framework, transport framework, agriculture, cultivating framework, traffic framework, security framework, and a lot more [1].

There will always be a demand for food all over the world. Due to a lack of integration and utilization of technology, there is a shortage of food in the world with the increase in the human population. Agriculture in straightforward words is the study of developing and cultivating the soil, creating yields and raising livestock, and lastly marketing the subsequent items [2]. The expanding demand for food as far as in amount and quality can be met by combining technology cultivating practices. The worldwide populace has been expanding and essentially thus there must be an expansion in crop creation to fulfill the world's need for food and nutrition. Simultaneously, agriculture is joined by a lot of different issues like atmosphere changes, ecological changes, an increase in urbanization, water shortage, soil dampness factors, deficiency of arable land for developing harvests [3, 4]. These variables influence the development of horticulture like harvest profitability, diseases, and yield production. Thus, there is a need to fuse innovation with agriculture to expand productivity. Current methods can be utilized to develop crops in a controlled situation [5] which can assist people with smart farming. Likewise, Cloud Computing gives adequate resources for continuous storage and analyzing the huge bulk of information produced by the gadgets which can be utilized in automating processes, foreseeing circumstances, and improving numerous exercises to progress cultivating.

IoT will have the option to assist farmers with getting a convenient and timely cultivation guideline regarding the seasonal plant disease, usage of pesticides and fertilizers, pest control, crop treatment, irrigation system, catastrophic events influencing crops and the recuperation strategies [4, 5]. With the mix of IoT with agriculture, it won't just be helpful to the farmers yet in addition to the progress of the country. With the issues referenced over in agriculture, one can comprehend that there is an interest in an adequate determination of yield types, an appropriate adjustment of cultivating practices, and manageability to save the scarce resources of the planet [4].

Fusing agriculture alongside IoT presumes that the connections will be remote and wireless dependent on the consumption of energy, the uplink and downlink of information rate, and gadget per success point, topology, size of the packet, and width of channel and data transfer capacity. For instance, diseases of plants are customarily recognized physically by horticulture specialists, which can be inaccurate at times and again and is likewise very tedious. To maintain a strategic distance from such inaccurate outcomes and tedious procedures, programmed and remote recognition of diseases of the crops can be applied through Wireless Sensor Networks (WSN) and IoT [2]. Other existing advances that are attainable with IoT are radio frequency identification (RFID), middleware technologies, and cloud computing and end-client applications [6]. Thus, these advances greatly affect cultivating with a great impact alongside a solid effect on the worldwide economy.

To cope up with climate changes and also to understand the growth of crops in customized small-scale environments, a wide range of research and study of the behavior of crop is needed. The growth pattern and environmental parameters of crop growth provide scientific guidance and optimum countermeasures for agricultural production. Main security threats which are faced by the farmers are unnecessary animal intruder, various crop wasting insects, and others.

Wireless Sensor Networks (WSNs) have been deployed in the agriculture domain for quite some time to improve the monitoring of the products and agricultural resources remotely. The maintenance and deployment of WSNs in the real world still face quite some challenges even though a lot of progress has been made in the past few years. The general challenges faced by WSNs are low power communication, hardware constraints of small sensor devices, and their power consumption. Keeping aside these problems, WSNs face additional challenges when deployed for a long term in outdoors. The natural environment holds a very strong impact on the operability of a WSN. Sensor nodes are usually exposed to harsh weather conditions during heavy rainfall and extreme temperature fluctuations.

Sensors placed on higher levels above the crops are sometimes covered or disturbed by birds. Some insects form nests in the sensor housing which has negative impacts. Humidity, soil moisture, dust during dry seasons, short circuits, corrosion, mud affect the growth of the crops and in turn, the productivity is affected. Along with these challenges, farmers face another main issue of an unnecessary animal intruder, various crop wasting insects, and others. Protection of the deployed devices from environmental damages and wildlife damages is a hence a very big challenge. Crop fields are usually located in the rural areas of the countries. When the ground-level sensors are deployed in the agriculture fields, they sometimes are moved from their respective locations due to local wildlife, the sensors are seen with bit marks on them or the cables are found with nibbles.

To overcome the security threats which are faced by the farmers due to unnecessary animal intruder, various crop wasting insects and others along with monitoring environmental conditions, a system is needed which will identify the unwanted objects near the crops and give an alert to the farmers along with keeping a check on the environmental conditions required to grow the crops. Such a system has been hence proposed in this book chapter which uses an array of sensors with a Raspberry Pi board to overcome these challenges.

Section 8.2 consists of a literature survey done on various existing systems mentioning the results, pros, and cons of these systems. In Section 8.3, the system design and the architecture of the proposed model have been elaborated. Section 8.4 has an explanation of the methodology of the proposed model. In Sections 8.5 and 8.6, the performance analysis and the future research direction of the proposed model are explained. Section 8.7 has a short conclusion of this book chapter.

8.2   Background & Related Works

Agriculture plays a very potential role in the growth of the country's economy since it is the main source of food grains and other raw materials. There are a lot of factors on which the farmers have to keep a tab on while cultivating crops in the fields. The crops need to be monitored daily. Crops have been monitored traditionally by farmers for ages. For example, finding which crop requires what type of pesticide for pest control was done by experts.

Along with monitoring the crops for their physical attributes, climatic conditions like extreme cold, storms, flood, hail, etc. affect the growth of crops. The change in weather conditions like the humidity, wind, rain, heat, etc. also challenges that farmers have to face regularly. The change in soil quality like the pH change, moisture in the soil, macronutrients like nitrogen, potassium, phosphorus needs to be paid attention by the farmers so that yield of crops is increased. Hence, we see the need for the development of IoT-based smart security and monitoring devices for agriculture. These systems not only help in identifying the change in soil parameters, topology change, and weather factors affecting crops but also help in monitoring the fields from animals, insects attacking the crops or the diseases that affect the crops and allow for remote access location by the farmers based on real-time data. Sensors are selected based on the problems faced by the farmers.

Wired and wireless sensors have been used in the agriculture fields widely in the past few decades. Most of the time, researchers have focused on climatic conditions in open-field deployments. Some researchers have also focused on soil monitoring. There are even some models which give us a development of the distributed monitoring system using wireless sensor networks (WSN) in a commercial greenhouse which helps in the uniform production of the quality and quantity of the products and at the same time minimizing the risk of diseases at certain problematic regions of the greenhouse.

Images of plants are captured by a camera interfaced by Raspberry Pi3 hardware periodically in a model proposed by Devi *et al.* [2] to classify diseases using a Random Forest Classifier technique. The extracted features are transferred to the cloud via Wi-Fi. This system achieved a 24% better classification accuracy, specificity, sensitivity, precision-recall when compared to the existing K-NN classifier, giving an accuracy of almost 99%. But this system's accuracy depends on the environmental conditions of the field like the angles of capturing the image. This system also lacks to see the soil conditions while growing the crops.

A system that focuses on leaf area index (LAI) continuously has been proposed by Bauer *et al.* [4], mainly comprising of a wireless sensor network (WSN) based monitoring system for precision crop growth. The monitoring system uses Public Land Mobile Network (PLMN) connectivity and a Message Queuing Telemetry Transport (MQTT) based IoT infrastructure to connect with the central server. Lack of any environmental sensors in the system makes it a little less enriched system.

In a model proposed by Gmur *et al.* [7], the sensor used to do a hyperspectral analysis of soil contents (carbon, nitrogen, organic matter) is a spectroradiometer. The range for this prediction model was limited as there were only three samples of soil carbonate concentrations greater than one percent. This model can be further developed with a drone integrated with a camera to take pictures of the fields.

The electrical conductivity, soil moisture, and temperature are analyzed using time domain reflectometry (TDR) in the designed model by Skierucha et al. [8], where the device is designed using eight channels of TDR, a General Packet Radio Service to collect data and two-rod probes. Lack of any image capturing sensor in the system makes it a little less enriched system. Jhuria et al. [9] proposed a system in which the image processing technique is used to monitor the diseases starting from plantation until harvesting on two fruits, grapes, and apples, using an artificial neural network concept. The system is effective for controlling disease spread and gives a 90% correct result. This system can be further developed using soil sensors to get better results for the growth of crops.

Jagannathan et al. [10] proposed a methodology in which a smart irrigator and a smart sensing system are linked through wireless communication technology. This smart sensing system is used to spray the necessary nutrients based on the requirements of the crops and adequate water spray based on the moisture content. This smart irrigation system can be developed further to check the intrusion of animals in the field using a sensor.

Balaji et al. [11] proposed a system which delivers real-time notifications to orient smart irrigation, after analyzing information without human interference. The pump is switched on to provide adequate water to the crops in this system based on the reading of the sensors deployed on the ground, helping in saving water and the power consumption of the motors. The image sensors can be incorporated into this system so that the monitoring of diseases of the crops can be done.

A Green House Management System (GHMS) has been presented by Mat et al. [12], where WSNs are used to measure air wetness, temperature, and soil moisture using the XBee technology. Irrigation efficiency is compared using this system through a comparison of automatic and scheduled irrigation. Lack of image capturing sensors makes this system a little less enriched.

The system proposed by Suma et al. [13] uses a microcontroller connected to various sensors to measure temperature, moisture, and to check if an object is near the vicinity of the crops. The system gives an output of the soil moisture, temperature, and intruder detection using PIC microcontroller 16F877A and also gives a result in the Android application about the same. The system can be further developed by integrating a drone to keep a track of the field by capturing images of the crops.

To do precision agriculture monitoring, the proposed approach by Murugan *et al.* [14] uses image statistics of a region received using satellite and drone to differentiate between a dense and a sparse field. Maia *et al.* [15] proposed a model in which an IoT device that monitors many agricultural parameters using sensors for humidity, soil, etc. has been discussed. In this system, the environmental changes can be detected in the soil. The future scope of the system mentions that an IoT device can be attached to detect fires in the crops.

A simulator that coordinates Unmanned Aerial Vehicles (UAV) in the presence of harmful insects in crops has been proposed by De Rango *et al.* [16], which would consider other factors of the drones also. In this system, the drones are set with related communication modules and sensors, parasites with their movements and plants with resistance characteristics. Two aspects are addressed in this system, monitoring the area to detect the parasites and the coordination of the drones to destroy these parasites. This simulator that is proposed can include other parameters for the monitoring approaches of the parasites. Other soil sensors or environmental sensors can be integrated to make the system more efficient.

Various plowing techniques are differentiated using an RGB-D sensor which is connected to drones in a model proposed by Tripicchio *et al.* [17]. The sensing technology that is presented in this system uses an RGB-D sensor to discriminate between the plowing depths and analyze the characteristics of the soil. Along with this, if soil characteristics are maintained using soil sensors, the model will be more efficient.

The usage of WSNs has increased the productivity and growth of crops and has reduced the waste significantly and hence these WSNs deployed are integrated with IoT more recently to monitor the resources and the agricultural products. Such a study has been discussed by Hartung *et al.* [18]. The challenges faced to incorporate such a system mentioned by are quite a few. A good amount of planning is required to deploy the nodes. It is also important to have an exact map of the nodes and directions so that reconstruction can be avoided. Another problem faced was the cut off cables and who caused it, that is, bitten by animals or cut by a human willingly was not exactly found out.

In a system proposed by López *et al.* [19], a remote automatic pest monitorization technology has been mentioned in which images of pests are sent to the host control via wireless one-hop communication using a low-power image sensor. The system can be further developed by integrating with other environmental or soil sensors.

The usage of drones has been mentioned in a model proposed by Reinecke *et al.* [20] in which the proposed mechanism helps in improving the quality of the crops. The system used a certain specific camera that is connected to the drones to detect the shortage of water and also harmful pests. These loopholes found through the drones help the farmers to increase the yield.

Nandurkar *et al.* [21] proposed an efficient wireless sensor network technique that is low in cost and acquires the temperature and the moisture of the soil from different segments of the farm. This helps the crop controller to decide if the irrigation is enabled or not. Image taking sensors if incorporated in drones with this WSN system will give a better accurate result for the productivity of crops.

Katsoulas *et al.* [22] proposed a system in which, powerful end-nodes and computationally demanding sensors like image sensors are used to monitor and control the agriculture. The images captured are used to process the image on-board or for plain monitoring of the crops on a cloud-based infrastructure or at the edge of the network. Along with these sensors, if soil sensors are used the system will help to yield a better production of the crops.

Some studies have shown that for WSNs, some of the popular wireless networking modules are Bluetooth, Wi-Fi, XBee modules, and nRF24L01 plus radio modules. These networking modules are embedded solutions that provide standard wireless connectivity. Among these, XBee modules and nRF24L01 plus radio modules are self-healing mesh networks and provide a longer range compared to Bluetooth and have lower power consumption than Wi-Fi networks [23].

Drones or UAVs (Unmanned Aerial Vehicles) with mounted cameras, integrated components, and sensors can be deployed in different areas of the region of fields, capturing real-time images and contributing to agricultural precision as well as crop safety issues. Some potential approaches [24] have been addressed that can be integrated into Unmanned Aerial Vehicles (UAV) or drones, such as hyperspectral imaging is significantly better than multispectral imaging. Using Support Vector Machine (SVM), an RGB-D camera can be mounted in drones to get real-time images that can be processed further for smart farming. These frameworks can have a built-in Global Positioning System (GPS), so that the controller, that is, the farmer can carry the right instruction across any location and keep a track on the UAVs [25].

So we can see that the potential applications of IoT in agriculture can be categorized into the utilization of sensing and control of agriculture (like multimedia sensor networks used in remote capturing of images to process and detect insects and plant diseases), scalar sensors' networks and RFID (Radio-Frequency Identification), NFC (Near-Field Communication) that are tag-based networks which allow to track and identify the products remotely. In the end, it is all about the sensors—weather stations, ground sensors, climate sensors the flow of data between the sensors, and the microprocessor that help in the increasing demand for the crops, the high quality of the agricultural products and also their safety.

From the above literature review, we can conclude that there are some systems developed that identifies the environmental conditions like the temperature and soil conditions of the crops, and necessary steps are taken in those systems to help in crop growth. Other certain systems are built to see the security of the fields. Some systems are built to keep the irrigation system in check. Existing systems also sometimes lack the potentiality to find out if any node is stolen, or any cable is cut by a human willingly or due to the biting of animals. The proposed system not only keeps a track of the soil contents but also keeps a track of the security of the crop field using sensors.

So, this book chapter proposes a model that will enable the farmers to know the conditions of the soil better using various sensors that are connected using a wireless connection and protect the crops from any intrusion made by and wildlife, humans with improper intentions, or any other objects. The system proposed also has a monitoring system attached to a drone to detect if the crops have any diseases. Images are captured using the drones and all data are stored in the cloud and are displayed on the website for the farmer to keep a track. An alert is sent to the farmer to take the necessary step if the sensor values cross the threshold values.

8.3   Proposed Model

The model (Figure 8.1) that has been proposed can guide the farmers about the conditions of the soil and give an alert if there is an intruder or animal near the crops through a series of sensors. The system also has Unmanned Aerial Vehicle (UAV) monitoring the entire field by clicking pictures using an RGB-D camera.

A PIR sensor is used in the proposed system to keep a check on any object/humans/wildlife/pest approaching the crops. The pH sensor and the dielectric soil sensor keep a track of the pH of the soil and the moisture content of the soil respectively maintains these soil factors by keeping the updated data in the cloud and showing the details on the website and the installed application on the phone.

The RGB-D sensor is used to protect the crops from environmental hazards like floods, etc. and also the pictures clicked shows the current condition

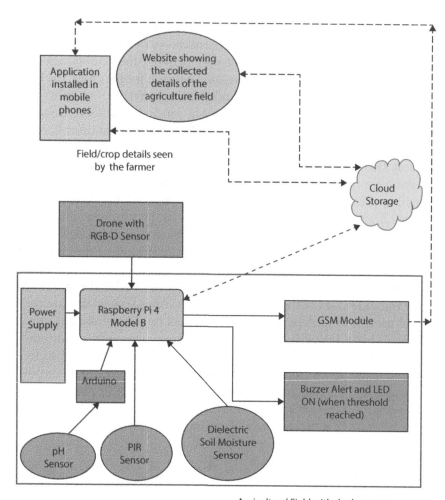

Figure 8.1 Framework of proposed system.

of the crops. For example, if a certain section of the field's crops turn yellow due to some disease and are reflected in the pictures clicked by the RGB-D camera, the farmer can treat that section before the entire field is affected. This in turn helps in keeping control of the crops efficiently and effectively.

8.3.1 Raspberry Pi 4 Model B

This is the latest model of the Raspberry Pi (RPi) used in the system. It was created by Raspberry Pi Foundation and is a tiny low-cost Single Board

Computer (SBC) based on an ARM. It has facilities for Bluetooth and Wi-Fi. The converted digital equivalents of the parameters obtained can be sent to any cloud-based storage area over the internet through this module. The sensors are connected with the Raspberry Pi 4 Model B through a secured wireless connection. This quad-core model is more capable and faster compared to its predecessors. This model has been chosen due to other benefits also like web browsing, which will allow us to visit the website built for this system, and with the additional memory, it can easily switch from mobile applications and heavy websites without lagging. The serial connection that is used here is the RS-232 connection which uses −10V and +10V for 1 and 0 respectively. But, the Universal Asynchronous Receiver/Transmitter (UART) pins of Raspberry Pi uses 0 and 3 Volts for logical 0 and 1 respectively. As this difference will cause the RPi to not survive, so an integrated circuit MAX3232CPE is developed which is a simple converter that converts voltage levels using the help of a few capacitors and allows connection to the RPi via RS-232. To build this integrated circuit a MAX3232CPE and 5× 100 nF capacitors are used. Python and Scratch can be used as the main programming language, but it also supports other programming languages. It also is beneficial as the Operating System to be used can be chosen by the user.

8.3.2   Passive Infrared Sensor (PIR Sensor)

Every object with a temperature above absolute zero emits heat energy in the form of radiation. A PIR Sensor is an electronic sensor, used in PIR-based motion detectors like the automatically activated lighting objects and security systems, which measures infrared light radiating objects in its field of view. PIR sensors detect the infrared radiation reflected or emitted from an object instead of measuring or detecting heat. PIR sensors usually detect the general movement. They do not give the details and information of what or who moved, but just movements of animals, humans, or any other objects. An active IR sensor can be used to get the details of who or what moves. When there is a presence of any wildlife or an unnecessary insect is present, or a human passes in the field, or there is an intruder sensed in the field, the temperature at that point in the sensor's field of view rises to the body temperature of the intruder from the room temperature and then back again. This resulting change in the incoming infrared radiation is converted by the sensor into a change in the output voltage which triggers the detection.

8.3.3   pH Sensor

A key factor for crop health is the soil content and its quality. So pH monitoring is a very important aspect. The best pH for plants is usually between 5.5 and 6.5. Some plants may need more acidic soil or some may need more alkaline soils. The efficiency of fertilizers is maximized by ph control by controlling the bioavailability of the nutrient of the soil. The presence of toxic elements, the structure of certain soils, and the activity of the soil bacteria are also affected by the pH of soil. A pH sensor relies on a voltage test to determine the level of hydrogen and then the pH, so there must be a flow of electricity. To do so, a complete circuit must be present. A test sample completes a pH sensor circuit. The sample soil comes into contact with the two electrodes (a part of a circuit that comes into contact with the non-metallic elements) present on the probe. A pH sensor has two electrodes—a reference electrode and a glass electrode. A chemical solution and a silver-based wire are housed in the glass electrode that has a permeable membrane which is made of specialized glass. The reference electrode acts as a buffer and is stable. In analog pH sensors, the signal obtained acts on an electromagnetic coil that causes a rotation on the needle which gives a pH reading on the scale. On the other hand, digital pH sensors require an analog-to-digital converter to display the number on the screen. This proposed system has used a digital pH sensor connected to Arduino to capture and record the pH data of the soil.

8.3.4   Dielectric Soil Moisture Sensor

There are two ways to measure the moisture of the soil. One is the contact-based in which the detection area of the sensor requires to be directly in touch with the soil, the detection media which is being detected. This type of sensor has many ways depending on the parameters of detection, like the capacitance sensors, fiber optic sensor, and the heat pulse sensor. The other way to measure soil moisture is the contact-free based. In this type of moisture sensor, the detection media, that is, the soil does not need to be touched directly to the detection area of the soil. Passive microwave radiometers, thermal methods, synthetic aperture radars are contact-free based moisture sensors. These sensors are used to determine the moisture of the soil by measuring the dielectric constant of the soil. This proposed system uses a dielectric soil moisture sensor. The dielectric constant of the soil is an electrical property that depends highly on the moisture content. The constant for water is 80, about one for air and dry soil is between 3 and 5. There is a substantial change in the dielectric constant of the soil when there is a change in the moisture content.

8.3.5 RGB-D Sensor

A specific kind of depth-sensing device, that is, depth sensor, is an RGB-D sensor, which works alongside an RGB camera. The proposed system uses a low-cost commercial RGB-D camera to visualize and analyze the soil. It can be implemented in rotary wings like a multi-rotor system or in a fixed-wing drone. A conventional image with depth information on the per-pixel is added. The depth data provided by the infrared sensor is coordinated with a calibrated RGB camera which in turn produces an RGB image with a depth associated with each pixel. Predefined dotted patterns are emitted by the IR projector. The depth of the region which is being examined is determined by the sidelong shift between the projector and the sensor of the pattern dots. The amalgamated data representation of the specific data is a collection of points in the three-dimensional space, the point cloud. So, there is an extra feature for every single point. In the case of an RGB-D sensor, it is the color. Asus Xtion PRO, Microsoft Kinect are commercially available sensors that use this technology.

8.3.6 GSM Module

A GSM (Global System for Mobile Communications) module is used to establish communication between a computing machine or a mobile device and a GSM. It is a circuit or a chip powered by a power supply and uses communication interfaces like the USB 2.0 or the RS-232 for the computer. A GSM modem acts like a mobile phone which has its unique phone number by accepting any GSM network operator SIM. Since it uses RS-232 protocol, hence our proposed approach uses this secured wireless connection between the sensors and the Raspberry Pi board. The Raspberry Pi is also connected to the GSM modem through RS-232. To use the RS-232 connection in Raspberry Pi, an integrated circuit is built as mentioned before. To interact with the controller or the processor, the modem requires AT commands. The SMSs sent and received to the terminal are done using AT commands. These AT commands are sent by the processor or the controller to control the GSM to get the desired results. It is used in this proposed model to send messages to the phones of the farmer as GSM cellular communication is ideal for sensor-based low-bandwidth-data projects as it sends low amounts of data over the Internet. The range for the GSM is

35 km maximum with a frequency of 900 MHz, thus covering a very large area and is advantageous for the farmer if he is not present in the agriculture field.

8.3.7   Unmanned Aerial Vehicle (UAV)

An agricultural drone allows a farmer to get an aerial view of his field. The advantage of a bird-eye view is that it reveals many issues like variations of soil, irrigation problems, pest control, etc. An agricultural drone is an Unmanned Aerial Vehicle (UAV) that allows the farmers to optimize agricultural yields, increase the production of the soil along with monitoring the growth of the crop. Sensors and cameras attached to these Unmanned Aerial Vehicles (UAVs) give the farmers a better picture of their fields. The capturing, localization, mapping, and analysis of high-resolution images give a detailed view to the farmers by differentiating between healthy and unhealthy crops. Such details may not be visible clearly to naked eyes. The farmers can set the survey of the crops using the UAVs according to their liking. Hourly, weekly or daily pictures captured by these UAVs can be uploaded to the cloud overtime to help the farmers identify the trouble spots on their fields and act accordingly.

8.4   Methodology

There are three main components in the proposed system: the cloud, the website, or the phone application, and the monitoring nodes. The methodology of the system, used in tomato fields, has been explained in Figure 8.2. An array of sensors, that is, the monitoring nodes—PIR sensor, pH sensor (connected to the Arduino first), and capacitance dielectric soil moisture sensor are deployed in the field to monitor the soil and intrusion.

The pH sensor and the soil moisture sensor are buried in the root zones of the crops so that they can accurately determine the moisture and pH level of the soil and transmit the readings to the Raspberry Pi. Python is the programming language used in Raspberry Pi. The Raspberry Pi requires a power supply of 5 V. The operating system that is used here to upload the Raspberry Pi is the Raspbian Jessie operating system which is a Debian based Linux distribution.

The PIR sensor is an electronic sensor, which is used for motion detection near the crops. It measures infrared light radiating objects in its field of view and hence can identify any unwanted objects or pests near the crops. There are two slots present in the PIR sensor and both the slots

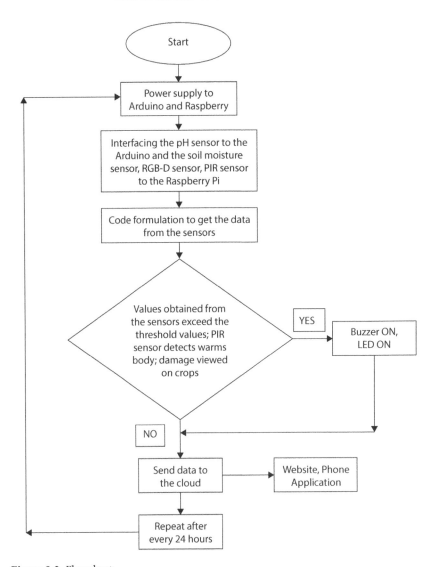

Figure 8.2 Flowchart.

are made up of special material that is sensitive to the IR. With the PIR sensor buried near the roots of the crops, it detects the same IR when it is idle, that is the ambient amount radiated from the near surroundings in the field. When a warm body, example, pest, insect, wildlife, or human crosses it, one half of the PIR sensor is intercepted which results in a positive differential change between the two halves of the sensor. The sensor generates a negative differential change when the warm body leaves the sensing area. These changes in pulses are detected and the data are sent to the Raspberry Pi board.

The pH sensor is connected to the Arduino that acts as an Analog-to-Digital Converter (ADC) this is connected to the Raspberry Pi using RS-232 connection. This is because Raspberry Pi is not compatible with analog values. To write the programming code for Arduino, Arduino IDE is used. The reference electrode acts as a reference to which the glass electrode can be compared. A small voltage is created when the glass electrode attracts the hydrogen ions, which is compared to the reference electrode. This voltage difference between the two electrodes is translated as a pH reading when sent as a signal to the indicator.

Capacitance dielectric soil moisture sensor is used which is attached to data loggers to maintain a continuous record of the soil moisture content. Two electrodes are separated by a material called the dielectric that does not conduct an electric current readily. When the sensor is inserted in the soil, the soil becomes a part of the dielectric. When an oscillator applies a frequency (between 50 and 150 MHz) to the electrodes, a resonant frequency is a result whose magnitude depends on the dielectric constant of the soil. The smaller is the frequency when the soil moisture content is greater. This frequency is then used to estimate the volumetric soil moisture content.

These sensors are connected and data is sent using the RS-232 connection to the cloud and also the GSM module. The cloud uses ThinkSpeak for storing and retrieving data from the Raspberry Pi board. The Raspberry Pi board is connected to the sensors and a power supply. The data collected from the array of sensors connected to the Raspberry Pi are sent to the board through a secured wireless connection RS-232. The system uses a Raspberry Pi board to send the control signals to the website.

To send data acquired through an RGB-D sensor connected to a drone or a UAV (Unmanned Aerial Vehicles), to the cloud storage, it is embedded in the Raspberry Pi model. The array of sensors keeps checking the moisture content of the soil, pH of the soil, the surrounding movements near the crops, and other parameters, and the readings are updated on the website. A GSM module is connected to the Raspberry Pi model using the same RS-232 secured wireless connection, which sends and receives messages to the farmer's phone.

A GSM module acts as a GSM network operator. It is like a mobile phone with its unique number and can be used to receive and send SMS and calls by the farmers to switch ON and OFF the Raspberry Pi automatically or manually. The website displays the soil parameters like moisture content, pH of the soil, and a widget of security status.

A monitoring system in which a drone or a UAV is equipped with the RGB-D sensor is deployed to check the status of the crops such that in case of pest attacks or when the crop health looks degraded or during veld fires, floods or landslides it can be efficiently noted and necessary steps can be taken. The UAV is equipped using a battery to provide the energy for flying and for moving in the required areas. The RGB-D camera captures real-time images and processes the images. To reduce the costing, the conventional multispectral technique has been used in the UAV instead of hyperspectral imaging. The advantage of this technique is that UAV suing multispectral imagery can be used throughout the crop cycle effectively by the farmers. With multispectral imaging capabilities, the farmers can estimate the yield of the crops. The UAVs movement is modeled through the usage of the local map of the field stored on-board. The received data is verified with the threshold values set for every sensor. The various data generated are stored in the cloud and will be used for further study to enhance the agricultural process. These data are updated on the website for the farmers to keep track of. A phone app that keeps track of all these data is installed on the farmer's phone.

The GSM module helps in sending and receiving texts to the farmers, when and wherever necessary. The threshold values for the respective sensors are set from beforehand. If the data received exceeds the threshold value, the buzzer is switched ON and the LED starts blinking. The buzzer and the LED light are used to alert the farmers. When the buzzer is switched ON and the LED blinks, it acts as an alarm which is sent as an alert message to the farmer. In such situations, the farmer also receives a text message on their phones to take the necessary step. For example, if soil nutrient is not at par with the requirements for a given crop the user will be notified to take action. The security system comprises the intermittent PIR sensor which gives the Raspberry Pi board a sense of intrusion by animals, any other human, or any other object. This system will help users to increase production output and mitigate the various risks of crop damage.

The mobile application and the website are built to show the pH content, soil moisture content, the detection of intruders, and the images clicked using RGB-D sensor. The ON/OFF status of the buzzer and the LED is also shown in both. The mobile application has a home screen (Figures 8.3(a) and (b)) in which the buttons for the respective sensors are present. The website interface also works similarly (Figure 8.3(c)). When we click one of those buttons, we can see the last updated status of that sensor. Some of the snapshots for the readings of data of the respective sensors are shown in Figure 8.4. Figure 8.5 shows some images taken from the UAV.

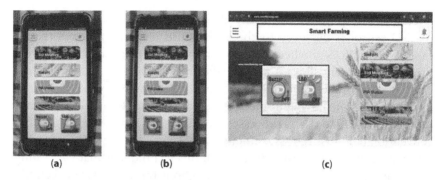

Figure 8.3 Snapshots of (a) home screen of phone application when buzzer and LED OFF; (b) the home screen of phone application when buzzer and LED ON (c) home screen of the website.

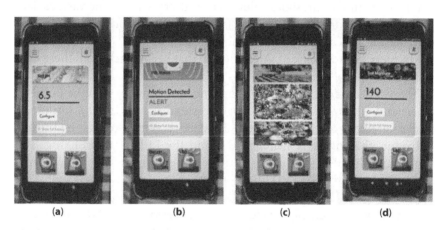

Figure 8.4 Snapshots of readings of sensors: (a) pH reading of soil using ph sensor; (b) motion detected alert using PIR sensor; (c) images clicked using RGB-D sensor, (d) soil moisture reading using capacitance dielectric soil moisture sensor.

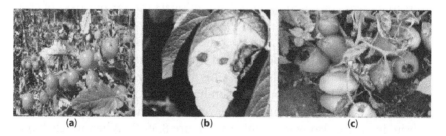

Figure 8.5 Some images of tomatoes taken using UAV. (a) image of healthy tomatoes; (b) image of a leaf from the tomato field turning yellow when affected by some pest; (c) image of pest affected tomatoes.

8.5 Performance Analysis

The model proposed has been used in tomato fields. This system gives us a better performance compared to the existing systems in terms of precision farming. The system is robust and gives better results when compared to the existing systems. This proposed system analyzes the conditions of the soil resulting in higher productivity by almost 15–20% (Figure 8.6) which ultimately increases the profit. There is a saving of almost 70–80% in terms of labor, chemic maltreatments as UAVs play a very crucial role to monitor the crops and indicate their health. RGB-D sensor is a typical commercial sensor used here because it is relatively cost-effective and also it does not require dedicated electronic acquiring devices. This sensor also is feasible to use as it can be embedded in many aerial vehicles, making it quite popular among the farmers. When the pH reading of the soil reaches less than 5.5, it is considered acidic. This alerts the farmer that the soil is deficient in nitrogen and phosphorous so that he can take the necessary action to improve the pH of the soil. This system is also advantageous and feasible for the farmers even when they are not close to the crop fields as they get all the real-time data on their phones and receive alert signals if the moisture content or the pH levels are different compared to the required levels.

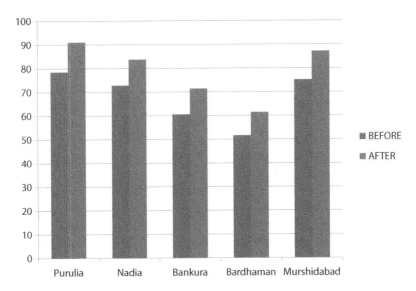

Figure 8.6 Graph shows the comparison of the production of tomatoes before and after the introduction of the proposed model. Approx. 15–20% increase in production of Tomatoes in different districts of West Bengal, India.

Using predictive analysis of the data captured by the sensors, the farmers can make better decisions related to the harvesting for the future. The sensors used in this system are broadly available, which allows this system to be built in any part of the world. The sensors chosen provide accurate measures that are useful to several types of soil modeling that are used in agriculture.

8.6   Future Research Direction

For future work, the system can be further developed to check other factors of the agriculture field like the weather parameters using the weather sensor along with the sensors used. The system can be enhanced into a smart irrigation system. The website can also show details of the water pump status. When water content becomes low, the user will be able to switch on the water pump directly from the website. In the case of waterlogging, the user can easily operate a water pump to drain out the excess water. For water management of the crops, ultrasonic sensors for water levels can be used which will send the details of the level of water to the website.

Location sensors that use the GPS satellite signals to find the latitude, longitude, and altitude in feet can be used to find the exact locations of issues if occurred in the fields. This system uses a Raspberry Pi board. A lot of other MCUs like the ESP8266, PIC16F877A, etc. are also available which can be used, and then a comparative study can be done. The Sensorex pH2200 spear tip pH sensor can be used in later stages in the future along with the pH which is specifically designed to penetrate the semi-solid surfaces for the effective measurement of the pH. It is easy to maintain and does not need refilling and is assembled with a bio-friendly Ultem body, which makes it safe to use in food and soil. The response time of this sensor is 90% or greater in 5–7 s which will make the system quicker in response.

The optical data captured by the Unmanned Aerial Vehicle (UAV) are stored in the cloud. Now, 'agricultural monitoring since performed in real-time can poses a problem if the cloud data is hacked. This might lead to misleading information caused due to altered values and can affect the productivity of the crops. Hence, there is a need to mask the data which are affected before analyzing. For such security, authentication of the user, access control, the confidentiality of data can be established. A middleware architecture that provides an end-to-end security solution for the farmers who upload the sensing data can be future work for this system. This can be extended to provide a multi-factor user authentication scheme at the middleware so the secured access is made to an authorized user, also providing a privacy solution that will prevent data breaches and data leakage at the middleware level. The system proposed is for crop fields, but smart greenhouses are also an application of IoT in which light sensors and actuators, temperature sensors, etc can be used to measure CO_2 level, water content, light level, etc. for efficient plant growth in controlled temperature. The model can be further developed to incorporate a smart GPS based remote-controlled robot along with the existing system. The aim will be to produce agriculture smart using IoT technologies and automation. The system will be able to perform tasks like detection of humans, sensing of moisture, keeping vigilance, weeding, and spraying.

The Unmanned Aerial Vehicle (UAV) used here is battery charged. For the future, they can get charged from solar energy during the day if solar panels are installed. The application of drones is not confined to the crops only. They can even identify which parts of the land are dry and can assess an irrigation plan much easier when embedded with hyper-spectral, multi-spectral, and thermal spectral. The system can be further extended with automated seed spraying. Such a device may be invented which can spread the seeds and with the change in weather conditions, the system can be intimated using intelligent systems to spread some other seeds.

8.7   Conclusion

The main objective of this book chapter is to help the farmers find out the pH level of the soil along with moisture of the soil content of the crops. This proposed system can be implemented in humid areas where the moisture of the soil keeps on varying. The UAVs will help in monitoring the crops by capturing real-time images using an RGB-D camera. The RGB-D sensor is advantageous as it is cost-effective compared to a prototype solution. It can also be embedded in several aerial vehicles and can be used in both the rotary-wing system and fixed-drone system. Protection of crops against insects, wildlife is an important task. Hence, the PIR sensor is used to sense intrusion by animals, insects, humans, or any other object which sends an alarm to the farmers. This helps the farmers in monitoring the crops from an unnecessary animal intruder, various crops wasting insects and others. In short, this proposed system comprises IoT and the cloud integrated with sensors attached to the Raspberry Pi board. The farmers can check the details updated on the website at regular intervals. It saves time and resources, along with reducing manual work that is required if the farmers wanted to do it manually. The information updated regarding soil also is more accurate compared to the manual observation when done by experts.

References

1. Chakraborty, S., Das, P., Pal, S., IoT Foundations and Its Application, in: *IoT and Analytics for Agriculture*, pp. 51–68, Springer, Singapore, 2020.
2. Devi, R.D., Nandhini, S.A., Hemalatha, R., Radha, S., IoT Enabled Efficient Detection and Classification of Plant Diseases for Agricultural Applications, in: *2019 International Conference on Wireless Communications Signal Processing and Networking (WiSPNET)*, IEEE, Chennai, India, pp. 447–451, 2019.
3. Masih, J. and Rajasekaran, R., Integrating Big Data Practices in Agriculture, in: *IoT and Analytics for Agriculture*, pp. 1–26, Springer, Singapore, 2020.
4. Bauer, J. and Aschenbruck, N., Design and implementation of an agricultural monitoring system for smart farming, in: *2018 IoT Vertical and Topical Summit on Agriculture-Tuscany (IOT Tuscany)*, IEEE, Tuscany, Italy, pp. 1–6, 2018.
5. Sowmiya, M. and Prabavathi, S., Smart Agriculture Using IoT and Cloud Computing. *IJRTE*, 7, 6S3, 2019.
6. Nayak, P., Kavitha, K., Rao, C.M., IoT-Enabled Agricultural System Applications, Challenges and Security Issues, in: *IoT and Analytics for Agriculture*, pp. 139–163, Springer, Singapore, 2020.
7. Gmur, S., Vogt, D., Zabowski, D., Moskal, L.M., Hyperspectral analysis of soil nitrogen, carbon, carbonate, and organic matter using regression trees. *Sensors*, 12, 8, 10639–10658, 2012.
8. Skierucha, W., Wilczek, A., Szypłowska, A., Sławiński, C., Lamorski, K., A TDR-based soil moisture monitoring system with simultaneous measurement of soil temperature and electrical conductivity. *Sensors*, 12, 10, 13545–13566, 2012.
9. Jhuria, M., Kumar, A., Borse, R., Image processing for smart farming: Detection of disease and fruit grading, in: *2013 IEEE Second International Conference on Image Information Processing (ICIIP-2013)*, IEEE, Shimla, India, pp. 521–526, 2013.
10. Jagannathan, S. and Priyatharshini, R., Smart farming system using sensors for agricultural task automation, in: *2015 IEEE Technological Innovation in ICT for Agriculture and Rural Development (TIAR)*, Chennai, India, pp. 49–53, IEEE, 2015.
11. Balaji, V.R. and Prakash, N., IOT Based Smart Security and Monitoring Devices for Agriculture. *Int. J. Pure Appl. Math.*, 116, 11, 121–129, 2017.
12. Mat, I., Kassim, M.R.M., Harun, A.N., Yusoff, I.M., IoT in precision agriculture applications using wireless moisture sensor network, in: *2016 IEEE Conference on Open Systems (ICOS)*, IEEE, Langkawi, Malaysia, pp. 24–29, 2016.
13. Suma, N., Samson, S.R., Saranya, S., Shanmugapriya, G., Subhashri, R., IoT based smart agriculture monitoring system. *Int. J. Recent Innovation Trends Comput. Commun.*, 5, 2, 177–181, 2017.

14. Murugan, D., Garg, A., Singh, D., Development of an adaptive approach for precision agriculture monitoring with drone and satellite data. *IEEE J. Sel. Top. Appl. Earth Obs. Remote Sens.*, 10, 12, 5322–5328, 2017.

15. Maia, R.F., Netto, I., Tran, A.L.H., Precision agriculture using remote monitoring systems in Brazil, in: *2017 IEEE Global Humanitarian Technology Conference (GHTC)*, IEEE, San Jose, CA, USA, pp. 1–6, 2017.

16. De Rango, F., Palmieri, N., Santamaria, A.F., Potrino, G., A simulator for UAVs management in agriculture domain, in: *2017 International Symposium on Performance Evaluation of Computer and Telecommunication Systems (SPECTS)*, IEEE, Seattle, WA, USA, pp. 1–8, 2017.

17. Tripicchio, P., Satler, M., Dabisias, G., Ruffaldi, E., Avizzano, C.A., Towards smart farming and sustainable agriculture with drones, in: *2015 International Conference on Intelligent Environments*, IEEE, Prague, Czech Republic, pp. 140–143, 2015.

18. Hartung, R., Kulau, U., Gernert, B., Rottmann, S., Wolf, L., On the experiences with testbeds and applications in precision farming, in: *Proceedings of the First ACM International Workshop on the Engineering of Reliable, Robust, and Secure Embedded Wireless Sensing Systems*, pp. 54–61, 2017.

19. López, O., Rach, M.M., Migallon, H., Malumbres, M.P., Bonastre, A., Serrano, J.J., Monitoring pest insect traps by means of low-power image sensor technologies. *Sensors*, 12, 11, 15801–15819, licensee MDPI, Basel, Switzerland, 2012.

20. Reinecke, M. and Prinsloo, T., The influence of drone monitoring on crop health and harvest size, in: *2017 1st International Conference on Next Generation Computing Applications (NextComp)*, IEEE, pp. 5–10, 2017.

21. Nandurkar, S.R., Thool, V.R., Thool, R.C., Design and development of precision agriculture system using wireless sensor network, in: *2014 First International Conference on Automation, Control, Energy and Systems (ACES)*, IEEE, Hooghy, India, pp. 1–6, 2014.

22. Katsoulas, N., Elvanidi, A., Ferentinos, K.P., Kacira, M., Bartzanas, T., Kittas, C., Crop reflectance monitoring as a tool for water stress detection in greenhouses: A review. *Biosyst. Eng.*, 151, 374–398, 2016.

23. Saha, H., Mandal, S., Mitra, S., Banerjee, S., Saha, U., Comparative Performance Analysis between nRF24L01+ and XBEE ZB Module Based Wireless Ad-hoc Networks. *Int. J. Comput. Netw. Inf. Secur.*, 9, 7, 2017.

24. Saha, A.K., Saha, J., Ray, R., Sircar, S., Dutta, S., Chattopadhyay, S.P., Saha, H.N., IOT-based drone for improvement of crop quality in agricultural field, in: *2018 IEEE 8th Annual Computing and Communication Workshop and Conference (CCWC)*, IEEE, Las Vegas, NV, USA, pp. 612–615, 2018.

25. Saha, H., Basu, S., Auddy, S., Dey, R., Nandy, A., Pal, D., Maity, T. *et al.*, A low cost fully autonomous GPS (Global Positioning System) based quad copter for disaster management, in: *2018 IEEE 8th Annual Computing and Communication Workshop and Conference (CCWC)*, IEEE, Las Vegas, NV, USA, pp. 654–660, 2018.

9

An Integrated Application of IoT-Based WSN in the Field of Indian Agriculture System Using Hybrid Optimization Technique and Machine Learning

Avishek Banerjee[1]*, Arnab Mitra[2] and Arindam Biswas[3]

[1]Department of Information Technology, Asansol Engineering College, Asansol, India
[2]Department of Computer Science & Engineering, Siksha 'O' Anusandhan (Deemed to be University), Bhubaneswar, India
[3]School of Mines and Metallurgy, Kazi Nazrul University, Asansol, India

Abstract

The goal of this chapter is to propose an integrated application of the Internet of Things-based Wireless Sensor Network in the arena of the Indian Agriculture System using the Hybrid Optimization Technique and Machine Learning. The IoT-based WSN can play a great role to collect various useful data from the ground level. In this chapter, we aim to do the area coverage optimization and this optimization will help to cover more areas to do the surveillance. The coverage area optimization of the target area surveillance in case of research in agriculture is always a major concern. A new Hybrid Algorithm, i.e., GA-MWPSO has been used for solving the non-linear constrained optimization problems. To test the competence of the proposed algorithms, a set of test problems has been taken, solved and compared with existing literature. The obtained dataset has been populated in a higher range to make the training set. This idea developed the concept of Machine Learning (ML). This concept became useful to take the decision-making tool in this research field. The data collected from the target area for year after year can be feed to the system to make a supervised machine learning system in this field.

*Corresponding author: avishekbanerji@gmail.com

Amitava Choudhury, Arindam Biswas, Manish Prateek and Amlan Chakrabarti (eds.)
Agricultural Informatics: Automation Using the IoT and Machine Learning, (171–188) © 2021
Scrivener Publishing LLC

Keywords: Genetic algorithm (GA), particle swarm optimization (PSO), mean weighted particle swarm optimization (MWPSO), wireless sensor network (WSN), internet of things (IoT), machine learning (ML), hybrid optimization technique (HOT), hybrid algorithm (HA)

9.1 Introduction

India is a vast country with 50% agriculture employed population. About 17.5% of national GDP is dependent upon Agriculture. India is the second-largest producer of rice and wheat according to FAO (Food and Agriculture Organization) as per 2014. The agricultural land of the country is very fertile due to many reasons. The country has many rivers like Ganga, Brahmaputra, Mahanadi, Godavari, Damodar, etc. The land surrounding different rivers are the most fertile land. The agriculture of India has been flourished during the green revaluation in the country. Indian Agriculture System is full of versatility and the Indian crops have a high demand in international markets due to the wide versatility. The sector is also growing day by day. But in the technological aspect, the sector is lagging behind. One of the major technical research aspects in the field of this sector is surveillance. The surveillance in the agriculture system can give extra mileage in the research field of the Indian Agriculture System. The monitoring will help to study different cops and collecting data related to the agricultural sciences including crop husbandry. Now the monitoring can be easily done with the aid of IoT-based WSN.

Wireless Sensor Network has a good range of applications in modern-day technology. WSN is a tiny device having sensing, communicative, processing, and storage units with power copy by a non-rechargeable battery. The WSN nodes are deployed within the target to collect various sorts of important information and transfer that information to the sink node. Nowadays this sort of network is getting used during a modern army, environmental monitoring [1], battlefield monitoring [2] body area network, intelligent household, etc. The Sink node [3] is the controller communicative node acting as an administrator node in the WSN.

Depending upon the moving nature of WSN, it is classified into two types and those are static WSN [4] and dynamic WSN [5]. In the case of static WSN, the whole unit is mounted and fixed to a certain fixed point (co-ordinate regarding the "sink node"). In the case of dynamic WSN, the node is dynamic, though the sink node is generally mounted to a fixed coordinate. Now depending upon the need and purpose the node is selected. In our experiment, static nodes were used where the coordinate of the sink node as well as typical nodes are fixed and permanent [6]. In the case of a typical WSN design, the sensor nodes are deployed to cover the target area [7]. The sensor nodes are positioned to sense the required data like weather information or enemy related information and transfer it to the "sink node" may be directly or via another sensor node. IoT-based WSN are equipped with different types of sensors, which can sense the environmental data from the target surveillance area. This type of surveillance will be helpful in the research field of the Indian agriculture system. The scope of surveillance can be enhanced with the help of maximizing the coverage area [8].

Coverage area optimization in Wireless Sensor Networks (WSN) is a necessity for achieving a reliable network because, by optimization, a WSN covering a large area or 3D space can have a reduced number of nodes covering the same space under a sink node. The total WSN power consumption, network cost, and efficiency throughput are directly related to its space coverage, and the WSN covering more space can secure more reliability. Therefore, if we can maximize the space coverage of the WSN, or more precisely if the covered range can be maximized for each individual node, then a more reliable WSN can be developed. Reliability improvement of WSNs is an important problem since only a more reliable network can ensure errorless, robust, and efficient communication. Reliability in WSNs depends upon a multitude of factors such as coverage optimization, cross-layer optimization, communication protocol optimization, packet size optimization, power optimization, duty cycle optimization, and topology control optimization. In this chapter, a new "Hybrid Algorithm (HA)" is proposed for solving the optimization problem of coverage maximization in WSNs.

The major contributions of this investigation as presented in this chapter are as follows.

a) A novel approach has been presented towards the maximization of area coverage optimization of the WSN(s);
b) an enhanced hybrid algorithm (GA-MWPSO) has been presented to support our proposed improvement;
c) A theoretical approach has been presented to make machine learning model.

9.1.1   Contribution in Detail

Modification in hybrid GA-MWPSO algorithm: At first a modified GA algorithm has been applied to 50% population solution. The major modifications in the GA algorithm are in crossover operator, mutation, and selection operator. As a crossover operator, we have user an updated power crossover, the uniform mutation operator, and "stochastic universal sampling" (SUS) as a selection operator.

Stochastic universal sampling (SUS) is a selection technique used in genetic algorithms. This operator is used for choosing possibly useful results for a crossover operator [9].

After the "selection process", a special "crossover operator" i.e., power crossover operation has been applied. The specialty of the operator is that the operator can be applied on two or more parent chromosomes simultaneously and it makes the offspring combining the properties of the "parent solutions". In this chapter, we have used the "power crossover" [10].

In case of "power crossover", components $\bar{s}_{kj}$ and $\bar{s}_{ij}$ $(j=1,2,\ldots,n)$ of two offsprings will be generated by

$$\bar{s}_{kj}^{(t)} = \left(s_{kj}^{(t)}\right)^{\lambda} \left(s_{ij}^{(t)}\right)^{1-\lambda}$$

$$\bar{s}_{ij}^{(t)} = \left(s_{kj}^{(t)}\right)^{1-\lambda} \left(s_{ij}^{(t)}\right)^{\lambda}$$

where λ is a "random number" which has been distributed uniformly in the interval $[0,1]$ and two "parent chromosomes" $s_k^{(t)}$ and $s_i^{(t)}$.

Introducing the random variations into the population is the main aim of mutation operator and it is also used to avoid the process from converging into the local optimum solution. In this work we have used "non-uniform mutation".

In case of non-uniform mutation the significant change is,

$$s_{ik}^{\prime(t)} \begin{cases} s_{ik}^{(t)} + \left(s_{ik}^{(t)} - l_k\right)* \rho_1 *(1-t/M_g)^2 \text{ if } \rho_2 < 0.5 \\ s_{ik}^{(t)} + \left(u_k - s_{ik}^{(t)}\right)* \rho_1 *(1-t/M_g)^2, \text{ otherwise} \end{cases}$$

where ρ_1 and ρ_2 be two random numbers which has been uniformly distributed in $[0, 1]$. Using u and l we represented upper and lower limit respectively.

Rest of the paper organization is as followed "Literature review" has been briefly described in Section 9.2; proposed "Hybrid Optimization Technique (HOT)" has been described in Section 9.3. "Reliability optimization and Coverage optimization Model" has been proposed in Section 9.4; "Problem Description" has been designed in Section 9.5. The numerical result analysis has been presented in Section 9.6 and concluding remarks and future research direction are described in Section 9.7.

9.2 Literature Review

A Wireless Sensor Network (WSN) architecture comprises numerous sensor nodes and they can spread over a geographic area for specified scientific or, engineering applications. These sensors have inadequate energy competence to be active for a long duration of time [11]. For the last few years, sensors have been upgraded with respect to their computing capability; unfortunately, the energy sources i.e., batteries are still not highly resourceful in contrast. Subsequently, to surge the life span of a sensor node, the investigation has been emphasized for a reduced demand for energy among nodes. The reason for doing this is to obtain a design to facilitate the WSN with enhanced reliability and improved energy efficiency [12]. By using Energy Efficient (EE) Routing, the life span of a sensor node can be extended [13]. During transmission, energy is exhausted, and energy-efficient routing will cost a minimal consumption of energy.

WSN routing protocols are classified into "flat", "location-based", and "hierarchical protocols" [14]. The Flat protocol ensures that the spreading of the sensor node is always uniform. The hierarchical scheme on the other hand ensures that nodes are distributed over several clusters [15]. On the other hand, the location-based protocol describes that each cluster is governed by a "Cluster Head". The cluster head is a high performing node with high computing capacity as compared to other nodes and is used to transmit data to a "sink node". Over a configuration of nodes, there may exist several routes from a source to destination. In our approach, we have used this type of protocol to achieve an efficient network.

Mathematical models were developed in [16] to explore the energy-efficient path in WSN under resource restriction. The mission of defining the most energy effective path is considered as a "hard optimization problem" [17]. Thus, several meta-heuristic techniques have been introduced to explore the most optimal energy-efficient path.

In 2013, Liao and Zhu [14] presented the primary purposes of the wireless sensor network routing protocol design. The main purpose of this protocol is to balance network energy consumption and to improve the efficiency of data transmission. Therefore, it will extend the lifetime of the entire network. The chapter investigates the usefulness of LEACH protocol towards a CH selection and further proposes an enhanced algorithm towards effective clustering. Said new algorithm considers the node's remaining energy and information related to the location and finally improves the selection method by using a threshold for choosing cluster-head, which further enhances the selection of optimal CH by announcing a cost function.

Evolutionary Algorithms (EAs) are an effective technique to acquire global optimality. EAs comprise of diverse population-based heuristic methods such as GA (Genetic Algorithm) EP (Evolutionary Programming) [18], ES (Evolutionary strategy) [19], GP (Genetic Programming) [20], SO (Swarm Optimization) [21], ACO (Ant Colony Optimization) [22], etc. Among these, GA is the most popular EA [23]. Genetic Algorithm (GA) is one of the most competent and influential heuristic search optimization approach primarily involving natural genetics and natural selection; the natural genetics and natural selection incorporate the philosophy of Charles Darwin's "Survival of the fittest". Prof. J. H. Holland first introduced the concept of GA. Thereafter, several works were presented by researchers to enhance further towards several scientific applications. The comprehensive works on the development Gas may further be found in the books of Goldberg [24], Michalewicz [25], Mitchell [26], Sakawa [27], and others.

The research focuses involving hybridization techniques towards optimization have received noteworthy interests in the recent years [28–31]. Past literature concludes that GA works most resourcefully when it is coupled with other local search approach or, another algorithm (s), rather than simple Genetic Algorithm (GA) [32–35]. To enhance the efficiency of GA, many researchers have been produced hybrid algorithms combining GA and various other algorithms. Combining binary-coded GA and SOMA [33] settled two different versions of algorithms, viz. SOMGA (Self-Organizing Migrating Genetic Algorithm) for unconstrained optimization problems [34] and Self-Organizing Migrating Genetic Algorithm (C-SOMGA) for constrained optimization problems [34]. However, to avoid the local optima for solving non-linear optimization problems, binary-coded GA is found to be a solution to robust search techniques. On the other hand, its computational cost is usually high. In addition, these methods have several complications for solving the optimization problems involving a high volume of search space and high precession. A novel genetic algorithm was proposed by Tsoulos [36] for solving constrained optimization problems with modified genetic operators.

To side step the complications result from C-SOMGA [34] and a novel GA of Tsoulos [36]. In this chapter, an attempt is made to improve them for solving constrained optimization. Like an Evolutionary Algorithm, it is related to a population of individuals. The recent works of Nolle et al. [37],

Deep and Dipti [33, 34], Coelho [38], Coelho and Alotto [39], Coelho and Mariani [40], Senkerik *et al.* [41] and others are also remarkable. To avoid the problems risen in C-SOMGA [34] and a novel GA of Tsoulos [36] (in this chapter we denote it as GA-MWPSO), we have proposed a new hybrid algorithm for solving nonlinear constrained optimization problem (NLCOP), by combining Genetic Algorithm (GA) with modified Particle Swarm Optimization (i.e. AQPSO and WQPSO).

9.3 Proposed Hybrid Algorithms (GA-MWPSO)

The proposed hybrid algorithms GA-MWPSO is a combination of two different algorithms i.e., genetic algorithm and specified types of particle swarm optimization i.e. Mean Weighted Particle Swarm Optimization (MWPSO). In this algorithm, GA has been applied for 50% chromosomes have been MWPSO has been applied for the rest 50% particles.

The different steps of the proposed hybrid algorithm (GA-MWPSO) are as follows:

Step-1: The population size is set to $2 \cdot NP$ where, $NP_{GA} = NP$ and $NP_{PSO} = NP$ where NP is population size; maximum count of generations is set to M_g, crossover probability is set to P_c, probability of mutation is set to P_m and the bounds of decision variables are also set.

Step-2: Set the iteration number $t = 0$.

Step-3: Random initialization of the chromosome for GA and particle for MWPSO of the population $P_{GA}(t) = \{x_i(t); i = 1,...,NP\}$ and $P_{PSO}(t) = \{x_i(t); i = NP + 1,...,2 \cdot NP\}$.

Step-4: Calculate the fitness function $f(x_i)$ for each chromosome x_i of $P_{GA}(t)$ and each particle x_i of $P_{PSO}(t)$.

Step-5: Evaluate the global best chromosome/particle (NP_g) consisting the best fitness value.

Step-6: Recurrence the following until the termination criterion is met.

A: Increase time (iteration): $t = t + 1$.

B: Apply GA for population $NP_{GA}(t)$.

– New Population generation using Crossover & mutation operators.

– Searching of the best chromosome (NP'_g)

– Comparison of new chromosome (i.e., NP'_g) with previous best chromosome P_g

– Restore the improved chromosome in NP_g.

C: Apply MWPSO for $P_{PSO}(t)$
- Select the best particle between NP_g and NP'_g
- Restore the best particle in NP'_g.
  - Calculate the velocity of each particle.
  - Get the new position of each particle by mean best position (*mbest*).
  - Update the best particle.

Step-7: Confirm termination condition.

If end conditions not encountered go back to Step-6 elsewhere go to Step-8.

Step-8: Print the result.

Step-9: End.

Now we are going to describe the update operator of MWPSO and due to this operator the algorithm is different than other traditional PSO i.e., calculation of Mean Best Position (*mbest*), which is recycled later to update particle positions x_i. *mbest* is defined as the average of the center of gravity of all particle positions [42] as in Equation (9.1):

$$mbest(t) = [m_1(t) \ m_2(t) \ldots m_n(t)] \qquad (9.1)$$

$$m_j(t) = \frac{1}{M} \cdot \sum_{i=1}^{M} P_{i,j}^{best}(t) \ j = 1, \ldots, n \text{ and } M = 2 \ NP \qquad (9.2)$$

where, $P_i^{best}(t) = \left[P_{i,1}^{best}(t) P_{i,2}^{best}(t) \ldots P_{i,n}^{best}(t) \right]$ is the personal best position of particle x_i. Now we are going to compute the fitness functions $f(x_i)$ where $i = 1, \ldots 2 \cdot NP$ and compare with P_i^{best}. If $f(x_i)$ is better than P_i^{best} then update P_i^{best} and make $P_i^{best} = f(x_i)$ and then update P_g^{PSO} such as $P_g^{PSO} = \max\left(P_g^{PSO}, P_i^{best} \right)$ and update the particle position x_i using the basic PSO. The new local and global best solution $\left(P_i^{best} \text{ and } P_g^{PSO} \right)$. On the contrary if P_i^{best} is better go to the next iteration and follow the same steps.

Thus, personal best positions are modified based on Equation (9.3):

$$P_i^{best}(t) = \eta \cdot P_i^{best}(t) + (1-\eta) \cdot P_g^{PSO}(t) \text{ where } \eta = \text{rand}(0,1) \qquad (9.3)$$

the new particle positions are found as:

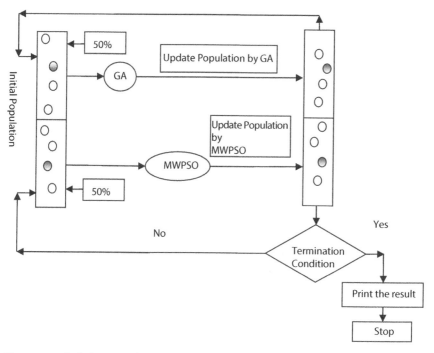

Figure 9.1 Block diagram of GA-MWPSO algorithm.

$$if\ (rand(0,1) > 0.5)\ then$$

$$x_i = P_i^{best}(t) - \beta \cdot |mbest(t) - x_i| \cdot \ln(1/u)\ \text{where } u = \text{rand}(0,1)$$

$$else$$

$$x_i = P_i^{best}(t) + \beta \cdot |mbest(t) - x_i| \cdot \ln(1/u) \tag{9.4}$$

Where β is a model coefficient.

The block diagram of the hybrid algorithm is shown in Figure 9.1.

9.4 Reliability Optimization and Coverage Optimization Model

In short reliability of a system can be explained as the probability of sustainability over a specified bounded system when similar results can be expected under constraint conditions. Here sustainability means the durability in its working condition. In this chapter, our approach aiming for reliability improvement with the help of a meta-heuristic hybrid algorithm [10] and this approach leads to reliability optimization technique.

Coverage problem [43] is one of the basic problems in WSN that means the reliability of the network can be increased if the range of coverage of WSN can be maximized. If sensor node can cover more area or 3D space that means with the help of less number of sensor node more equivalent area of the monitoring region can be covered and energy can be saved and the sustainably of the network can be increased. But here the coverage optimization problem encounters the restriction, in order to increase the "signal strength" of WSN communication to cover the maximum space. The energy efficiency reductions exponentially while the energy supply to a simple sensor node is limited to certain range [44]. On the other hand, increasing the power supply has also another drawback i.e., it makes the network unreliable. If the power consumption is high there is a chance of breakdown also for high voltage. Therefore, the optimal reliability for the WSN cannot be achieved if those constraints are going to be maintained in its feasible range. Therefore, the coverage space should be optimized with respect to those constraints, which affect the power consumption rate.

In this chapter, the entire process of network development has been done through the following steps:

Step1: *Indexing for Sensor Nodes*: The sensor nodes must be indexed virtually before deployment just to denote or keep track of each sensor nodes before and after the deployment. The indexing is generally a sequential number.

Step 2: *Clustering*: Here clustering means separating target area into some uniform or equal chunks. The aim is to construct an efficient network. The structure of cluster cells has been chosen as a square. It can be proved [45] that using square cluster-cell the target area can be covered properly.

Step 3: *Different strategies of the deployment of WSN nodes*:
A. *Random deployment of sensor nodes*: The deployment is done randomly means the sensor nodes are deployed to the target area from a certain distance.
B. *S pattern deployment*: In this type of deployment, deploymentship follows the S-pattern movement at the time of deployment of sensor nodes.
C. *Spiral deployment*: In this type of deployment, deploymentship follows the Spiral-pattern movement at the time of deployment of sensor nodes.

9.5   Problem Description

Supposing the area of the bounded network area or the monitoring area is represented as D in two-dimensional rectangular planes. As we are interested to maximize the coverage area therefore two-dimensional space has been considered. We also assume that the network contains the N numbers of WSN nodes. Here, WSN nodes can be considered as the chromosome in case of GA and particles in case of MWPSO of the hybrid algorithm. Using the iterative property of the hybrid algorithm the maximization problem has been solved to find the optimal coverage area.

We also assume that the wireless sensor network nodes have the "communication radius"—"r" i.e. the length of the range of each sensor node to make data transmission with neighborhood nodes. The definition of coverage ratio [46]: "It is the ratio of the entire nodes covered with a total area to the total monitoring area. The coverage area is the sets of all nodes and the coverage ratio is less than or equal to 1".

In this chapter detection probability or probability of availability of a Sensor Node can be represented by $A(i,j)$ it can be formulated as,

$$A(i,j) = \begin{cases} 1 & d(s_i, p_j) \leq r \\ 0 & otherwise \end{cases} \tag{9.5}$$

Where r is the radius of sensing range, $d(s_i, p_j)$ is the Euclidean distance of the sensing range. The "detection probability" of sensor i on the point j is given as (s_i, p_j). Furthermore, it is assumed that all WSN nodes are homogeneous, and their locations are predefined. In this chapter, the coverage ratio is considered as objective function. The coverage ratio is the ratio between the total number of covered point and the total number of discrete points. Here covered point indicates the covering target point of the wireless sensor network.

Now coverage ratio [46] i.e. A can be represented as follows,

$$A = \max\left(\frac{\bigcup_{i=1}^{N} SC_d(si, pj)}{S} \right) \tag{9.6}$$

Here, S is the scope of the bounded are. $C_{d(si, pj)}$ is the coverage requirement for the Euclidean distance [47] of the sensing range. In addition to "geometric coverage", the coverage requirement can be included parameters such as the "potential threats" that rises in the case of "insufficient coverage problem", and/or the insufficient population that will be pretentious.

9.6   Numerical Examples, Results and Discussion

9.6.1   Case Example

In this case study, different values of the Coverage ratio with respect to the range [48] have been depicted obtained by different algorithms [49]. Here a Hybrid algorithm is introduced and compared with the Mean Weighted PSO (MWPSO) and the Genetic Algorithm (DE) algorithm. In order to verify the hybrid and individual algorithms, iterative optimization techniques performed with some fixed environmental constraints [49]. Result obtained through simulation by the MWPSO algorithm, GA algorithm, and the hybrid algorithm is depicted in Figure 9.1.

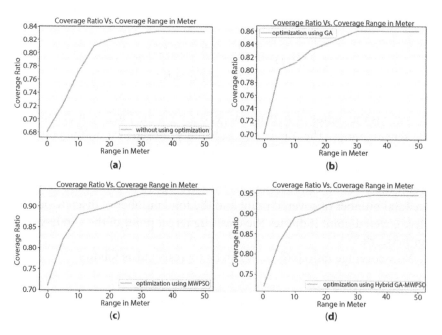

Figure 9.2 (a) Plotting of coverage ratio vs. coverage range without using optimization. (b) Plotting of coverage ratio vs. coverage range using GA. (c) Plotting of coverage ratio vs. coverage range using MWPSO. (d) Plotting of coverage ratio vs. coverage range using hybrid GA-MWPSO.

The proposed algorithm has been implemented for 20 independent runs for the same sets of population and after that again the population set is changed for different generations. We have used python to code the program in Linux environment. In this simulation, a complete run is measured to be "successful" if the solution originates is either the same or better than the known "best-found solution". A comparison between different algorithms has been depicted in Figure 9.2.

9.6.2 Theoretical Approach to Make Machine Learning Model

In this chapter, we have discussed a Metaheuristic approach (GA-MWPSO). We have discussed in this chapter about coverage area optimization using this Metaheuristic algorithm. The main aim to use the Metaheuristic approach is that we can update as well as retrieve various data related to the field of agriculture using this approach. The WSN is deployed to the agricultural area and the related data will be captured using various sensors of WSN. The area coverage optimization is the main aim of the research, side by side the WSN will be used to collect various useful data. As the Metaheuristic approach uses many iterations by generating many populations on many generations therefore the concept of machine learning can easily be adopted. Here we can use a machine learning model named as reinforcement learning. With the help of this type of learning the system will be capable to auto adapt many situations due to its machine learning capability and able to take the decision [44] according to the situation and modify itself in case of any mistake and will not repeat the same mistake next time.

9.7 Conclusion

In this chapter, coverage ratio has been maximized with respect to a range of coverage of WSN and it has been defined as "maximum sensing coverage region problem" for randomly distributed WSNs over a specified bounded region. Here a hybrid algorithm using GA and MWPSO is proposed to resolve this problem. The simulation results show a satisfactory improvement of coverage ratio over the range which implies the improvement of reliability. In this approach of a hybrid algorithm, in each step of iteration/generation of the GA-MWPSO algorithm, the "particle best position" has been calculated by comparing both populations from GA and MWPSO algorithms. For further research, the proposed hybrid approach can be better using advanced crossover, mutation, and selection operators for GA and different update operators of advanced MWPSO. In this chapter, we have used a special crossover operator i.e., power crossover operator [10]. The theoretical approach of the machine learning model can be formalized in the near future.

References

1. Wu, M., Tan, L., Xiong, N., Data prediction, compression, and recovery in clustered wireless sensor networks for environmental monitoring applications. *Inf. Sci.*, 329, 800–818, 2016.
2. Jaigirdar, F.T. and Islam, M.M., A new cost-effective approach for battlefield surveillance in wireless sensor networks. *2016 International Conference on Networking Systems and Security (NSysS)*, IEEE, 2016.
3. Wang, J. *et al.*, Energy-efficient cluster-based dynamic routes adjustment approach for wireless sensor networks with mobile sinks. *J. Supercomput.*, 73, 7, 3277–3290, 2017.
4. Ahmad, A. *et al.*, Data transmission scheme using the mobile sink in the static wireless sensor network. *J. Sens.*, 2015, 279304, 1-8, 2015.
5. Elhoseny, M. *et al.*, An energy-efficient encryption method for secure dynamic WSN. *Secur. Commun. Netw.*, 9, 13, 2024–2031, 2016.
6. Alnawafa, E. and Marghescu, I., New energy efficient multi-hop routing techniques for wireless sensor networks: Static and dynamic techniques. *Sensors*, 18, 6, 1863, 2018.
7. Han, G. *et al.*, Analysis of energy-efficient connected target coverage algorithms for industrial wireless sensor networks. *IEEE Trans. Ind. Inf.*, 13, 1, 135–143, 2015.
8. Banerjee, A. *et al.*, Reliability improvement and the importance of power consumption optimization in wireless sensor networks. *2015 9th International Symposium on Advanced Topics in Electrical Engineering (ATEE)*, IEEE, 2015.
9. Smith, J., *Self adaptation in evolutionary algorithms*, Diss, University of the West of England, Bristol, 2020.
10. Sahoo, L. *et al.*, An efficient GA–PSO approach for solving mixed-integer nonlinear programming problem in reliability optimization. *Swarm Evol. Comput.*, 19, 43–51, 2014.
11. Pantazis, N.A., Nikolidakis, S.A., Vergados., D.D., Energy-efficient routing protocols in wireless sensor networks: A survey. *IEEE Commun. Surv. Tut.*, 15, 2, 551–591, 2013.
12. Zenia, N.Z., Aseeri, M., Ahmed, M.R., Chowdhury, Z.I., Kaiser, M.S., Energy-efficiency and reliability in MAC and routing protocols for underwater wireless sensor network: A survey. *J. Netw. Comput. Appl.*, 71, 72–85, 2016.
13. ECE, S.F., A Survey on Energy Efficient Routing in Wireless Sensor Networks. *Int. J.*, 3, 7, pp 184–189, 2013.

14. Liao, Q. and Zhu, H., An energy balanced clustering algorithm based on LEACH protocol, in: *Applied Mechanics and Materials*, vol. 341, pp. 1138–1143, Trans Tech Publications, Switzerland, 2013.

15. Gajjar, S., Sarkar, M., Dasgupta, K., FAMACRO: Fuzzy and ant colony optimization based MAC/routing cross-layer protocol for wireless sensor networks. *Procedia Comput. Sci.*, 46, 1014–1021, 2015.

16. Lee, J.H. and Moon, I., Modeling and optimization of energy efficient routing in wireless sensor networks. *Appl. Math. Modell.*, 38, 7–8, 2280–2289, 2014.

17. Wang, X., Li, Q., Xiong, N., Pan, Y., Ant colony optimization-based location-aware routing for wireless sensor networks, in: *International Conference on Wireless Algorithms, Systems, and Applications*, 2008, October, Springer, Berlin, Heidelberg, pp. 109–120.

18. Holland, J.H., *Adaptation in Natural and Artificial Systems*, University of Michigan Press, Ann Arbor, MI, 1975.

19. Rechenberg, I., *Evolutions strategie: Optimierung technischer Systeme nach Prinzipien der biologischen Evolution*, Frommann-Holzboog, Stuttgart, 1973.

20. Koza, J.R., *Genetic Programming*, MIT Press, Massachusetts, United States, 1992.

21. Beni, G. and Wang, J., Swarm intelligence in cellular robotic systems. *Proc. NATO Adv. Workshop on Robots and Biol. Systems*, Tuscany, Italy, 1989.

22. Colorni, A., Dorigo, M., Maniezzo, V., Distributed Optimization by Ant Colonies. *Actesde la Première Conférence Européenne Surla vie Artificielle*, Elsevier Publishing, Paris, France, pp. 134–142, 1991.

23. Back, T. and Schwefel, H.-P., An overview of evolutionary algorithms for parameter optimization. *Evol. Comput.*, 1, 1–23, 1993.

24. Goldberg, D.E., *Genetic Algorithms in search, Optimization and Machine Learning*, Addison-Wesley Publishing Co. Inc., MA, 1989.

25. Michalewicz, Z. and Schoenauer, M., Evolutionary computation for constrained parameter optimization problems. *Evol. Comput.*, 4, 1–32, 1996.

26. Mitchell, M., *An Introduction to Genetic Algorithms*, MIT Press, Cambridge, MA, 1996.

27. Sakawa, M., *Genetic algorithms and fuzzy multiobjective optimization*, Kluwer Academic Publishers, Norwell, MA USA, 2002.

28. Pedamallu, C.S. and Ozdamar, L., Investigating a hybrid simulated annealing and local search algorithm for constrained optimization. *Eur. J. Oper. Res.*, 185, 1230–1245, 2008.

29. Renders, J.M. and Flasse, S.P., Hybrid methods using genetic algorithms for global optimization. *IEEE Trans. Syst. Man Cybern.—Part B: Cybern.*, 26, 243–258, 1996.

30. Fan, S.-K.S., Liang, Y.-C., Zahara, E., A genetic algorithm and a particle swarm optimizer hybridized with Nelder–Mead simplex search. *Comput. Ind. Eng.*, 50, 401–425, 2006.

31. Salhi, S. and Queen, N.M., A hybrid algorithm for identifying global and local minima when optimizing functions with many minima. *Eur. J. Oper. Res.*, 155, 51–67, 2004.

32. Deb, K., An efficient constraint handling method for genetic algorithms. *Comput. Methods Appl. Mech. Eng.*, 186, 311–338, 2000.
33. Deep, K. and Dipti, A new hybrid self organizing migrating genetic algorithm for function optimization. *Proc. IEEE Congr. Evol. Comput*, Singapore, pp. 2796–2803, 2007.
34. Deep, K. and Dipti, Self-organizing migrating genetic algorithm for constrained optimization. *Appl. Math. Comput.*, 198, 237–250, 2008.
35. Chelouah, R. and Siarry, P., Genetic and Nelder–Mead algorithms hybridized for a more accurate global optimization of continuous multiminima functions. *Eur. J. Oper. Res.*, 148, 335–348, 2003.
36. Tsoulos, I.G., Solving constrained optimization problems using a novel genetic algorithm. *Appl. Math. Comput.*, 208, 273–283, 2009.
37. Nolle, L., Zelinka, I., Hopgood, A.A., Goodyear, A., Comparison of a self organizing migration algorithm with simulated annealing and differential evolution for automated waveform tuning. *Adv. Eng. Software*, 36, 645–653, 2005.
38. Coello, C.A., Theoretical and numerical constraint handling techniques used with evolutionary algorithms: A survey of the state of the art. *Comput. Methods Appl. Mech. Eng.*, 191, 1245–1287, 2002.
39. Coelho, LdS and Mariani, V.C., An efficient cultural self-organizing migrating strategy for economic dispatch optimization with valve-point effect. *Energy Convers. Manag.*, 51, 2580–2587, 2010.
40. Coelho, LdS and Alotto, P., Electromagnetic optimization using a cultural self organizing migrating algorithm approach based on normative knowledge. *IEEE Trans. Magn.*, 45, 1446–1449, 2010.
41. Senkerik, R., Zelinka, I., Davendra, D., Oplatkova, Z., Utilization of SOMA and differential evolution for robust stabilization of chaotic Logistic equation. *Comput. Math. Appl.*, 60, 1026–1037, 2010.
42. Salkin, H.M., *Integer Programming*, Edison Wesley Publishing Com., Amsterdam, 1975.
43. Bin, Z., Jianlin, M., Haiping, L., A hybrid algorithm for sensing coverage problem in wireless sensor netwoks. *2011 IEEE International Conference on Cyber Technology in Automation, Control, and Intelligent Systems*, IEEE, 2011.
44. Banerjee, A. *et al.*, Decision making in assessment of RRAP of WSN using fuzzy-hybrid approach. *2015 IEEE International Conference on Advanced Networks and Telecommuncations Systems (ANTS)*, IEEE, 2015.
45. Katz, J.E., *Handbook of mobile communication studies*, The MIT Press, Massachusetts, United States, 2008.
46. Maheshwari, A. and Chand, N., A survey on wireless sensor networks coverage problems. *Proceedings of 2nd International Conference on Communication, Computing and Networking*, Springer, Singapore, 2019.
47. Vural, S. and Ekici, E., On multihop distances in wireless sensor networks with random node locations. *IEEE Trans. Mob. Comput.*, 9, 4, 540–552, 2009.

48. Habib, S. and Safar, M., Sensitivity study of sensors' coverage within wireless sensor networks, in: *2007 16th International Conference on Computer Communications and Networks*, August, pp. 876–881, IEEE, 2007.

49. Tao, D., Ma, H.-D., Liu, L., Virtual potential field based coverage-enhancing algorithm for directional sensor networks. *Ruan Jian Xue Bao (J. Software)*, 18, 5, 1152–1163, 2007.

10

Decryption and Design of a Multicopter Unmanned Aerial Vehicle (UAV) for Heavy Lift Agricultural Operations

Raghuvirsinh Pravinsinh Parmar

Department of Farm Machinery and Power Engineering, Punjab Agricultural University, Ludhiana, India

Abstract

A multicopter Unmanned Aerial Vehicle (UAV) was made by combinations of several components and sensors. Multicopter UAV can be classified into different systems like airframe, propulsion system, and command and control system. This system was made of several components and sensors in a very complex way due to their matching and compatibility with each other. So, the developer should know each and every component of multicopter UAV in depth. The knowledge of flying multicopter UAV and working of other components should be strong while developing UAV; otherwise, the design and assembling of UAV leads to poor performance or even fail design. Configuration of UAV includes the size and shape of UAV and the proper matching of BLDC motors and propellers. Therefore, it is essential to have a deep knowledge about each and every component and its designing and selection requirements. This chapter gives all answer regarding basic introduction to UAV, its several systems and components, and its design related basic principle.

Keywords: Drone, unmanned aerial vehicle, design, heavy lift drone

---

Email: parmarraghuvir1@gmail.com

Amitava Choudhury, Arindam Biswas, Manish Prateek and Amlan Chakrabarti (eds.)
Agricultural Informatics: Automation Using the IoT and Machine Learning, (189–222) © 2021 Scrivener Publishing LLC

189

10.1   Introduction

A vehicle without a pilot onboard controlled by a dedicated computer and/ or by operating through the remote control from a ground control station (GCS) is called Unmanned Aerial Vehicle (UAV), commonly known as drone. Small Unmanned Aerial Vehicles (UAVs) (i.e., less than 25 kg payload capacity) are classified into three categories viz. fixed wing UAV, single rotor helicopter, and multicopters UAV [1]. Earlier in the field of aerial photography, fixed-wing UAVs were used. Nevertheless, recently multicopters were popular due to its ease of use and mobility [2]. Recently in the market, all necessary components of multicopter were available so, professionals started assembling and completing the market requirement. Moreover, the components must be compatible with each other and perfectly tuned according to the required specifications, for that sound knowledge of the UAV design is necessary [3]. Globally multicopter market value is increasing day by day due to factors like farmer success stories, new advanced precision technology, availability of open-source autopilot units, positive feedback from scientists, and capital investment of manufactures. This chapter aims to answer following questions:

Why was multicopter UAV selected for agriculture operation?
What are the components of a multicopter UAV?
What is the working principle of the multicopter UAV?
What are the assumption and considerations while designing multicopter?

10.1.1   Classification of Small UAVs

As shown in Figure 10.1, UAV can be classified into three categories as per the following:

(i) Fixed wing UAV: As shown in Figure 10.1(a), these types of UAV's wings are fixed to the UAV frame similar to the civil and fighter aircraft. In this type of UAV, certain forward speed should be maintained to glide in the air. Due to that principle, this type of UAV cannot take off and land in a vertical direction, and they needed a dedicated runway area for safe flights. Also, it was observed that payload capacity was also less compared to other types of UAVs [4].

(ii) Single rotor helicopter: As shown in Figure 10.1(b), one big rotor provides lift force to the helicopter frame, and it can Vertical Take-Off and Landing (VTOL). This type of UAV does not require a dedicated runway area. Its time of endurance was less then fixed-wing aircraft. Moreover, it

(a) Fixed wing UAV   (b) Single rotor helicopter   (c) Multicopter UAV

Figure 10.1 Different types of UAV.

has more moving parts, and complex frame structure requires considerable maintenance time to time [5].

(ii) Multicopter UAV: As shown in Figure 10.1(c), it has three or more propellers which provide thrust to the airframe of UAV. Generally, it is also called a multirotor or drone. Recently it becomes popular due to its ease maneuverability, hovering, and VTOL ability. Multicopter UAV has a simple structure and less moving parts; that is why it required low maintenance as compared to others. Nevertheless, it has limited payload carrying capacity and less flight time; that are the significant challenges in this type of UAV [6].

The overall comparison with each other is shown in Table 10.1 (more '*' means much better). According to Ref. [3], mainly four types of performance parameters are considered in the selection of the type of UAV. The first one is the ease of use, i.e., flying of multirotor UAV is more easier; it can hover at one-point, easy to maneuver, and no large dedicated area required for take-off and landing. The second one is reliability. Due to the solid structure multirotor UAVs, are highly reliable to perform a task. Less number of moving parts makes it more reliable. Whereas in fixed-wing UAV and single rotor helicopter, there are more moving and

Table 10.1 Comparison of user experiences of three types of small aircraft [3].

Performance factors	Fixed-wing UAV	Single rotor helicopter	Multicopter UAV
Ease of use	**	*	***
Reliability	**	*	***
Maintainability	**	*	***
Time of endurance	***	**	*

mechanical parts in their frame. The third one is the maintainability of UAV. Multicopter UAV is easy to maintain as compared with fixed-wing UAV and single rotor helicopter since they have more components and complex structures. The fourth and last one is the time of endurance. It is less in multicopter because it consumes more energy as compared with others. However, ease of use, reliability, and maintainability are on high priority. That is the reason for selecting the multicopter UAV for agricultural operation.

10.2   History of Multicopter UAVs

The reason for selecting of multicopter UAV for agriculture operation has been discussed in the previous section. Recently, multicopter UAVs are popular because of the new and efficient multicopter related technology are widely available and easily accessible.

Building multicopter was started in early 1907; the first human-carrying quadcopter was built under the guidance of Charles Richet, the Breguet Brothers. The quadcopter was also famous as Breguet–Richet Gyroplane No. 1, as shown in Figure 10.2 [7]. In 1956, the first successful flight was taken by Convertawings Model "A" quadcopter (Figure 10.2(b)) designed by Marc Adman [3]. Before 1990, technology and components availability was limited for the development of the multicopter. At that time single rotor helicopter have more considerable advantages.

From 1996 to 2004, the researchers [8–11] tried to find out the weakness of the multicopter and started working on it. They work on the development of Inertial Measurement Unit (IMU), efficient propellers,

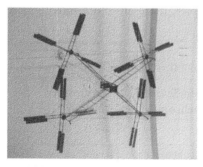

(a) Breguet- Richet Gyroplane No. 1   (b) Convertawings Model "A"

Figure 10.2 Early-stage development of multicopter.

(a) AR Drone   (b) DJI phantom

Figure 10.3 Recent successful multicopter products available in the market.

flying algorithms, and Flight Controller Units (FCUs). This research provides a significant push in the development of a multicopter area, but there was a major problem of stability and control of multicopter.

During 2006 to 2010, some searchers [12–18] worked on the altitude and control algorithms. AR Drone which was a quardcopter was launched in the Japanese market. As shown in Figure 10.3(a), AR drone was smart and used advanced technology for its control and maneuverability. It has one onboard camera to provide a flying or hovering point of view. Furthermore, it can be controlled by smartphone and tablet [19]. Secondly, it was light in weight and made from foam for the safety point of view. A smartphone or a tablet could control the drone and also give a bird eye view using three axis gimble fitted camera on the drone. In 2012, DJI Phantom quadcopter was available in the market, as shown in Figure 10.3(b). Phantom is easy to operate and it can hold and hover in one position by using GPS sensor. It is mounted with high-resolution camera for aerial photography.

10.3   Basic Components of Multicopter UAV

The multicopter UAV comprised of several components but, mainly it had basic systems like, airframe, propulsion system, command and control system. Hierarchy of the multicopter system is shown in Figure 10.4. Airframe includes fuselage, landing gear and arms. Battery, motor, electronic speed controller (ESC) and propellers belongs to propulsion system. Radio controlled (RC) transmitter and receiver, flight controller unit, global position system (GPS) receiver, ground control station (GCS) and radio telemetry belongs to the command and control system.

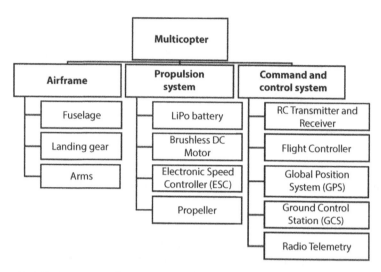

Figure 10.4 Basic system and components of multicopter UAV.

10.3.1　Airframe

Frame design of UAV platform affects flight stability, reliability, payload capacity and overall endurance time. For the multirotor UAV platform supported different kind of frame configurations are shown in Figure 10.5.

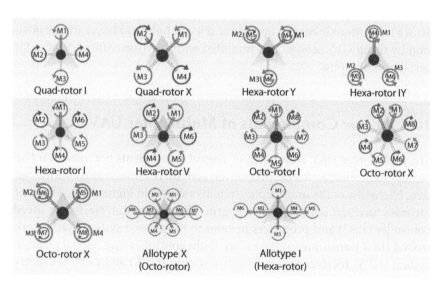

Figure 10.5 Common frame configurations in multirotor UAV platform.

According to Ref. [3] Quadrotor (quadcopter) type of configuration has four number of rotors, and it can generate less amount of thrust. Hexa-rotor configuration has six number of rotors. This type of frame config-uration can generate a decent amount of thrust, and generally, it is used for medium payload capacity task. Octo-rotor (octocopter) configuration has eight numbers of rotors, and it can generate a good amount of thrust. Generally, this type of configuration was used for higher lifting tasks. The hexacopter and octo-rotor configuration is the best suitable configuration for lifting pesticide payload for agricultural spraying. They had more lifting capacity, more stable flight, and wider frame size. It had more downward air wash along with its swath width, which could be utilized to settle down droplets more quickly and reduced chance of drift.

10.3.1.1   Fuselage

The fuselage of multicopter UAV provides physical structure, and it is com-monly known as a frame or main body, as shown in Figure 10.6. Fuselage houses all the other essential components and sensors of a multicopter UAV. For stable multicopter UAV, the material of fuselage, its scale, shape, and weight were taken into consideration, for the same thrust produced by multicopter UAV lesser the fuselage weight higher the payload capacity. It held all other electronic parts like power distribution board (PDB), flight controller, water pump module, radio transmitter, and its components,

Figure 10.6 Airframe of multicopter UAV.

global position system (GPS) sensor and other electronics parts. Batteries were also fixed on it during a flight of UAV.

10.3.1.2   Landing Gear

Landing gear supports the whole multicopter UAV and also supports when UAV is going to land or taking off. So, it absorbs the impact energy while landing. It keeps multicopter UAV in level and balanced so that the propellers do not touch the ground.

10.3.1.3   Arms

Multicopter UAV had more than three arms fixed on the fuselage. Arms are generally made of aluminum, hard plastic tubing, and carbon fiber tubing. Strong and sturdy arms in multicopter design is necessary; otherwise, it causes unnecessary vibration and other related issues.

10.3.1.4   Selection of Material for UAV Airframe

Various properties of different materials are shown in Table 10.2. The carbon fiber has low density, high young's modulus and higher tensile strength but, it is costly and difficult to process. The acrylic plastic material is lightweight, cheaper and easy to process but, its rigidity and tensile strength was less. So, the carbon fibre material was found suitable in the design and development process of UAV platform [20].

Table 10.2 Different materials and its properties [20].

Different materials	Density (kg/m³)	Young's modulus (GPa)	Tensile strength (MPa)	Cost (10: cheapest)	Producibility (10: simplest)
Carbon fibre	1,383.99	64.11	827.37	1	3
Fiberglass	1,937.59	18.61	103.42–344.73	6	7
Polycarbonate	1,383.99	5.17	55.15–420.58	9	6
Acrylic	1,107.19	2.61	55.15–75.84	9	7
Aluminium	2,767.99	71.00	103.42–517.10	7	7
Balsa	74.73–224.20	1.10–6.20	6.89–31.71	10	10

10.3.2 Propulsion System

The propulsion system includes Lithium Polymer (LiPo) battery, electronic speed controller (ESC), brushless DC (BLDC) motor, and propellers. This system had the most important impact on the performance of multicopter UAV, like endurance time, payload capacity, and flying speed and flying height. All the components must be compatible with each other; otherwise, it fails the system.

10.3.2.1 Lithium Polymer (LiPo) Battery

The battery is the main source of energy. Time of endurance is directly relying on the capacity of batteries. There are different types of batteries available in the market but, Lithium Polymer (LiPo) and Nickel Metal Hydride (NiMH) batteries are mostly used due to its good performance and stable voltage for longer duration without much fluctuations. Nominal voltage of LiPo battery (Figure 10.7) is 3.7 V of a single cell but at fully charged voltage is about 4.2 V [21]. LiPo batteries gives constant voltage in liner relationship and at later stage voltage drops sharply. It is clear from the graph shown in Figure 10.8. Therefore, battery must have enough capacity at later stages so that the landing or returning to home during the operation can be done without battery ran out [22, 23].

The buzzer was used to check the remaining voltage of the battery in real-time (Figure 10.9). Buzzer make loud noise when voltage is less to a certain limit. So, that UAV pilot can get an idea while operating it if the

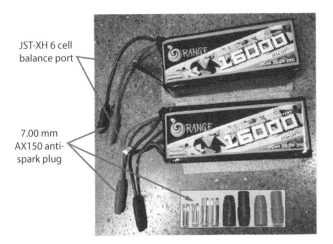

Figure 10.7 LiPo 16,000 mAh batteries with anti-spark plug connectors.

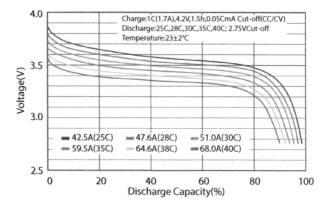

Figure 10.8 Discharge curve of LiPo battery (Source: http://learningrc.com).

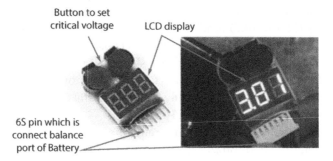

Figure 10.9 6S voltage sensor (Buzzer).

battery's remaining voltage is low. Moreover, the pilot can plan UAV's return journey or landing.

10.3.2.2 Propeller

Propeller produces thrust and torque to lift the multicopter UAV with a payload. The selection of appropriate propeller and motor is necessary, which resulting in high efficiency, less power consumption, and more flying time to the overall UAV system. Propellers are available in many sizes and materials. A carbon fiber propeller is shown in Figure 10.10. Nominucultutre of the propeller was written by four-digit number, e.g., 2255 (or 22 × 55) carbon fibre propeller means 22-inch diameter and 5.5-inch pitch. As shown in Figure 10.10(b), the chord located at the 2/3 of the propeller's radius is chosen as the nominal chord length [24]. Moment of

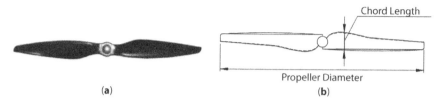

(a)   (b)

Figure 10.10 Carbon fiber two blade propeller (a) 22X55 carbon fibre heavy duty propeller (b) Schematic top view of propeller.

inertia of the propeller is also an important factor for the control and performance of multicopter UAV. A propeller which is having less moment of inertia gives higher speed response to the BLDC motor.

Generally, propellers were available in carbon fiber, plastic, and wood material. The carbon fiber propeller was costlier than the plastic one. Wooden propellers were costlier and much heavier. But, carbon fiber propeller had advantages like high rigidity; it generates less vibration and noise, durable and lighter.

10.3.2.3   Brushless DC (BLDC) Motor

Motor is used to convert stored electric energy into mechanical work. Each propeller is fitted on separate BLDC motors which spins and yields the required lift or thrust to the multicopter UAV (Figure 10.11). Generally, brushless DC motors are used in the multicopter UAV because they provide good thrust to weight ratio than brushed DC motor, and highly efficient [25]. Brushed motors overheat more quickly, but brushless motors have no overheating issues. Each DC brushless motor required a separate electronic speed controller (ESC) to gain control over the spin of the motor.

The outer rotor types brushless DC motor has an outer spin case which is durable and can withstand high temperature. Recently, new BLDC motors

Figure 10.11 BLDC motor mounted on arm.

follow splash and dustproof (IP34) standards. For bigger size propeller to improve efficiency and stability, outer rotor type motor performs better as compared to inner rotor type motor [25].

10.3.2.4   Electronic Speed Controller (ESC)

The function of the electronic speed controller (ESC) is to control the spin speed of the brushless DC motor according to the signal received from the flight control unit (FCU). FCU's direct signal is not strong enough to drive DC brushless motor directly, so each motor need to equip with separate ESCs. The detailed connection of ESC is shown in Figure 10.12.

The maximum input current and maximum peak current for ESC is very important to consider while selecting multicopter UAV components. BLDC motor needs to be fitted with appropriate matched ESCs. Each ESC has a specific value, such as 70, 80, 100 A, which indicate the maximum input current allowed. The selection of appropriate ESC is mainly based upon maximum input current. The range of input voltage for ESC is also an important parameter and needs to be checked with the battery [3].

Another parameter of ESC is the refresh rate, which is directly related to a motor response. So, if we want a faster response, a higher refresh rate is required. There were three methods of calibration, i.e., programmable cards, computer software via USB and remote control (RC) transmitters. RC transmitter method was used to calibrate ESC.

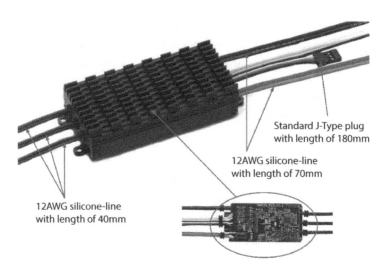

Standard J-Type plug
with length of 180mm

12AWG silicone-line
with length of 70mm

12AWG silicone-line
with length of 40mm

Figure 10.12 Detailed connection diagram of ESC.

10.3.3   Command and Control System

10.3.3.1   Remote Controlled (RC) Transmitter and Receiver

A remote controlled (RC) transmitter (Figure 10.13(a)) was used to send commands to the flight control unit (FCU) through the RC receiver (Figure 10.13(b)), which was fitted inside the fuselage of UAV. After decoding the RC receiver command sent to autopilot, which was directly connected via the S.BUS module. Mostly, Nickel Metal Hydride (NiMH) battery was used in the remote control.

The radio wave communication is done between RC transmitter and RC receiver; and 72 MHz and 2.4 GHz are two frequencies commonly used. In 72 MHz frequency, the interference between the channels is very high. While 2.4 GHz has advantages like low power consumption, very less chance of channel interference, small antennas, fast response, and great control accuracy. So, 2.4 GHz frequency was widely used in multicopter UAV [26].

By controlling sticks on the RC transmitter, the potentiometer inside RC changes the value accordingly. And then, these values decoded into a pulse coded signal, like Pulse Pulse Module (PPM), Pulse Width Module (PWM), or serial bus (S.BUS) module, which is transmitted to RC receiver. Among PPM, PWM, and S.BUS. S.BUS module was reliable, cheaper, less susceptible to interference, and also compatible with most of the flight controller unit. RC shown in Figure 10.13(a) supports 18 channels, which is sufficient for a multicopter UAV platform for pesticide application.

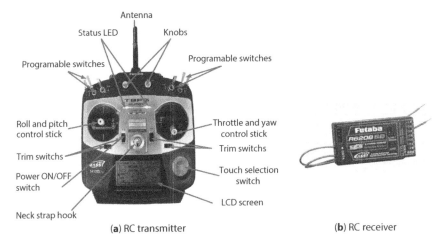

(a) RC transmitter   (b) RC receiver

Figure 10.13 18 channel remote controller transmitter and receiver.

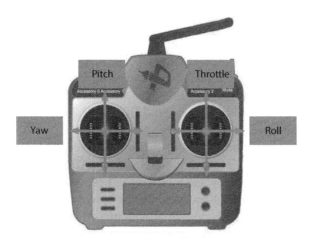

Figure 10.14 Control mode of RC transmitter.

Generally, there are two modes, i.e., MODE1 and MODE2 are available in RC. MODE1, i.e., the right-hand model, was used in which pitch/yaw was on the left stick, and throttle/roll was on the right stick (Figure 10.14) [26].

10.3.3.2   Flight Controller Unit (FCU)

In multicopter UAV, a flight controller was used to control the attitude, position, and flight path. Flight Controller Unit (FCU) is the brain of multicopter UAV, and it is used to do all complex calculations and send/receive information or data, as shown in Figure 10.15. With FCU, different hardware was used to operate multicopter UAV successfully [27]. Those hardware were GPS receivers, it was used to obtain the latitude and longitude of a particular location of multicopter UAV. For altitude measurement, Inertia Measurement Unit (IMU) was used. IMU had a three-axis gyroscope, three-axis accelerometer, and an electric compass. Multicopter UAV exact position, control, and complex decision were solved by FCU, GPS receiver, and IMU combinedly [28]. The best position for FCU was near the geometric center of octacopter. It was observed that if the flight controller unit was installed far from the center, octacopter produced an error in the accelerometer while flying. Theoretically, an ideal position should

Figure 10.15 Pixhawk open-source flight controller.

be the coincident point of the center of geometry and the center of gravity. According to UAV frame configuration generally, the FCU unit was installed with arrow matching with forwarding flight direction, and FCU was fixed by using an anti-vibration damper to reduce vibration. IMU was used to estimate the real-time position and altitude during the flight. Some open source flight controller units were shown in Table 10.3 [3, 29].

10.3.3.3   Ground Control Station (GCS)

Ground Control Station (GCS) consisted of a computer/tablet or smartphone with a software/application and radio telemetry system that was connected to a laptop via USB port. The software was used for the setting of waypoints and a new mission in advance by the pilot. GCS was also doing monitoring and maintaining flight status and data in real-time [20].

Communication between the telemetry system, remote controller (RC), and UAV was done, as shown in Figure 10.16 [30]. In the UAV radio telemetry receiver was connected via the circuit. So that communication was established between laptop and UAV. One RC receiver was connected to the UAV circuit, and they communicated via a wireless radio communication link. The field setup of the system and GCS software window is shown in Figure 10.17. There are many open-source GSC software are available. Figure 10.18 shows a screenshot of the popular Mission Planner (Ardupilot) GSC software.

Table 10.3 Details of open source FCUs [3].

Available FCU in market	Size (mm)	Weight (g)	Processor	Frequency (MHz)
Arducopter	66 × 40.5	23	AT mega2560	16
Openpilot	36 × 36	8.5	STM32F103CB	72
Paparazzi (Lisa/M)	51 × 25	10.8	STM32F105RCT6	60
Pixhawk	40 × 30.2	8	LPC2148	60
Mikrokopter	44.6 × 50	35	AT mega644	20
Kkmulticoptcr	49 × 49	11.7	ATmcgal68	20
Multi wii	N/A[a]	N/A[a]	Arduino[b]	S-20
Aeroquad	N/A[a]	N/A[a]	Arduino[b]	S-20
Crazy flic 2.0	90 × 90	19	STM32F405	168
CrazePony-II(4)	38.9 × 39.55	20	STM32fl03T8U6	72
Dr.R&D(20l5)IV	33 × 33	300 (the whole)	STM 32 FI 03	72
Anonymous(V2)	75 × 45	40	STM32F407	168

10.3.3.4   Radio Telemetry

As shown in Figure 10.19, radio telemetry was used to transmit data through wireless media using digital signal processing (DSP) technology. It was doing modulation/demodulation and radio transmission between multicopter UAV and laptop in real time with high accuracy. Digital radio telemetry can transmit the data at a rate of 19.2 Kbps in less than 10 ms [31].

10.3.3.5   Global Positioning System (GPS)

Global Positioning System (GPS) was used to locate the UAV in real-time. GPS module was directly connected to the electronic circuit to provide real-time data to the UAV system and GCS software. The GPS module (Figure 10.20) was fitted on the top side of the fuselage with the help of a foldable aluminium stand or on an anti-vibration damper.

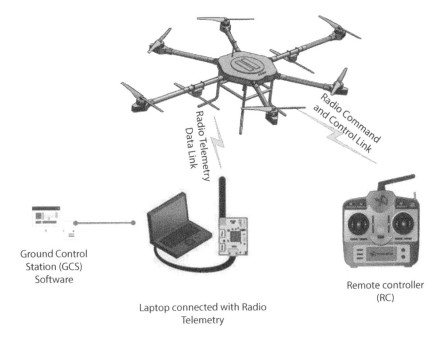

Figure 10.16 Wireless communication of GCS (Source: [30]).

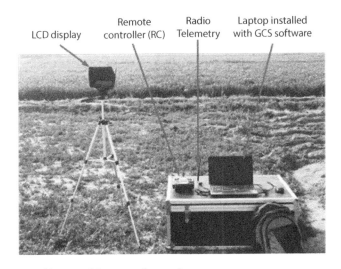

Figure 10.17 Field setup of the ground control system.

Figure 10.18 Screenshots of Mission Planner GCS software.

Figure 10.19 Radio telemetry module.

Figure 10.20 Alpha GPS 13 module for multicopter UAV.

10.4   Working and Control Mechanism of Multicopter UAV

We use the octacopter alloy X type configuration of UAV for easy under-standing. The octacopter UAV was controlled by eight motors by chang-ing the propeller's angular speed, which resulted in a change in thrust and moments of UAV. As a result, continuous thrust and moments is being reg-ulated about its center. Altitude and position of the UAV were controlled by changing in thrust and moment.

At a hovering state of octacopter (Figure 10.21), all eight motors spin-ning at the same angular speed with motor M2, M4, M6, and M8 rotating counter-clockwise while, motor M1, M3, M5, and M7 rotating clockwise. That balanced the UAV and hovered in mid-air. Essentially, the movement of an octacopter falls into one of the following four basic types [30].

10.4.1   Upward and Downward Movement

With the increase of angular speeds of all motors (Figure 10.22(a)) by the same amount, the thrust force increased without any overall moments. The movement of UAV was controlled by the RC transmitter (Figure 10.22(a)). When the throttle stick moved upward resulted in the spinning of all motors, and it lifted upward once the thrust force generated by the propel-ler was greater than the weight of the octacopter UAV. When throttle stick

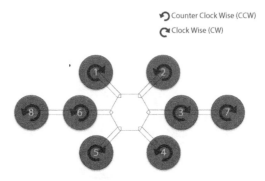

Figure 10.21 An octacopter in hovering state.

moved downward, that resulted in the reduction of spinning of all motors, and octacopter will move downward.

10.4.2   Forward and Backward Movement

When the angular speed of the motors M1 and M2 were decreased, and angular speed of motors M3, M4, M5, M6, M7, and M8 were increased by the same value (Figure 10.22(b)); it created a moment which made octa-copter to move forward. At that point, the thrust had two components one was a forward component, and the other was a vertical component. When the octocopter moved in the forward direction, the vertical component of the thrust decreased, which was not equal to the weight of the octocop-ter. So, all previously changed motors again change the angular speed by the same amount to count the self-weight of the octocopter. Similarly, the

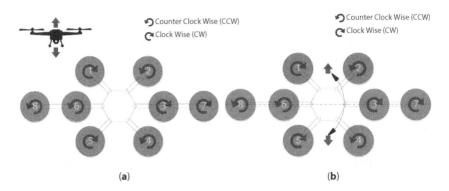

Figure 10.22 Movement of an octacopter (a) upward movement, (b) forward movement.

backward moment of the octacopter could be attained by reducing motor speed M4 and M5.

10.4.3   Leftward-and-Rightward Movement

When the angular speed of the motors M2, M4, and M7 were decreased and of motors M1, M3, M5, M6 and M8 were increased by the same value, that created a moment which made octacopter roll to rightward (Figure 10.23(a)). The thrust had two components, which were a right and verti-cal component. When the octocopter changed its position to rightward, at that time vertical component of the thrust decreased and was not equal to the self-weight of the octocopter. So, all previously changed motors again changed the angular speed by the same amount to count the self-weight of the octocopter. Similarly, the leftward moment of the octacopter could be attained.

10.4.4   Yaw Movement

The angular speed of the motor M1, M3, M5, and M7 were decreased, and the angular speed of the M2, M4, M6, and M8 were also increased by the same value, that created zero moments in the forward-backward and leftward-rightward directions (Figure 10.23(b)). Due to the reduction of angular speed of motors M1, M3, M5, and M7, clockwise yaw moment increased. Simultaneously, the counterclockwise yaw moment of the octa-copter decreased due to an increase in the angular speed of the motor

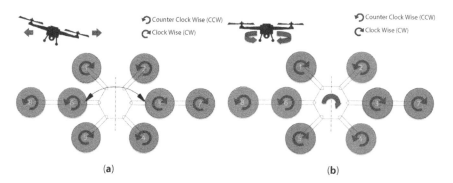

Figure 10.23 Movement of an octacopter (a) rightward movement, (b) Yaw movement.

M1, M3, M5, and M7 in the clockwise direction so, as a result, octacopter turned clockwise direction and changed its orientation.

10.5   Design Calculations and Selection of Components

Selection of different components related to multicopter UAVs are as per the following:

1. The UAV must be capable of vertical take-off and landing (VTOL) because in field conditions, there is no runway available.
2. The landing and take-off of UAV from the ground should be very stable because of the liquid payload is there.
3. While designing the UAV platform, major parament to consider is the maximum take-off weight (MTOW). The expected payload capacity of the UAV should be approximately more than 10 kg in for heavy-lift agricultural operations like pesticide spraying.
4. The UAV must have electric motors that draw power from a battery. That makes the environment pollution-free.
5. The communication range of the UAV should be more, for our case, it should be about 2 km, and the minimum range is 1,000 m.

10.5.1   Fuselage Configuration

There are different possible fuselage configurations. The first one was plus or I configuration (Figure 10.24(a)), second was X configuration (Figure 10.24(b)), and third was ring configuration (Figure 10.24(c)). According to Ref. [3], X-configuration had higher maneuverability compared to plus or I configuration. X-configuration had higher control over roll and pitch. While ring configuration was considered as more rigid frame and also there was less vibration in the frame but, its cost was higher and had less control over maneuverability. For heavy lifting operation, X configuration is more prevalent in the market.

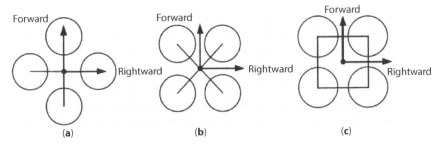

Figure 10.24 Various fuselage configuration (a) Plus or I configuration, (b) X-configuration, (c) Ring-configuration (Source: [3]).

10.5.2   Propeller Selection

Propellers having different numbers of blades were already available in the market (Figure 10.25). According to Ref. [24], the performance characteristics of the two-blade propeller were best comparing with the three-blade propeller and four-blade propeller. Single-blade propeller had the poorest performance among them. For the same thrust, a two-blade propeller required less power compared with other types of blades (Figure 10.26(a)). For the same power coefficient, the two-blade propeller gave the highest thrust coefficient as compared with the different number of blade propeller (Figure 10.26(b)). Therefore, a two-bladed propeller was widely used in the multicopter UAV.

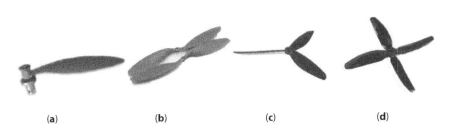

(a)   (b)   (c)   (d)

Figure 10.25 Propeller with different number of blade (a) single-blade propeller, (b) two-blade propeller, (c) three-blade propeller, (d) four-blade propeller.

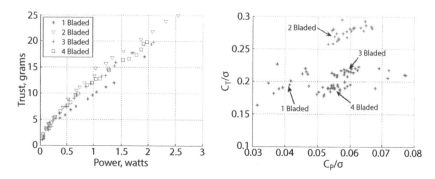

Figure 10.26 Performance graphs of different number of blades (a) Thrust v/s Power, (b) Thrust coefficient v/s power coefficient. C_T = thrust coefficient, C_p = power coefficient and σ = rotor solidity (Source: [24]).

10.5.3 Motor Selection

The motor efficiency changes with type and size of propeller. Therefore, a good match of motor and propeller combination was a must to operate the BLDC motor for high efficiency and less power consumption for the same lift capacity.

For understanding, a 350 KV brushless DC motor had the ability to spin 350 rpm with an application of 1V with no load. The maximum continuous current, i.e., 42 A per 30 s, means the BLDC motor can spin safely with a continuous current of 42 A beyond which for more than 30 s, the BLDC motor may burn out.

Motors are rated according to continuous draw current and KV value. Continuous draw current (A) shows how much current the motor uses in normal operation, and KV indicates the number of revolutions per volt.

Electrical power and motor efficiency and overall specific thrust were calculated using the following formulas [25], and overall specific thrusts are given in Table 10.4.

$$\text{Mechanical Power (W)} = \text{Torque(N} \cdot \text{m)} \times \text{Propeller Speed (rad/s)} \tag{10.1}$$

$$\text{Propeller specific thrust}\left(\frac{g}{W}\right) = \frac{\text{Thrust(g)}}{\text{Mechanical power(W)}} \tag{10.2}$$

$$\text{Electrical power (W)} = \text{Effective current (A)} \times \text{Rated voltage(V)} \\ \times \text{Motor efficiency} \tag{10.3}$$

Table 10.4 Overall specific thrust of motor XM7015HD-11 (Source: http://www.dualsky.com).

Voltage (V)	Propeller (RPM)	Throttle (%)	DC current (A)	DC voltage (V)	El. power (W)	Efficiency (%)	Thrust (g)	Specific thrust (g/W)
22.2 V (6S LIPO)	2,000	30	2.2	22.2	49.5	75.0	641	13.0
	2,400	36	3.7	22.2	81.2	79.0	923	11.4
	2,800	43	5.7	22.1	125.1	81.5	1,257	10.0
	3,200	49	8.3	22.1	183.4	82.9	1,641	8.9
	3,600	56	11.8	22.1	258.6	83.7	2,077	8.0
	4,000	63	16.1	22.0	353.1	84.1	2,564	7.3
	4,400	70	21.5	21.9	469.2	84.3	3,102	6.6
	4,800	77	28	21.9	609.5	84.2	3,692	6.1
	5,200	85	35.9	21.8	776.6	84.0	4,333	5.6
	5,600	92	45.2	21.7	973.1	83.8	5,026	5.2
	5,970	100	56.1	21.6	1,199	82.7	5,712	4.8

$$\text{Motor efficiency} = \frac{\text{Mechanical Power}(W)}{\text{Electrical Power}(W)} \qquad (10.4)$$

Matching the right propeller with a motor for higher efficiency was very important in the propulsion system. For that overall specific thrust was calculated as:

$$\text{Over specific thrust}\left(\frac{g}{W}\right) = \frac{\text{Thrust}(g)}{\text{Electrical power}(W)} \qquad (10.5)$$

10.5.4   Maximum Power and Current Requirement

A lower KV motor has higher torque; that allows the BLDC motor to spin larger propellers and provide larger lifting capacity, but higher KV motor has lower torque. Still, it is more reactive, providing better control so, smaller size propellers are recommended. Our main objective was to lift heavy objects for pesticide application, so lower KV BLDC motor was suitable. The maximum power of BLDC motor was calculated for the following equation.

$$\text{Maximum power of BLDC motor } P = I_{motor} \times V \times \eta_m \qquad (10.6)$$

Where,

I_{motor} = continuous draw current of the motor (A)
V = rated voltage of the battery (V)
η_m = BLDC motor efficiency (faction)

An ESC controls rpm of each BLDC motor. The selection of ESC for the UAV platform had been done by keeping the following points in mind.

1. Must exceed the current draw of the selected BLDC motor (A).
2. Must match the wattage of the selected battery (W).

For safety, 20% extra amperes were considered, to avoid any damage in ESC. The required ESC current for the BLDC motor was calculated as per the following equation.

Required ESC current for BLDC motor = $1.2 \times I_{motor}$ (10.7)

For an understanding point of view, two 16,000 mAh batteries were used to last for an hour with the current of 16,000 mA when the voltage dropped from 4.2 to 3.0 V for a single cell. Discharge rate was calculated using the following equation,

$$\text{Discharge rate}(C) = \frac{\text{Current of discharge}(A) \times 10^3}{\text{Capacity (mAh)}} \quad (10.8)$$

Battery nominal capacity was 16,000 mAh, and the discharge current was 400 A, substituting values in Equation (10.8), the discharge rate of selected batteries was 25 C.

Power requirement to spin for propeller can be calculated by the following equation

Propeller power requirement (W) = $k \times R^3 \times D^4 \times p$ (10.9)

Where,
k = design factor depends on propeller blade thickness, width, air foil profile, etc. A typical value is 5.3×10^{-15}.
R = propeller revolutions (rpm)
D = propeller diameter (inches)
P = propeller pitch (inches)

Current requirement for the propeller,

$$I = \frac{\text{propeller power required}(W)}{\text{nominal voltage of battery}(V)} \quad (10.10)$$

So, ESC must be able to supply more current than the current obtained from Eqn. (10.10) otherwise, it will overheat.

10.5.5 Thrust Requirement by Motor [32]

$$\text{Required thrust (kg)} = \frac{\text{Total weight of setup (kg)} \times 2}{\text{Number of motors}}. \quad (10.11)$$

Total weight of setup without payload = frame + ESC + batteries + other parts.

UAV platform required to lift 5–10 kg of pesticides.

Total weight of setup with payload = weight of setup without payload + payload weight of spraying system.

According to Refs. [32, 33] the thrust generated by the motor,

$$T = \left[\frac{\pi}{2} \times D^2 \times \rho \times (Eta \times P)^2 \right]^{\frac{1}{3}} \tag{10.12}$$

Where,

Eta = Propeller hovers efficiency. Generally, its range is 0.7 to 0.8.

D = Diameter of propeller (m)

ρ = Air density (1.22 kg/m^3)

P = Maximum power

The thrust generated by each BLDC motor should be greater than required thrust with payload.

10.5.6   Thrust Requirement by the Propeller

Weight of UAV platform itself was 12.020 kg and the UAV platform had to carry 10 kg of pesticides. Therefore,

$$\text{Payload capacity+ the weight of UAV platform} = \text{Thrust+ hover throttle\% [33]} \tag{10.13}$$

The thrust provided by a single motor [33],

$$T = \frac{\text{total thrust}}{8}. \tag{10.14}$$

The thrust produced or generated by each motor should be greater than the thrust required so that the UAV platform system was supposed to run without any problem.

10.5.7   Endurance or Flight Time

Hover endurance time based on the battery capacity and motor current with a margin of error [33],

$$T_{max} = \frac{60 \times \left(\dfrac{C}{1000} \right) \times N_{Battery}}{I_{Hover}}. \tag{10.15}$$

Where,

T_{max} = Maximum hover time (min)
C = battery capacity (mAh)
$N_{battery}$ = Number of batteries in parallel
I_{Hover} = Total current of motor @50% throttle (A)

Full throttle endurance time based on the battery capacity and motor current with margin of error [33],

$$T_{min} = \frac{60 \times \left(\dfrac{C}{1000} \right) \times N_{Battery}}{I}. \tag{10.16}$$

Where,

T_{min} = Minimum hover time (min)
C = battery capacity (mAh)
$N_{battery}$ = Number of batteries in parallel
I = Total current of motor @100% throttle (A).

10.5.8   Maximum Airframe Size

From the radius of the propeller overall size of multicopter UAV can be define as shown in Figure 10.27. Assuming that the angle between two arms is θ, then for alloy type X configuration θ = 60°.

$$\theta = 360°/n \tag{10.17}$$

where,

n = the number of arm of multicopter UAV
θ = angle between two arms

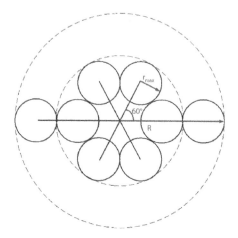

Figure 10.27 Alloy type X-configurations and their geometry parameters.

then Refs. [24, 34] define the relationship between the maximum radius of a propeller (r_{max}) and airframe radius (R) is as follows,

$$R = \frac{r_{max}}{sin\dfrac{\theta}{2}} = \frac{r_{max}}{sin\dfrac{60°}{n}} \qquad (10.18)$$

According to Ref. [34] thrust generated by propellers is reduced because of the aerodynamic interference when propellers are too close. Additionally, Ref. [24] concluded that as a thumb rule (Equation 10.19) so that multi-copter UAV can be compact without losing the efficiency.

$$r_{max} = 1.05r_p - 1.2r_p \qquad (10.19)$$

Earlier, we already select propeller size (r_p) based on the payload capacity so, now airframe radius can be calculated by using Equation 10.18.

10.6 Conclusion

This chapter decrypt each and every component in all the system in multi-copter UAV. It describes every component or sensor very deeply with their function and its various design paraments. The new technology for multicopter UAV viz. auto flight control unit (FUC) was also well descried. Different design consideration for BLCD mots and propellers were discussed with their design equations and criteria. Design parameters for airframe of multicopter UAV were also explained. If components of multicopter UAV were not design and not well matched then the design will fail. All designing theories were explain in perspective of heavy lift multicopter UAV for agricultural operation. This chapter may be helpful for the students and researchers.

References

1. Austin, R., *Unmanned aircraft systems: UAVS design, development and deployment*, pp. 1–205, Wiley, NY, 2010.
2. Christie, K.S., Gilbert, S.L., Brown, C.L., Hatfield, M., and Hanson, L., Unmanned aircraft systems in wildlife research: current and future applications of a transformative technology. *Frontiers in Ecology and the Environment*, 14,5, 241-251, 2016.
3. Quan, Q., Introduction to multicopter design and control, pp. 1–70, Beijing: Springer, 2017.
4. Fan, P.H., Design and control of multi-rotor aircraft, Dissertation, Beihang University, Beijing, China, 2010
5. Zhang, R.F., A study on quadrotor compound helicopter oriented to reliable flight control, Dissertation, Beihang University, Beijing, China, 2011.
6. Q. Quan, J.S. Fu, K.Y. Cai, A compound multicopter, Chinese patent, ZL201220708839.7, 2012.
7. Leishman, J.G., The Breguet–Richet quad-rotor helicopter of 1907, *Vertiflite*, 47, 3, 58–60, 2001.
8. Hamel, T., Mahony, R., and Chriette, A., Visual servo trajectory tracking for a four rotor VTOL aerial vehicle, in: *Proceedings of IEEE International Conference on Robotics and Automation*, Washington, DC, pp. 2781–2786, 2002.
9. Altug, E., *Vision based control of unmanned aerial vehicles with applications to an autonomous four rotor helicopter, quadcopter*, Dissertation, University of Pennsylvania, Philadelphia, Pennsylvania, 2003.
10. Kroo, I., and Printz, F., *Mesicopter project 1999: A Miniature rotocraft concept*, Project report published by Standford University, California, 30-138, 2001.
11. Bouabdallah, S., Murrieri, P., and Siegwart, R., Design and control of an indoor micro quadcopter, in: *Proceedings of IEEE International Conference on Robotics and Automation*, New Orleans, USA, pp. 4393–4398, 2004.
12. Tayebi, A., and Mcgilvray, S., Attitude stabilization of a VTOL quadrotor aircraft. *IEEE Trans. Control Syst. Technol.*, 14, 3, 562–571, 2006.

13. Bouabdallah, S. and Siegwart, R., Full control of a quadcopter, in: *Proceedings of international conference on intelligent robots and systems (IROS)*, San Diego, USA, pp. 691–699, 2007.
14. Pounds, P., Mahony, R., and Corke, P., Modelling and control of a large quadrotor robot. *Control Eng. Pract.*, 18, 7, 691–699, 2010.
15. Huang, H., Hoffmann, G.M., Waslanderet, S.L. *et al.*, Aerodynamics and control of autonomous quadrotor helicopters in aggressive maneuvering, in: *Proceedings of IEEE International Conference on Robotics and Automation*, Kobe, Japan, pp. 3277–3282, 2009.
16. Madani, T., Benallegue, A., Backstepping sliding mode control applied to a miniature quadrotor flying robot, in: *Proceedings of 32nd IEEE International Conference on Industrial Electronics Society*, France, Paris, pp. 700–705, 2006.
17. Zhang, R.F., Wang, X.H., Cai, K.Y., Quadcopter aircraft control without velocity measurements, in: *Joint 48th IEEE Conference on Decision and Control and 28th Chinese Control Conference*, pp. 817–822, 2009.
18. Soumelidis, A., Gaspar, P., Regula, G., Control of an experimental mini quad-rotor UAV, in: *16th IEEE Mediterranean International Conference on Control and Automation*, pp. 1252–1257, 2008.
19. Bristeau, P.J., Callou, F., Vissire, D. *et al.*, The navigation and control technology inside the AR Drone micro UAV, in: *18th IFAC World Congress*, Milano, Italy, pp. 1477–1484, 2011.
20. Lim, H., Park, J., Lee, D. *et al.*, Build your own quadrotor: Open-source projects on unmanned aerial vehicles. *IEEE Robot Autom. Mag.*, 19, 33–45, 2012.
21. Plett, G., Extended Kalman filtering for battery management systems of LiPB-based HEV battery packs, part 1 Background. *J. Pwr. Scr.*, 134, 252–261, 2004.
22. Plett, G., Extended Kalman filtering for battery management systems of LiPB-based HEV battery packs, part 2 Modeling and identification. *J. Pwr. Scr.*, 134, 262–276, 2004.
23. Plett, G., Extended Kalman filtering for battery management systems of LiPB-based HEV battery packs, part 3 State and parameter estimation. *J. Power Sources*, 134, 277–292, 2004.
24. Harrington, A.M., *Optimal propulsion system design for a micro quad rotor*, Dissertation, University of Maryland, College Park, MD 20742, U.S., 2011.
25. Chapman, S.J., *Electric machinery fundamentals*, 4th edn. McGraw-Hill Higher Education, Boston, 2005.
26. Buchi, R., *Radio control with 2.4 GHz*, BoD—Books on Demand, 2014. https://www.amazon.in/Radio-Control-2-4-Roland-Buchi/dp/3732293408
27. Aguiar, A.P., and Hespanha, J.P., Trajectory-tracking and path-following of underactuated autonomous vehicles with parametric modeling uncertainty. *IEEE Trans. Automat. Contr.*, 52, 8, 1362–1379, 2007.
28. Roza, A., and Maggiore, M., Path following controller for a quadrotor helicopter, in: *Proceedings of American Control Conference*, Montreal, pp. 4655–4660, 2012.

29. Lee, T., Leoky, M., and McClamroch, N.H., Geometric tracking control of a quadrotor UAV on SE (3), in: *Proceedings of 49th IEEE Conference on Decision and Control*, Atlanta, pp. 5420–5425, 2010.

30. Parmar, R.P., *Development of an agricultural spraying system for unmanned aerial vehicle*, Ph.D. Dissertation. Department of Farm Machinery and Power Engineering, Punjab Agricultural University, Ludhiana (141004), Punjab, India, 2019.

31. Fahlstrom, P., and Gleason, T., *Introduction to UAV systems*, 4th edn. Wiley, UK, 2012.

32. Suprapto, B.Y., Heryanto, M.A., Suprijono, H., Muliadi, J., and Benyamin, Design and development of heavy-lift hexacopter for heavy payload. *International Seminar on Application for Technology of Information and Communication*, pp. 242–46, 2017.

33. Saheb, S.H. and Babu, G.S., Design and analysis of light weight agriculture robot. *Global J. Res. Eng.*, 17, 6, 22–40, 2017.

34. Hwang, J.Y., Jung, M.K., Kwon, O.J., Numerical study of aerodynamic performance of a multirotor unmanned aerial-vehicle configuration. *J. Aircr.*, 52, 3, 839–846, 2014.

11

IoT-Enabled Agricultural System Application, Challenges and Security Issues

Himadri Nath Saha[1]*, **Reek Roy**[2], **Monojit Chakraborty**[3] and **Chiranmay Sarkar**[3]

[1]Department of Computer Science, Surendranath Evening College, Calcutta University, Kolkata, India
[2]Department of Computer Science, Belda College, Vidyasagar University, Paschim Medinipur, India
[3]Department of Information Technology, RCC Institute of Information Technology, Kolkata, India

Abstract

The growing demand for food in quantity and quality has increased the need to modernize the agricultural sector. In the present scenario, IoT applications in agriculture include real-time monitoring of crops, croplands, environment, precision farming, smart greenhouse, data analytics, etc. Sensors and smart controllers help to estimate soil moisture or plants' water needs, detect diseases of the crops, monitor weather conditions, etc. Challenges faced in the IoT-enabled agricultural systems are software simplicity, secure data generation, and transmission, lack of supporting infrastructure. But the biggest obstacle is lack of smooth integration with the agricultural industry at present and lack of optimally skilled human workforce along with the need for sensors to work wirelessly and consume low power, better connectivity, remote management, the rectification of complexity in the software, and security. There is also a high demand for fail-proof systems to mitigate the risk of data loss in any faults during operation. A short description of challenges, limitations, future developments and security issues of IoT-enabled agricultural system are presented in this book chapter along with a small comparison of the existing recent works has been presented to show in which areas the IoT-enabled agricultural system are progressing.

Corresponding author: contactathimadri@gmail.com

Amitava Choudhury, Arindam Biswas, Manish Prateek and Amlan Chakrabarti (eds.)
Agricultural Informatics: Automation Using the IoT and Machine Learning, (223–248) © 2021
Scrivener Publishing LLC

Keywords: IoT-enabled agricultural system, smart agriculture, wireless sensor networks, security, soil parameters, cloud computing, smart farming challenges

11.1   Introduction

The word "Internet of Things" (IoT) was first proposed by Kevin Ashton, a British visionary, in 1999. Internet of Things has been broadly applied in different fields for quite some time like home, industry, and many other applications acquiring attention all over the world. It is very clear from the term itself that the IoT network will provide us with a technological world in which day-to-day tools, sensors, equipment enhanced by computing power and network functionalities, in short, physical objects that can be classified as "Things" will be able to play a role as individual components or as distributed collaborations of inter-connected devices [1]. The computer, the Internet and mobile Internet technology have brought a lot of great changes in human society in the last few decades.

In this present technical era, it is quite impossible to think of a single moment in our daily lives without any device and the Internet. IoT has been changing the meaning and dimensions of our lives for quite some time by connecting different parts of our lives. To put simply, IoT is ruling the technical world and hence enables us to connect with anything at anywhere and at any time. The interconnectivity, ubiquitous, heterogenic, dynamic changes, interoperability, sensing and actuation, and enormous scalability characteristics of IoT make it very powerful to integrate everyday objects through the Internet [1]. The present and upcoming technology of IoT have the huge potentiality of connecting machine-to-machine, human-to-human making it a global smart communication through smart technologies like wireless sensor networks, mobile computing, etc. IoT is serving worldwide smart environments in everyday life domains such as the farming system, transport system, agriculture, healthcare system, traffic system, security system, and many more [1].

Agriculture in basic terms is a science of soil cultivation, crop production, animal husbandry, and, ultimately, the marketing of the resulting products [2]. The increasing demand for food in quantitative and qualitative terms can be met by fusing technology with farming practices. The global population has grown dramatically, and so there needs to be such a rise in crop production to satisfy world demand for food and nutrition. With the integration of IoT with agriculture, it will not only be beneficial to the farmers but also the development of the nation. Thus, the development of efficient smart agricultural systems will revolutionize the agricultural industry.

Integrating agriculture along with IoT presumes that the connections will be wireless classified based on energy consumption, the uplink and downlink data rate, and device per success point, topology, packet size, and channel width and frequency bandwidth. IoT-enabled agricultural systems help in finding accurate details about the environmental conditions, soil conditions, etc. to get better productivity. The sensors, when properly installed and maintained, save water while also increasing production output. At the same time, Cloud Computing offers ample tools and solutions for managing, storing, and analyzing the vast amount of data produced by devices that can be used to automate tasks, predict scenarios, and enhance several real-time activities that allow farmers to decide on different factors for crop improvement. For example, diseases of plants are conventionally detected manually by agriculture experts, which can be inaccurate at times and is also very time-consuming. To avoid such inaccurate results and time-consuming processes, automatic and remote identification of crop diseases can be applied through Wireless Sensor Networks (WSN) and IoT [2]. At the same time, agriculture is accompanied by a lot of other problems like climate changes, environmental changes, increment in urbanization, water scarcity, soil moisture factors, shortage of arable land for growing crops [3, 4]. Given the problems faced in agriculture mentioned above, it can be understood that there is a need for a sufficient range of crop varieties, a proper adaptation of agricultural practices, and sustainability to conserve scarce resources [4]. Such factors affect agricultural growth, such as crop productivity, diseases, and yield generation. Hence, there is a need to incorporate technology with agriculture to increase production.

Modern techniques can be used to grow crops in a controlled environment [5] which can help humans to lead wise and smart agriculture. Since, Cloud Computing also provides sufficient resources and facilities for handling, processing, and evaluating the vast volume of data collected from sensors; so it can be used to optimize operations, forecast scenarios, and improve broad-based real-time activities for smart farming. IoT will be able to help farmers get a timely cultivating guideline related to the parameters like the seasonal plant diseases, pesticide usage, pest control, crop treatment, irrigation management, natural disasters affecting crops and the recovery methods [4, 5]. Other existing technologies along with WSNs that are feasible with IoT are radio frequency identification (RFID), middleware technologies, and cloud computing and end-user applications [6]. Hence, these technologies have a great impact on smart farming or agriculture along with a strong impact on the global economy.

This chapter of the book focuses mainly on the implementation of the IoT-enabled agricultural system, that is, which modern technologies are integrated with the agricultural sector that are benefitting the farmers and increasing the quality of the products, productivity's volume, and the profitability of a business. The chapter also aims at the challenges and the security issues along with the scopes and trends faced by these systems as many of the current surveys at present focuses on the constraints, pitfalls, and benefits of the agricultural food sector on large scale.

Section 11.2 consists of a literature survey done on various existing systems mentioning the results, pros, and cons of these systems along with a table showing the survey analysis. In Section 11.3, the challenges to implement IoT-enabled systems have been elaborated. Section 11.4 has an explanation of the security issues of IoT systems and measures that can be taken. In Section 11.5 the future research direction of the IoT-enabled systems are explained. Section 11.6 has a short conclusion of this book chapter.

11.2   Background & Related Works

Agriculture is the primary source of food grains and other natural resources, and food is the basis of human life. This area, therefore, plays a very key role in the rate of economic growth of the country. Enhancing the agricultural sector with the implementation of new technology is also one of the major challenges faced by developing countries. Unfortunately, several farmers in developing countries still use conventional farming methods, resulting in low yields of crops and fruit. Some of the characteristics of agriculture that affect the quality and production of the crops and are different for every crop are enormous, dynamics, complexity, and spatiality. IoT-enabled agriculture system application enables the farmers to not only monitor the cultivating crops better but also to scan the soil along with access to the GPS. Access to remote locations can be established to track and manage agricultural fields. Plant disease is a very big threat to cultivation. Conventionally, these diseases are detected manually by experts, which other than being time-consuming are also inaccurate at times. The identification of plant diseases is possible through WSN and IoT. Raspberry Pi3 hardware interfaced with wireless sensors when deployed in the agricultural fields can measure the parameters of the environment and also monitor the agriculture field.

A Random Forest Classifier technique is used to classify the diseases in a system proposed by Devi *et al.* [2]. Plant images are collected repeatedly and continuously via a camera sensor that is integrated with Raspberry Pi3 hardware and Gray Level Co-occurrence Matrix (GLCM) features are extracted to be transmitted to the cloud via Wi-Fi. In this system, plant disease is identified at an early stage so that the spread of such disease can be avoided. The system consists of five phases to detect plant diseases using image processing techniques and IoT-image acquisition (captured using sensor cameras which are interfaced with Raspberry Pi3 hardware model), image pre-processing (resizing captured image to 256×256 size and converting color image to gray image to calculate the histogram equalization), image segmentation (segmentation is done on the obtained equalized image using k-means clustering technique), feature extraction (Texture features such as energy, dissimilarity, contrast, correlation are retrieved from the segmented image and the features are determined from the GLCM matrix) and finally image classification (Random Forest Classification (RFC) technique is used to classify and analyze finally). The proposed system is capable of identifying diseases with increased accuracy of 24% compared to the current K-NN classifier.

In some other recent studies have been done on the growth of the monitoring system developed for the crops and the real-world deployments [4], and the main focus has been kept on the leaf area index (LAI) in this study which is a specific crop parameter. Bauer *et al.* [4] proposed a system that focuses on the LAI, a well-known key parameter that provides details about the performance of the photosynthesis and the plants' vital conditions. The architecture [4] developed mainly comprises of a WSN based monitoring system which is tailored for *in-situ* LAI assessment. The key approaches of the architecture are simplicity of the software, redundancy of the hardware, and control of the entire system. A holistic IoT-based agricultural framework to track crops continuously and evaluate the LAI appropriate for the accurate monitoring of crop growth based on an *in-situ* WSN that is optimized to collect sensor information is presented in Ref. [4]. This sensor network is linked to the central server using an IoT-based MQTT infrastructure and the networking used is the Public Land Mobile Network (PLMN).

Some systems propose that real-time notifications can be delivered to orient smart irrigation based on analyzing information and without the intervention of humans, for example, systems proposed by Balaji *et al.* [7]. Hartung *et al.* [8] explained that WSNs have been deployed in the agricultural sector for some time to enhance the remote control of agricultural products and resources. The capability of WSNs to improve efficiency and reduce waste has improved remarkably. More recently, with the increase in the potentiality of WSNs, these deployments have been integrated with IoT successfully as shown by Vasist *et al.* [9].

Mat *et al.* [10] presented a system of Green House Management System (GHMS) in which Wireless Sensor Networks (WSNs) have been used. The system will measure soil moisture, the wetness of air, the temperature of air by using a soil moisture sensor, a humidity sensor, and a temperature sensor respectively. The XBee technology [10] has been selected for WSN. A GUI is connected by XBee which can be a computer or a mobile phone. The GreenHouse Management System (GHMS) uses various sensors to collect environmental data like temperature, humidity, and soil moisture. The readings of the sensors will decide which device (fan or water pump) will be switched ON or OFF. Here, the moisture was being used to monitor the input measured in Volumetric Water Content (VWC). The data values decide which device should be ON or OFF. The system uses wireless technology.

Suma *et al.* [11] proposed a system that uses a microcontroller connected with various sensors (temperature, moisture, and PIR sensor) through RS232. The system receives data and it contains a buzzer and LED light which is set ON and the LED starts to blink if the value received exceeds a threshold value. This system uses sensors, a microcontroller, and RS232 to check incoming sensor values with threshold values. If the sensor value exceeds a certain threshold, the buzzer is switched on and the LED immediately begins to blink. This sends an alarm to the farmer and the power is switched off immediately. The system contains two modes manual and automatic. The system also contains an android application. In the manual mode, the user must manually turn on and off using the built android program. In automatic mode, it is done automatically. In both modes, the implementation is done using a GSM module.

Drought is a major serious problem that limits crop yield productive capacity. Many areas of the world face this problem with varying degrees of severity. To address this problem, remote sensing, especially in very rural areas, is used to acquire frequent soil moisture data that help to assess agricultural drought in remote regions. For this reason, the Soil Moisture and Ocean Salinity (SMOS) satellite was launched in 2009, which offers global soil moisture maps every one to two days. SMOS L2 was used in the framework proposed by Martínez-Fernández *et al.* [12] for the measurement of the Soil Water Deficit Index (SWDI) in Spain. They used various methods and compared the data derived from *in situ* data on soil water metrics with the SWDI. An autonomous, sensor-based, and vision-based robot named Agribot was developed for seed sowing by Santhi *et al.* [13]. The robot can execute on any crop yields as long as the robot's self-awareness is verified via the global and local maps created by the Global Positioning System (GPS) and the on-board vision system is equipped with a personal computer.

On the other hand, more data collection functions, such as environmental monitoring, plant health, and pest problems, can be provided by field sensors in every corner of the crop cycle. Approaches such as vehicle precision spraying and automated VRT chemigation was proposed by Oberti *et al.* [14], which are widely used in smart fertilization, can also be used to treat diseases and other pesticide concerns. Some IoT-based automated traps are advantageous over remote sensing as they can count, track, identify insect types, and export data to the cloud for further evaluation. New approaches are also provided through the advancement of robotic technology. An agricultural robot with multi-spectral sensing systems, under the guidance of a remote IoT disease management system, configured with accurate spray nozzles, can locate and deal with pest challenges more precisely. This type of IoT-based pest management system hence supports the restoration of the natural climate along with reducing the overall expenditures.

Some crops that are grown indoors are less likely to be affected by the climate and the environment. This is called Greenhouse farming in which crops are not limited to receive lights only during day time. Such farming allows crops to grow under suitable conditions in any part of the world and at any time. Greenhouse farming proposed by Akkas *et al.* [15] has also gained well acknowledgment as it allows the successful production of various crops under a controlled environment like ventilation system, the accuracy of monitoring parameters, covering materials to control the wind, etc. An original routing protocol was developed and integrated into an IoT-based internally accessible agriculture application using MicaZ off-the-shelf wireless nodes [15] programmed in nesC. XServe is the primary gateway for wireless networks and other applications. The data obtained can also be processed on a server and day- and time-based reports are available for analysis. The specific data collected using the adjustable sensor nodes allows the farmers to study intricate trends of the farming process. The long term collected data allows agriculture specialists to make timetables that can grow specific crops in any controlled conditions.

From the literature review above, we can draw the conclusion that certain systems have been developed that identify environmental conditions such as crop temperature and soil conditions. Many systems are designed to keep inspection of the irrigation system. Many existing networks often lack the ability to find out whether any node is being hacked, or whether any cable is being cut by a human knowingly, or by animal scratching. Some systems not only keep a record of soil content but also use sensors to keep track of crop field safety. Many other systems are designed to see field protection.

The book chapter focuses on the challenges and security problems along with the scopes and developments these systems face, as many of the existing studies are currently centered on the large-scale limitations, risks, and benefits of the agricultural food field. The chapter focuses on those aspects of IoT-enabled agricultural systems that need to be considered very keenly while implementing these systems. This chapter of the book also emphasizes how the IoT-enabled agricultural system is applied, that is, what technological innovations are incorporated with the agricultural industry that favors the farmers and increases the quality of the goods, the volume of production and the profitability of a business. Table 11.1 shows the survey analysis of the existing systems in smart agriculture.

Table 11.1 A survey analysis.

Field of work	Technology/devices used	Outcomes/future scopes
IoT–enabled disease detection system of plants [2]	Various sensors—Soil moisture sensor, pH sensor, camera sensor, Temperature sensor, Raspberry Pi 3, Wi-Fi, Image Processing Techniques— Random Forest Classification (RFC), Gray Level Co-occurrence Matrix (GLCM).	• On average, 24% increased accuracy compared to the current model • Accuracy depends on the environmental conditions (image capturing angle, lighting in the field)
A comprehensive IoT-based agricultural monitoring system that focuses on continuous evaluation of the LAI (leaf area index) [4]	Wireless Sensor Networks— TelosB1-based platform, Linux-based Raspberry Pi 3, MQTT-based IoT infrastructure, PLMN connectivity.	• Gives accurate temperature and humidity readings • Data in the central server is persistent for analysis • The system helps farmers to take decisions • Additional environmental sensors can be added

(Continued)

Table 11.1   A survey analysis. (*Continued*)

Field of work	Technology/devices used	Outcomes/future scopes
Efficient irrigation in Green House Management System (GHMS) [10]	Wireless Sensor Networks-Wireless Moisture Sensor Network (WMSN), temperature sensor, humidity sensor, XBee technology, Irrigation methods— Irrigation by schedule, Feedback based irrigation.	• More effective automatic irrigation compared to scheduled irrigation • Optimizes water, fertilizers and retains soil moisture • Average savings of 1,500 ml per tree per day
Smart agriculture irrigation system using sensors deployed in the field [11]	Wireless Sensor Networks— moisture sensor, temperature sensor, PIR sensor, PIC16F877A microcontroller, GSM module, RS-232, buzzer.	• The buzzer is switched ON and LED starts to blink when the threshold value exceeded in both manual and automatic mode • Communication with the farmer through a GSM module • The system can be enhanced for large areas of land
Calculation of Soil Water Deficit Index (SWDI) for drought areas [12]	Soil Moisture and Ocean Salinity (SMOS) satellite, 4 methods used to calculate SWDI— pedotransfer functions (PTF), laboratory analysis (exp), soil moisture series (p5, p95, and gsmm) and linear regression analysis	• Correlation coefficient high for all 4 methods (R, 0.86) • Analysis of results obtained using the Crop Moisture Index (CMI) and Atmospheric Water Deficit (AWD) • Good results obtained in both, but AWD was better • SMOS found to be a feasible tool for agriculture • SWDI of SMOS can be applied to different environmental conditions and spatial scales • The issue is the requirement of the parameters FC (field capacity) and WP (wilting point)

(*Continued*)

Table 11.1 A survey analysis. (*Continued*)

Field of work	Technology/devices used	Outcomes/future scopes
Sensor and Vision-based autonomous agricultural robot for sowing seeds [13]	Controller (Arduino), Sensors—Ultrasonic sensors, IR sensors, Image Processing Technique, and morphological features, Global Positioning System (GPS)	• Errors and imprecision removed, calibration completed • The suspension mechanism can withstand bumps of up to 3 cm • Ultrasonic sensor and IR sensor sow seeds at optimum depth • For the future, multi-robot swarming technology can be integrated
Green House Monitoring System using a wireless sensor network (WSN) [15]	MicaZ off-the-shelf wireless modules, TinyOS, 802.15.4 wireless network, XServe	• Saves the cost of cabling and overcomes the difficulty of the relocation of nodes if connected by cables • Measures greenhouses' temperature, light, humidity, and pressure • The one-way flow of information—from the greenhouse to end-user • The system can be extended to include actuators

11.3   Challenges to Implement IoT-Enabled Systems

All technologies have their boon and their curse. Though smart farming is very effective and helps in the increase of productivity of the crops for the farmers, IoT-enabled agricultural systems do have their challenges and drawbacks. Some of the challenges in IoT-enabled agricultural system are discussed below.

11.3.1   Secured Data Generation and Transmission and Privacy

IoT-based agriculture systems have a lot of security issues while implementing. It is very important to keep in mind that there can be data loss while implementation. With the Internet being accessed more and more nowadays, access to raw information, on-field information can be easily hacked without proper security. The sensor nodes can lead to destruction without adequate security [16]. The security challenge is one of the main factors that affect the success of IoT. With the up-gradation of the technology, the environment of IoT is becoming way more complex making privacy issues more complicated. The transition of data to the interconnected internet of smart things should ensure that the security, privacy, and authenticity of the data involved in the network are preserved.

11.3.2   Lack of Supporting Infrastructure

The lack of sufficient infrastructure does not allow farmers to take advantage of the IoT technology even if they implement it. Many farms are concentrated in remote areas and far from the Internet. A farmer needs to be able to access crop data securely from any position at any time, so issues with networking will make an advanced monitoring system ineffective. Also, a lot of remote locations in India do not have proper electricity supply and since electricity is the engine for IoT-enabled smart agricultural systems this is one of the greatest obstacles in integrating IoT technology with the existing agricultural industry. Developing countries face major challenges in the availability and connectivity of the internet and hence the adoption of IoT becomes quite difficult for farmers [17]. There is a shortage of IoT services, such as smart grid and smart metering, in the agriculture sector. In addition to this, the cost of infrastructure modernization and maintenance will be a major obstacle for farmers who are already suffering from high costs and low incomes. Lack of knowledge on IoT infrastructure in agriculture would be detrimental to productivity. It can therefore be recognized that rural agricultural areas are not developed in terms of overall infrastructure. The capacity of the user to incorporate new core-related functionality is diminished by the unanticipated development tool. Many of the infrastructures that are far from ready for use in Indian agriculture are smart water supply, smart power grid, smart drainage, a system of sanitation, etc.

11.3.3   Technical Skill Requirement

For years, agriculture was completely based on manual labor. Farmers, hence have abundant knowledge when it comes to doing farming manually, but integrating technology with farming is not something that they are familiar with. For smart farming to be successful, data analytics should be at the core of every smart agriculture solution. One of the essential keys to the survival of agricultural extension is the capacity building [17].

Adequate knowledge of know-how is required for agriculture, and the lack of operational skills affects the overall agricultural output. The capacity building focuses on solving challenges and resolving the need for development [17] to increase the capacity of an institution so that the functions of agriculture can be carried out. Technological development has also developed to increase the demand for high skilled labor across various working environments. Motor skills, cognitive skills, and communication skills are the three stages of skills needed by the operator in the agriculture industry. The educational gap is one of the primary problems for the farmers in the path of adopting new practices and effective technologies. Technical manpower is expected to be needed in a high number. It will tend to be inadequate with time over the horizon.

The technical, skilled manpower in the agricultural sector has played a crucial role in achieving self-sufficiency in the growth of food grains. Studies have shown that technical manpower shortage is present at various levels especially related to IoT. There is a shortage of manpower, resources, technology-related skills, and access to the latest technologies to improve infrastructure in most of the rising economies. Interoperability, ensuring data protection and sourcing the skills needed are some of the main concerns that are growing in emerging economies. Also in the developed world, the spectrum of IoT problems has not been specific and has faced a range of challenges. Some of the challenges related to the IoT in many sectors are the incentives of market and investments, resources of policy, infrastructure readiness, and technical skill requirements [17]. Interoperability has produced a huge effect on the IoT with an economic impact beyond technological aspects.

11.3.4   Complexity in Software and Hardware

The complexity of software and the interpretation of data are identified as one of the main critical problems of the IoT-based agricultural framework. Some other problems associated with the IoT-based agricultural system are scalability, self-configuration, interoperability, energy-optimized solutions storage capacity, and fault tolerance [17]. Adequate software infrastructure is needed to support the network. Software running in smart sensors should be able to operate with minimal resources, as in traditional embedded systems, and the server should be able to support the network of these smart devices in the background. Software performance, complexity, design, and dynamics are some of the variables that have a significant effect on the quality and production of the crop. At the same time software should be such that it is easily operable by the user to perform various functions involved in agriculture. User-friendly applications have paved the way for big data to be implemented on the various data acquired by the smart devices to understand the growth and behavior of plants in customized environments, effectively implement precision farming techniques, and increase production output. But even so, a lot of problems persist and much detailed analysis is needed to cope with these problems in a better way.

Devices used for smart farming must be robust so that they can protect them from temperature fluctuations, heavy rainfall, humidity, heavy winds, solar radiation, and extreme cold, and also from other dangerous issues that can destroy these devices. To run for longer periods, these IoT devices must be battery powered. Solar panels and turbines are power harvesting modules that can help in the implementation of IoT. Data for IoT–enabled agriculture systems are usually in bulk and so they must be compatible with lower-power capabilities powering tools and small-scale infrastructure servers. The costly equipment must be provided with physical protection in different climates to ensure the efficiency of the transmission of data. The current gateways and protocols and networks may not handle a wide variety of IoT devices or nodes deployed on the agricultural platform. With the IoT devices deployed, scalability and localization of the devices must be considered so that good communication with other IoT devices is possible.

The fault tolerance is also a major challenge and it requires redundancy on several levels depending on various conditions. Hence better systems need to be developed which can tackle hardware and systemic faults while also decreasing the risk of data loss such that the maximum amount of data can be retrieved even in worst-case scenarios.

Complexity, spatial–temporal variation, and complexity are some of the characteristics of agriculture that need to be addressed when designing the right types of services. In addition to these, the actuators, cameras sensors, software, and positioning technology (GPS), wireless communication, and radio frequency identification (RFID) technology are some of the technologies which have been used for the development of IoT-enabled smart agricultural systems. Due to all these factors, the complexity of the system increases in certain sectors of agriculture. With time the system complexity will increase even further as agricultural systems will be needed to be developed more which means considering and monitoring more parameters and operating more number of functions. Thus, a proper in-depth understanding of the software and operating it is needed.

11.3.5   Bulk Data

A secure IoT system or service relies not only on the efficiency of the entire system and on each layer of the network but also on cooperation between layers in terms of protection, privacy, and other assets linked to trust [17]. The trustiness of the entire system has to be achieved. New issues continue to emerge in the area of IoT due to their specific characteristics. Data collection, usually in bulk, is a key problem in IoT. The overwhelming amount of data obtained from the physical perception layer must be accurate. In the event of harm to the data collected or malicious feedback of any sensors, the output of the IoT sensors would be significantly affected [17]. The collection of data needs to be assured. Data mining and merging involve accurate, stable, confidential, and reliable data processing and analysis. On the one hand, IoT systems are focused on data mining, processing, and analysis and, at the same time, users need to reveal their data or privacy to benefit from advanced services. Intelligently delivering context-aware and customized services while preserving consumer privacy at the expected stage, is a significant obstacle in current IoT research and practice [17]. Many small scale farmers who are not aware of the system are thus skeptical to disclose such huge bulk of data about their farming.

11.3.6   Disrupted Connectivity to the Cloud

In most locations, poor third or fourth-generation (3G/4G) connectivity coverage is present [18] practically, 5G is not implemented at most of the remote places. SIGFOX, LoRa are low power wide area 9LPWA technologies which provide an opportunity to overcome the poor connectivity issue [18]; but they do not handle bulk datasets. So, internet connectivity in farmhouses is still not efficient enough to send Big Data to the cloud for review. There may also be examples of field interference that may have damaging effects on cloud connections. These disruptions in connections between the smart devices in the farm and the cloud can be overcome in several ways. These include offline capabilities, the presence of specific IoT gateways, enhanced deep learning through cloud services, and system migration. These technologies provide end-to-end IoT connectivity that enables systems to provide a variety of agricultural services, such as precision farming methods, pH monitoring, productivity forecasting, and microclimate prediction, even when the cloud computing system is not continuously interconnected.

To reduce operational costs, ensure environmental sustainability, and improve yields, farmers need to implement technologies that promote data-driven operations. These and other features are still under development and are slowly empowering farmers to take advantage of precision farming techniques to operate a more productive and profitable enterprise. Thus, there is a high demand for much better technologies; systems, and connectivity which would make farmers recognize all the benefits of farming using data analytics.

11.3.7   Better Connectivity

In general, most farms are located in different areas where Internet access might not be good enough to allow rapid data communication. Rural areas face a lot of problems in the domains of connectivity, communication infrastructure, environmental management, etc. For all the rural and remote areas, the barriers that are to be addressed by broadband information and communication technologies (ICTs) are economic, social barriers, and most importantly distance barriers [19]. Also, communication lines in remote areas can be disrupted by trees, canopies, and other physical obstacles. These factors drive up the cost of data transmission and have been responsible for the sluggish implementation of highly precise technology in agriculture. Such costs will increase exponentially after the advent of Big Data.

These problems can be overcome by the use of vacant TV frequencies. Vacant TV frequencies can be used to transfer information. It is especially helpful in remote areas, as poor reception of TV also contributes to the presence of White Spaces in TV broadcast frequencies, which are then available for use. Ultra-High Frequency (UHF) and Very High Frequency (VHF) broadcast bands are both capable of multiplying the power of Wi-Fi signals, rendering them stronger. Such advantages would reduce expenses and increase networking, thus expanding the adoption of precision agricultural techniques.

11.3.8   Interoperability Issue

Interoperability is a crucial concern for the application of IoT technology. Millions of devices are linked in IoT and need to communicate with each other in which interoperability plays an important role. Technical interoperability, syntactic interoperability, and organizational interoperability are various types of interoperability problems that need to be addressed in IoT. Technical interoperability aims to provide seamless information exchange between the systems, associated with the software and hardware [20]. Data formats such as the syntax of messages exchanged in systems, high-level languages (HTML, XML, etc.) or table formats are subject to syntactical interoperability. Semantic Interoperability deals with the human interpretation, experience, and understanding of IoT applications and hence has special importance for end-users. For IoT scalability, organizational interoperability is of very great importance for the success of distributed IoT infrastructures; so that data can be transferred effectively and there is meaningful communication in different geographical regions and varying systems [20].

11.3.9   Crop Management Issues

Along with monitoring the climatic conditions like hail, flood, extreme cold, drought, snowfall, storms, crop management issue is also a challenge. Weather parameters keep on changing like the rain, wind, temperature, barometric pressure, global warming, which in turn affects the crops. Also, the change in soil should be paid heed to so that managing the crops and sowing the seeds at the proper time can be done. Macronutrients like the potassium, nitrogen, phosphorus of the soil need to be monitored. Keeping track of these manually involves human intervention which is very time consuming and a very tedious process. As we know, temperature, humidity, wind are parameters of the environment which affect types of soil, change in topology, weather change and vegetation, so, having IoT-based agricultural system will help in identifying the soil requirements and can also help in suggesting the amount and type of fertilizers which are to be used. Diseases in the crop can be detected earlier and suitable fertilizer and pesticide can be organized as a collection of data, along with soil parameters, of the particular crop to be planted so that the correct pesticide can be sprayed to the field to save the crop in advance.

11.3.10   Power Consumption

The concept of IoT is to connect numerous smart devices via the Internet and transfer and exchange information in bulk which as a result leads to very high power consumption and high bandwidth. So, there is a need to minimize the consumption of power as well as the bandwidth [21] as in many rural areas abundant power supplies are not available and internet connectivity does not provide high bandwidth.

11.3.11   Environmental Challenges

Wireless Sensor Networks (WSNs) have been deployed in the agriculture domain for quite some time. While many improvements have been made in the last decade, the maintenance and deployment of WSNs in the physical world still face some difficulties. Keeping aside the general challenges of WSN, that is, their power consumption, the hardware limitations of small sensor devices, and sometimes low power communication, WSNs face additional challenges when deployed for the long term outdoors. The natural environment has a very strong effect on the WSN's operability. Sensor nodes are usually exposed to severe weather conditions during extreme temperature variations and heavy rainfall. Humidity, moisture content, dust during dry seasons, short circuits, corrosion, mud has a major impact on WSNs if they are deployed directly in the field.

11.3.12   High Cost

The equipment required to incorporate IoT in agriculture is extremely expensive. Bigger and capital intensive farms are usually much more receptive to the concept of IoT-based agriculture systems and interested to invest continuously in new equipment. The main challenge remains is to attract small scale farmers who have limited resources for newer technology and are scared of misuse of data. Nonetheless, sensors are the least expensive part, but it would cost more than a thousand dollars to equip all farmers' fields with them.

Automated machinery expenses are more than manually controlled machinery, as it requires the cost of the farm management software and cloud access to record data. Added to these are cloud service costs and other technology costs like regular monitoring, data analysis, and prediction, and of course, material cost directly associated with agriculture like crop seeds, fertilizers, and other utility costs. Even though agricultural processes are automated in the proposed system but human labors are needed for certain functions like manually checking plant health and detecting any faults or anomalies or maintenance purposes all of which come at a cost. On top of these are the electricity costs, since the whole system will be powered by electricity. Hence cost is a major hiccup in IoT-enabled smart agricultural systems.

Farmers are currently relying on a sparsely distributed network of sensors to gather farm conditions data. Apart from the physical constraints of these sensors, they are costly. As a result, farmers tend to rely on less sophisticated farming technologies that reduce their yield and productivity. To reduce these costs, the use of unmanned aerial vehicles (UAVs) increases spatial coverage and helps to enhance control. Tethered Eye helium balloons may also be used in places where there are limitations on the use of drones, including government controls, poor battery life, and high costs. Such aerial sensors produce a stream of uninterrupted images of farm situations that are used to refine the data obtained by sensors on the ground. As a result, this strategy helps to minimize hardware costs while promoting more accurate data collection. Also if this is not possible then cameras can be implemented to monitor the crops from time to time. But again initial installation cost for all these may be too expensive for farmers. To make higher profits, the farmers must invest in these technologies, but it would be difficult for them to make an initial investment to set up IoT technology in their farms. Added to these will be extra charges in case the system needs some repair. A solution to this problem is quite complex. The technological firms should be able to offer these technologies and equipment to the farmers at a lower price and the government should also have lucrative financial schemes for farmers which encourage them to embrace IoT-enabled smart agricultural systems.

11.4 Security Issues and Measures

Security has always been an essential component and a challenge in the implementation of IoT solutions. Improper access and privacy are the main issues on the list. With the advent of new technology, the IoT world has become more challenging and complex, making problems of privacy and protection more complicated.

Some of the security threats in IoT are the modification of data, data leakage, device modification, protocol hijacking, software vulnerabilities data gathering, and many more. Other factors affecting the security measures of IoT are network structure, terminal equipment, etc. The implementation of mobile nodes and wireless sensor networks enhances the role of wireless infrastructure in IoT applications. Wireless sensor networks become vulnerable to hackers from all over the world if they are left open to internet connectivity. Several reports have shown that IoT systems and users are seriously impacted by various security threats. Many of the major security concerns in IoT include an unsafe mobile interface, unprotected web interface, unsafe network infrastructure, inadequate authorization and authentication, insecure cloud interface, lack of security specifications, etc.

The security threats listed above are as general in the field of smart farming as in other IoT fields. Therefore, as with any other sector, farmers need to think about safety and security to use technology in the right way. The agricultural sector involves the challenges of hacking and theft of data brought about by the concept of precision farming. Organized crime or cyber terrorism can cause huge damage to the system, infrastructure, and business. Malware attacks may cause huge data loss. Less expensive machines in compromised locations are much more susceptible to cyber-attacks. Also, other modern and complex higher-level security threats are triggered by middleware integration, several software layers, APIs, machine-to-machine communication, etc.

Front-end sensors and devices, network, and back-end IT services are referred to as security threats of IoT. A few of the aspects associated with the back end of IT systems are the replacement of an operator and management of the safety of code resources. Since data is the brain of IoT-based smart agricultural systems, they are extremely valuable. Somebody might have unauthorized entry to the IoT provider database and can hence steal and manipulate the information. If anyone alters the data then even the smallest alterations may have disastrous consequences like if someone alters the data about the precise use of fertilizers or pesticides on plants then a huge amount of crops will be damaged and the farmer may incur huge losses. If the plants survive, excess amounts of fertilizers, pesticides, or chemicals may be consumed by humans and animals leading to more fatal outcomes. Thus data security is a top priority in IoT-based agricultural systems. There has been a lack of information significantly about data protection in IoT-enabled agricultural systems additionally. To make farming more efficient, IoT devices and data analysis practices are used by farm equipment providers.

Traditional agriculture with old technologies still prevails which often does not include a robust data backup along with a proper security concept. Let us take an example, farms equipment is connected via some field monitoring drones which are often linked to the internet and general channels. However, these types of equipment do not include basic security mechanisms such as employee logins monitoring or two-factor verification or authentication for remote access sessions. Nevertheless, these types of equipment do not have specific security features, such as employee log-ins monitoring or two-factor remote access session authentication. Major security standards must therefore be developed, such as network access control, identity authentication, 2-way verification, the confidentiality of data to improve protection. One of such systems developed to secure agri-cultural data from hackers uses AES 128 cryptography method [22]. The data obtained by the sensors is stored safely in the cloud in this system. The device which gathers the sensor data from the cloud gets the information framed into the JSON format at the encryption side in the device system. An extension of the AES 128 cryptography method has been proposed which gets the data encrypted. The reverse order is followed at the decryp-tion side. The JSON parser is used to obtain the raw data at the decryption side of the server system. Other systems that define precision agriculture technologies, uncover security threats, devises lightweight encryption, and decryption method to facilitate a robust authentication solution in P2P communications of smart farming have also been proposed. A system that constructs the Common Vulnerability Scoring System (CVSS) score has also been predicted which calculates the score based on the technologies that are used in the farm for smart farming. Such a system can be used to focus on assessing the cyber-attack vulnerabilities in the technologies along with the smart farming environment.

The security issue is not only confined to the resources but also the agri-cultural products. For example, crops are often damaged due to rodents or insects as mentioned before. To detect the motion of insects, pests, or rodents, an Infrared (IR) Sensor can be used which can calculate the dis-tance of the pests or insects and capture their images. These data can be stored in the websites so that the farmers can retrieve them and can get an idea as to how to protect the crops. Such systems can use web cameras to take the images, hence reducing manpower and usage of pesticides.

Drones or UAVs (Unmanned Aerial Vehicles) with equipped cameras, integrating modules, and sensors can be deployed in various sections of the field which can capture real-time images and contribute towards pre-cision agriculture and also towards security issues of the fields. Some pro-posed solutions [23] which can be incorporated into Unmanned Aerial Vehicles (UAV) or drones have been discussed such as hyperspectral imaging is much better than multispectral imaging. RGB-D camera can be installed in drones to obtain real-time images that can be processed further using Support Vector Machine (SVM). These systems can have Global Positioning System (GPS) [24] built in it so that it can carry the right instruction by the operator across any location. The use of thermal or heat-seeking cameras can aid agriculture in a significant way by tracking the thermal properties of plants and crops and also by identifying the presence of harmful wildlife in agricultural fields. Thermal imaging also allows us to track plant pests, lack of water, and other physiological processes.

11.5   Future Research Direction

The future of IoT-based agricultural farming is the interconnected farm known as smart farming. Precision agriculture applications are usually targeted at large and conventional farming, but in the future, there will also be new levers to enhance the changing trends in agricultural investments, such as organic farming, family farming, etc. The coming years of agriculture lie in linking, gathering, and analyzing the vast majority of data to maximize efficiency and productivity. Licensed low-power wireless access (LPWA) is believed to be the new era of sustainable agriculture because of its good geographical coverage and also because it is cost-effective.

The use of drones can help to keep track of rainfall and environmental information, as well as the crop species that can be harvested in a particular environment. The historical information can be found out about an area and sent to agricultural experts to make better decisions as to which crop suits which environment. The identification of the type of fertilizers which is suitable for a specific crop is an important challenge that can be overcome if a device can say the change in soil type or weather change through intelligent systems.

Protection of the deployed devices from environmental damages and wildlife damages is a big challenge. Along with the sensor networks, the connectivity of the entire network is affected by adverse weather effects. Ground-level sensors when deployed in rural areas get moved sometimes due to wildlife, sometimes the cables get nibbles or even bit marks on sensors are seen. Sensors on higher levels are sometimes disturbed by birds. These challenges could be mitigated by the usage of solar energy equipment, more robust and shielded cables, and professional uninterrupted power supply (UPS) systems or by electric fences.

As data security is one of the critical problems in this field, local networks should be protected from interference by other networks. If the server is infected once, it will be very difficult to debug it. Reinstalling the software or shutting down a compromised system is not a feasible option and takes a major toll on the entire process. The devices can be authorized and authenticated if the middleware of IoT can manage a trust relationship with these devices. Middleware helps in promoting data interoperability (technical interoperability) and becomes the bridge between the heterogeneous applications in the cloud and the things.

Autonomous systems will always be more efficient according to the market situation, minimizing the cost and maximizing the profits. But in some cases, many small individual users can use the same IoT integrated agriculture process. In such cases, the technologies and the specifications of the sensors used by the different users may be different. So we need local network security along with making difference in the interoperability, the semantic annotation, and filtering of data coming from each user. Security, command over access rights to information, anonymity is hence important and should be maintained in such a system as many of these data stored by these users can be related to commercial enterprise, strategic thinking and are not to be disclosed to non-authorized entities.

11.6 Conclusion

In today's world, every aspect of human life is connected by IoT devices such as automotive and logistics, remote monitoring of health and fitness, smart homes, industrial IoT, smart cities, alarm systems, etc. [25]. In the last decades, there has been a major technological transformation in the domain of agriculture and farming and this field has become more industrialized and technology-driven. IoT-enabled agricultural system applications have made farmers gain better control over growing crops by saving scarce resources like water, increasing scale efficiencies, decreasing production risks, and cutting down costs. The weather patterns, crop production, soil conditions, and all other data can be managed using smart sensors from remote locations, i.e. without the presence of humans. Climate-based controllers alter climatic factors to facilitate plant growth. This critical data collected can be recorded and stored in the cloud and later retrieved to monitor equipment output and staff results. Automation is an important IoT approach to achieve greater control over the production cycle while retaining higher growth potential and higher crop quality standards.

Hence we see that crop management devices make farming more precise by tracking factors like precipitation, temperature, leaf water capacity, and overall crop safety, which as a result makes it possible to avoid diseases or infestations that could adversely affect crop yields. In this book chapter, we see that there are quite a several challenges that are faced to implement such IoT-based agricultural systems. With the future moving towards and farming being the major source of survival in this world, a continuous study and research are going on to make the IoT-based agricultural system more and more feasible to all sectors of the farmers.

References

1. Chakraborty, S., Das, P., Pal, S., IoT Foundations and Its Application, in: *IoT and Analytics for Agriculture*, Springer, Singapore, pp. 51–68, 2020.
2. Devi, R.D., Nandhini, S.A., Hemalatha, R., Radha, S., IoT Enabled Efficient Detection and Classification of Plant Diseases for Agricultural Applications, in: *2019 International Conference on Wireless Communications Signal Processing and Networking (WiSPNET)*, Chennai, India, pp. 447–451, IEEE, 2019.
3. Masih, J. and Rajasekaran, R., Integrating Big Data Practices in Agriculture, in: *IoT and Analytics for Agriculture*, pp. 1–26, Springer, Singapore, 2020.
4. Bauer, J. and Aschenbruck, N., Design and implementation of an agricultural monitoring system for smart farming, in: *2018 IoT Vertical and Topical Summit on Agriculture-Tuscany (IOT Tuscany)*, Tuscany, Italy, pp. 1–6, IEEE, 2018.
5. Sowmiya, M. and Prabavathi, S., Smart Agriculture Using IoT and Cloud Computing. *IJRTE*, vol. 7, issue 6S3, 2019.
6. Nayak, P., Kavitha, K., Rao, C.M., IoT-Enabled Agricultural System Applications, Challenges, and Security Issues, in: *IoT and Analytics for Agriculture*, pp. 139–163, Springer, Singapore, 2020.
7. Balaji, V.R. and Prakash, N., IoT-Based Smart Security and Monitoring Devices for Agriculture. *Int. J. Pure Appl. Math.*, 116, 11, 121–129, 2017.
8. Hartung, R., Kulau, U., Gernert, B., Rottmann, S., Wolf, L., On the experiences with testbeds and applications in precision farming, in: *Proceedings of the First ACM International Workshop on the Engineering of Reliable, Robust, and Secure Embedded Wireless Sensing Systems*, pp. 54–61, 2017.
9. Vasisht, D., Kapetanovic, Z., Won, J., Jin, X., Chandra, R., Sinha, S., Stratman, S. *et al.*, Farmbeats: An IoT platform for data-driven agriculture, in: *14th {USENIX} Symposium on Networked Systems Design and Implementation ({NSDI} 17*, pp. 515–529, 2017.

10. Mat, I., Kassim, M.R.M., Harun, A.N., Yusoff, I.M., IoT in precision agriculture applications using wireless moisture sensor network, in: *2016 IEEE Conference on Open Systems (ICOS)*, Langkawi, Malaysia, pp. 24–29, IEEE, 2016.

11. Suma, N., Samson, S.R., Saranya, S., Shanmugapriya, G., Subhashri, R., IoT based smart agriculture monitoring system. *Int. J. Recent Innovation Trends Comput. Commun.*, 5, 2, 177–181, 2017.

12. Martínez-Fernández, J., González-Zamora, A., Sánchez, N., Gumuzzio, A., Herrero-Jiménez, C.M., Satellite soil moisture for agricultural drought monitoring: Assessment of the SMOS derived Soil Water Deficit Index. *Remote Sens. Environ.*, 177, 277–286, 2016.

13. Santhi, P.V., Kapileswar, N., Chenchela, V.K., Prasad, C.V.S., Sensor and vision based autonomous AGRIBOT for sowing seeds, in: *2017 International Conference on Energy, Communication, Data Analytics and Soft Computing (ICECDS)*, Chennai, India, pp. 242–245, IEEE, 2017.

14. Oberti, R., Marchi, M., Tirelli, P., Calcante, A., Iriti, M., Tona, E., Ulbrich, H. et al., Selective spraying of grapevines for disease control using a modular agricultural robot. *Biosyst. Eng.*, 146, 203–215, 2016.

15. Akkaş, M.A. and Sokullu, R., An IoT-based greenhouse monitoring system with Micaz motes. *Procedia Comput. Sci.*, 113, 603–608, 2017.

16. Thirukkumaran, R., Survey: Security and trust management in internet of things, in: *2018 IEEE Global Conference on Wireless Computing and Networking (GCWCN)*, Lonavala, India, pp. 131–134, IEEE, 2018.

17. Khan, S.F. and Ismail, M.Y., An Investigation into the Challenges and Opportunities Associated with the Application of Internet of Things (IoT) in the Agricultural Sector—A Review. *JCS*, 14, 2, 132–143, 2018.

18. Gupta, K. and Shukla, S., Internet of Things: Security challenges for next generation networks, in: *2016 International Conference on Innovation and Challenges in Cyber Security (ICICCS-INBUSH)*, Noida, India, pp. 315–318, IEEE, 2016.

19. Dlodlo, N. and Kalezhi, J., The internet of things in agriculture for sustainable rural development, in: *2015 International Conference on Emerging Trends in Networks and Computer Communications (ETNCC)*, Windhoek, Namibia, pp. 13–18, IEEE, 2015.

20. Tzounis, A., Katsoulas, N., Bartzanas, T., Kittas, C., Internet of Things in agriculture, recent advances and future challenges. *Biosyst. Eng.*, 164, 31–48, 2017.

21. Talwana, J.C. and Hua, H.J., Smart world of Internet of Things (IoT) and its security concerns, in: *2016 IEEE International Conference on Internet of Things (iThings) and IEEE Green Computing and Communications (GreenCom) and IEEE Cyber, Physical and Social Computing (CPSCom) and IEEE Smart Data (SmartData)*, Chengdu, China, pp. 240–245, IEEE, 2016.

22. Vidyashree, L. and Suresha, B.M., Methodology to secure agricultural data in IoT, in: *Emerging Technologies in Data Mining and Information Security*, pp. 129–139, Springer, Singapore, 2019.

23. Saha, A.K., Saha, J., Ray, R., Sircar, S., Dutta, S., Chattopadhyay, S.P., Saha, H.N., IOT-based drone for improvement of crop quality in agricultural field, in: *2018 IEEE 8th Annual Computing and Communication Workshop and Conference (CCWC)*, Las Vegas, NV, USA, pp. 612–615, IEEE, 2018.

24. Saha, H., Basu, S., Auddy, S., Dey, R., Nandy, A., Pal, D., Maity, T. *et al.*, A low cost fully autonomous GPS (Global Positioning System) based quad copter for disaster management, in: *2018 IEEE 8th Annual Computing and Communication Workshop and Conference (CCWC)*, Las Vegas, NV, USA, pp. 654–660, IEEE, 2018.

25. Saha, J., Saha, A.K., Chatterjee, A., Agrawal, S., Saha, A., Kar, A., Saha, H.N., Advanced IOT based combined remote health monitoring, home automation and alarm system, in: *2018 IEEE 8th Annual Computing and Communication Workshop and Conference (CCWC)*, Las Vegas, NV, USA, pp. 602–606, IEEE, 2018.

12

Plane Region Step Farming, Animal and Pest Attack Control Using Internet of Things

Sahadev Roy[1]*, Kaushal Mukherjee[2]† and Arindam Biswas[3]

Department of ECE, NIT Arunachal Pradesh, Yupia, India
Department of Physics, The University of Burdwan, Burdwan, India
School of Mines and Metallurgy, Kazi Nazrul University, Asansole, India

Abstract

The cost of agriculture in plane region grows rapidly in recent years due to less rainfall, animal and pest attack. In this paper, we present an advance step farming method applied for the plane region with the help of the IoT. The step farming done in hilly areas in terms to increase production rate, less maintenance, etc in the paddy field. By considering step farming in the plane region, we can increase the production of the crop to the next level. Moreover, by applying the network of various sensors like humidity, temperature, rain detection sensor, water level detection sensor, an ultrasonic sensor for detecting animals invading to the field, etc. These sensors are connected to the internet by using IoT network for closed monitoring. By using the IoT, we can maintain proper scheduling of the irrigation as per the weather information of the field area. We are using cayenne drag and drop IoT builder to design sensor networks for the proposed agriculture farm to observe and control various sensors and actuators from anywhere in the world through a laptop, desktop, and Android Smartphone. Here we present a prototype of a irrigation field and validated our model in the real world.

Keywords: Agriculture, internet of things, sensor network, irrigation, pest and animal attack control

*Corresponding author: sahadevroy@nitap.ac.in
†Corresponding author: mukherjeek95@gmail.com

Amitava Choudhury, Arindam Biswas, Manish Prateek and Amlan Chakrabarti (eds.)
Agricultural Informatics: Automation Using the IoT and Machine Learning, (249–270) © 2021
Scrivener Publishing LLC

12.1 Introduction

Recent study reveals that the worldwide population is about to reach 10 billion within 2050 [1]. To feed this substantial population, the agriculture farm is bounded to implement the IoT-based smart farming. In crop growing, the IoT has brought the utmost impact [2]. IoT is eliminating challenges like climatic changes, extreme weather conditions, environmental impact and improves the supporting the entire agriculture system by observing the field in real-time. IoT-based smart farming is helping us to meet the demand for required food. The help of the IoT in agriculture has not only saved the time of the farmers but has also reduced the excessive use of resources such as electricity, fertilizer and water. Agriculture is no doubt the largest sustenance providers in India. It also gives a very vital contribution in GDP (Gross Domestic Product). But the farmers who are known as the backbone of India are subjected to many personal as well as field-related problems. So we need to advance agriculture system and modify current farm structure so that farmers get more yield and they can easily manipulate the crop and observe each and every activity from home itself without a physical presence in the farm [3]. Due to this, they will get more relief from mental stress as well as stress from work. Also, by using an advanced technique, we can save rain water for the next crop, when the water scarcity problem arises [4]. This automation is possible by using the internet of things which is the network of various sensors, actuators and physical devices which are well installed on the advanced farm structure mentioned above [5]. All the sensor devices are connected to internet and user can access data from anywhere in the world.

Internet plays the main role in observation of the digital data from every part of the world that is available electronically. The world is now working based on the internet. With the help of internet connectivity people can monitor their work from anywhere in the world from their PCs or Smartphones [6]. Internet service help is the collection and exchange of digital data around the globe. The achieved data can be compared with the specific area location and earlier data analysis or with any predefined model. The data achieved from the sensor can be monitored and managed from any part of the world with the help of IoT, where the internet service is accessible. In this way, IoT helps in the enhancement of effectiveness, accurateness and facilitate the nation to attain an enormous tip in this digital world [7]. Although, IoT is totally a fresh concept, it becomes an attractive subject in several industries because of its most up-to-date trending technology. The foremost theory of IoT was proposed by Kevin Ashton, in the early 2000s [8]. According to Verizon, IoT has definitely risen above its early life and is in good health to achieve some definite momentum in the world of digital system. Verizon issued in their "State of the Market" that, nearly 1.2 billion various smart devices are using the IoT services and it will be increased up to 5.4 billion within 2020 [9].

As the population grows, it looks like it will reach a billion by 2050, from this point of view of population growth, according to the United Nations Food and Agricultural Organization, we need to increase food production up to 60%, to feed this growing population.

IoT is transforming the farming sector by assisting the farmers to tackle their huge challenges. The organization must overcome rising water shortage, limited land resources, tricky-to-manage expenses while addressing the increasing needs of world's population which is predicted to increase about 70% before 2050 [10].

New, innovative IoT technologies solve these problems and increase the quality, quantity, productivity and price-effectiveness of crop production. For example, modern wide as well as rural farms could utilize IoT that dynamically control sensors, capable of detecting moisture levels, seed production as well as animal feed rate, remotely monitor and control their intelligent embedded excavators and irrigation infrastructure, and use robotics-based analysis to efficiently evaluate functional information coupled with data from external parties, like weather systems, to have different insights, as well as to strengthen judgment-making.

The population of the world is increasing at a rapid pace but the sum of wealth or resource does not prosper as well as that. There is a certain amount of money in our possession and we need to manage our available resources properly. The price of fertilizer, electricity is increasing, but the amount of irrigation is set, so farmers need to make wise use of their resources in farming. If both the infield and the field-to-shelf monitoring management are handled properly, crop wastage can be minimized to some extent.

Everybody in this world has to face problems in their lives, such as deadline pressure, lack of knowledge available, time and distance challenges etc. that can be solved with the help of IoT.

This is the current generation where the internet is a daily need of people, which the development of agriculture without internet is not feasible in any way. Modern agricultural work rapidly became an information-intensive industry, where farmers desperately need to collect data from various sources or devices such as sensors, farming machinery, meteorological tendering, etc., and analyze the information obtained from all these objects in order to cultivate crops efficiently. Hence these processes are required to train the farmers which is turn would increase the rate of crop production. The initiatives deals with a number of issues such as environmental impact, food safety, labor welfare, plants and animals safety and security, existence of regional market, etc. A portable sensor network is a custom transducer system which provides a surveillance system for controlling and capturing parameters at various locations. A WSN framework integrates a gateway by directly providing mobile connectivity into the wired network and centralized nodes [11]. The wireless device may be chosen based on the program's specifications.

Step farming is the process of cutting steps or flats on the sidewalls of mountains for cultivation. Cultivation through step farming is implemented on the hilly regions which can be controlled by the farmers without using any kind of technical features. Farmers get experienced from a lot of emotional stress and therefore more physical labor because of this. Although despite implementation of internet of things to track soil, water and weather conditions in this field, we're not going to get that much of the output that we're getting done in the plane zone. Step farming can be divided into two categories namely plane region step farming and hilly region step farming. One example of step farming is the cultivation of paddy on the mountains of Asia. The main objective of this research work is to discuss the plane region step farming procedure and how animal as well as pest attacks can be controlled with the help of IoT. Mountainous rice paddies in Asia are the most popular examples, where generations of farmers have held the same parcels of land.

12.1.1 Possible Various Applications in Agriculture

Horticulture: Even without weather monitoring, we can use wireless sensors to observe various aspects like soil temperature, air moisture, solar radiation, greenhouse temperature, humidity levels, rainfall intensity, etc. We can turn from the different information gathered from the sensors whenever we need grain maintenance. This is one of saving time as well as money.

Livestock: From identifying animals to their footprints, Radio-Frequency Identification (RFID) is quite fast to find statistics of each species, including their birth as well as selling information, etc.

Security: Agriculture is the economic backbone of developing countries therefore, security in agricultural sector is essential. As can be seen, with the aid of IoT, the entire cycle from production of agricultural products to market sales can be tracked and managed completely.

Water management: It is seen that after we use water, we do not turn off the faucet properly and water continues to flow from the faucet. So in many areas sensors are installed in the faucet. When we don't use water from the faucet, the water from the faucet will stop flowing automatically, thus wasting water.

It's seen that we don't shut off the faucet properly after the use of water and the water continues to flow from the faucet. Thus sensors are mounted in the faucet in many places to avoid waste of water. If we don't use water from the faucet, the water from the faucet will immediately stop flowing, thereby reduces the water wastage. It is therefore obvious that with the aid of IoT, we can retain water in various ways. The same idea can also be put into action with the agricultural fields, with the help of IoT the need for water for the crops at what time and in what amount can be remotely controlled which in turn reduces water wastage.

Health application: Monitoring has a unique function in health issues. IoT is mainly a network system that consists of a network of surrounding life support devices. WSN sensor plays a significant role in integrated patient monitoring, disability tracking, diagnosis and rehabilitation, proper drug distribution and several facts such as physician and patient monitoring in the hospital.

Agricultural sector: Use the wireless sensor network allows farmers to produce crops in tricky condition. Most crops, for example, are rain-fed but agriculture in arid areas disrupts certain crops, but the use of this network determines how much irrigation is required. As a result, it will become reasonably profitable in a fair way and sufficient quantity in agriculture.

Area monitoring: Sensor nodes are set up in an area where certain events are observed. These nodes then monitor the events such as its pressure, temperature etc., and then generates a report, based on that Administration with the help of local people takes necessary action.

Industrial monitoring: The use of these sensors has become quite an important part of the industrial sectors. These sensors act as an indicator of the industry i.e. if any part of a large device is faulty so that we do not need to inspect the whole part, only by examining that part we can know which part of the machineries is defective or damaged. This saves us both time and money.

Environmental monitoring: Earth Science research relies on a variety of studies on the environment. As can be seen in several cities such as Stockholm, London, etc., to determine how dangerous the gas concentration is for the citizens of that region. As a result, it is possible to monitor the air pollution in the area and maintain civic awareness. Also

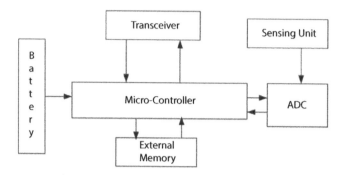

Figure 12.1 Architecture of sensor node.

other environmental parameters such as forest fires, landslides, etc. can be sensed.

The design of the sensor node is comprised of several tracking points called sensor nodes, including transducers, microcomputers, transmitters and receivers and power source; all of which are compact, lightweight and versatile as shown in Figure 12.1. Transducer produces electrical signals on the basis of perceived physical effects and condition. The microcomputer analyses the sensor data, and stores it. The transceiver collects instructions from a central database and sends information on to that computer. For each sensor node the power is extracted from a battery.

12.1.2 Cayenne IoT Builder

Cayenne offers the first function-built IoT architecture planned to meet today's unique technological world requirements [12]. Cayenne has the protection and functionality to manage millions of regular operations as the leading IoT platform [13]. In a fraction of the time of other approaches, one can deliver effective, new IoT solutions for smart agriculture with Cayenne.

12.2 Proposed Work

12.2.1 Design of Agro Farm Structure

In agriculture, to perform more effective farming we need to cut the plane surface into series of the successively step-like structure as shown in

Figures 12.2 and 12.3. These types of farming are commonly found in hilly or mountainous terrain [14].

But in this paper, we have designed this type of model for the plane region to obtain greater production with the full support of sensor network control through the internet of things.

Here, the designed farm structure is worked as follows. During the rainy season, the quantity of water available is more, but the crop required less quantity of water. Excess water must be transferred from farm 1 to farm 2 and farm 2 to farm 3 and so on. Here the main point is an election of crop according to the water required at the different step of the farm. According to that crop will be placed and excess water at the end of all is stored in

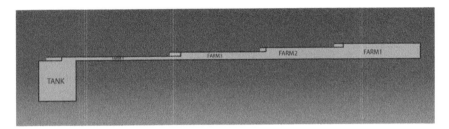

Figure 12.2 Side view of the designed agro farm structure for the Plane region.

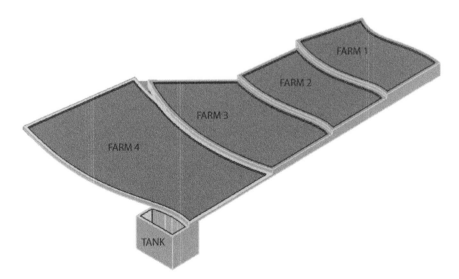

Figure 12.3 Full view of the designed agro farm structure for the Plane region.

the water tank reservoir for the future need of water. During winter and summer, the water collected during rainy season as well as from external source is to be utilized for the feed purpose by continuously monitoring the moisture level of the soil.

The water reservoir also receives water from the external source such as a canal, waste water from the village and small drainage system. The size of the water reservoir depends on the farmers land. If the land is more storage tank is required and vice versa.

Currently, step farming procedure is only implemented in the mountainous regions which are controlled by the farmers with little or no technical feature being used. Farmers get experienced from a lot of emotional

Table 12.1 Advantage of step farming in-plane region versus hilly region.

Sl. No.	For plane region	For hilly region
1.	The in-plane region, we can expect more production because of large step size.	In the hilly region, we can expect less production as compared to the plane region because of small step size.
2.	Big area with big step size.	Small area with small step size.
3.	The cost of digging to make step is same as that of the hilly area because the no of the step is less and depth is also small.	The cost of digging is nearly same because we have to create more steps with more depth than plane region.
4.	Easy maintenance using sensor network and can be controlled and observe effectively by using internet of things.	Hard to implement because of the unavailability of the network problem so, create some hindrance between sensor and signal.
5.	By using rainwater harvesting, we can increase the production rate. Also, by using proper irrigation using IoT, we can take crops in all the three season i.e., summer, winter, and rainy.	In this reason also, we can increase production rate by using rainwater harvesting, but the problem is the storage of water. If we store water at the bottom, then more force is required by the motor to pull water upward so, chances of the burning of the motor.

stress and therefore more physical labor because of this [15]. Despite implementation of internet of things to track soil, water and weather conditions in this field, we're not going to get that much of the output that we're getting done in the plane zone. Some advantages of step farming over in plane regions in contrast with hilly regions have been tabulated in Table 12.1.

12.3   Irrigation Methodology

Irrigation takes a really crucial part in the expansion of crop production. Production of food relies significantly on the irrigation quality supplied to the crops. We can just get 55% of crop production from irrigated fields, so the irrigation method needs to be stressed more to solve water scarcity problems [16].

The irrigation network for the farming field is shown in Figure 12.4.

Selection of plant species is according to the water requirement in that area. Plant breeding and plant species selection play a very important role to increase the productivity of the available water in the respective region.

The way in which planting is done in the field is a very considerable factor to capture sufficient solar energy from the sun for photosynthesis and for better evaporation process. It mainly employs two types of planting pattern practices, i.e. plant density and row spacing.

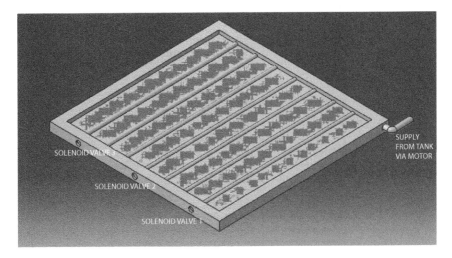

Figure 12.4 The structure of farm by applying suitable irrigation network of pipes.

Selection of optimum months and dates for good germination and placement of seeds in the optimum moisture zone is a necessary and optimum condition for good root growth and root penetration and take maximum nutrient content from the soil [17].

We need to remove weeds from the crop because weeds can challenge with the crop by taking light, soil nutrient and water. So by utilizing effective weed control technology, we can increase water use efficiency of the plants.

Several hybrid varieties of the crops are available in the market which is pest resistant and certain diseases which are common to the area so, efficient crop and water management includes the rational use of chemical pesticides [18]. We can increase water use efficiency by the managing crop in the field.

12.3.1   Irrigation Scheduling

It is the processes which suggest to the farmer in deciding the time to start irrigate and specify the quantity of water needed for irrigation. Proper scheduling is necessary to use water effectively and proper manner. Irrigation scheduling gives the estimated water requirement of the crop [19].

By regularly monitoring the water in soil and crop development condition and future forecasting of the need of water by the crop based on the

Table 12.2 Water requirement (mm) of different crops.

Crop	Water requirement (mm)
Rice	900–2,500
Wheat	450–650
Maize	500–800
Sugarcane	1,500–2,500
Groundnut	500–700
Cotton	700–1,300
Soya bean	450–700
Tobacco	400–600

daily data obtained by the sensor (as shown in Table 12.2), efficient irrigation is possible [20].

12.3.2   Two Critical Circumstances Farmers Often Face

- *Under-irrigation:* In summer and winter, a limited quantity of water is available so scarcity of water may arise. To get a ride from this we need to feed water to the crop from the external source.
- *Over-irrigation:* In the rainy season, more water is available, so crop always submerged in the water so there is a chance of damage to the crop. So, to move excess water from that field here, we used a solenoid valve to pass water from field to reservoir.

12.3.3   Irrigation Indices

Irrigation technique is based on the observation of plant–soil–water–atmospheric calamities. The radiation received from the sun fall directly on the leaf during daylight which is utilized for transpiration. The remaining energy is used to heat the plant's leaf tissue and the air surrounded by them. So we need to periodically check the temperature and according to that moisture level is maintained. The status of water can be visualized by the color of leaves and curved leaves etc. Also, we find the requirement of water by measuring leaf water content and leaf water potential.

We can calculate the amount of water required for the irrigation which is calculated as follows:

Water requirement per Irrigation = (DRZ(MCAI − MCBI))/IE

Where,
DRZ—depth of root zone
MCAI—soil moisture content after irrigation
MCBI—soil moisture content before irrigation
IE—Irrigation Efficiency.

12.4   Sensor Connection Using Internet of Things

Figure 12.5 shows the sensor interconnection for fields 1 and 2 using the internet. We use cayenne as fast drag and drop IoT builder platform to control and manipulate the entire sensor network which is applied at the

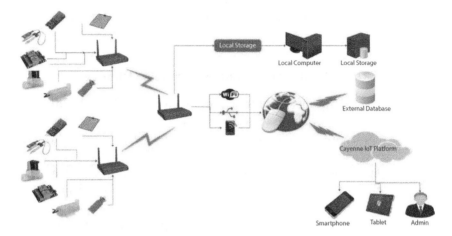

Figure 12.5 Sensor interconnection through the Internet of Things.

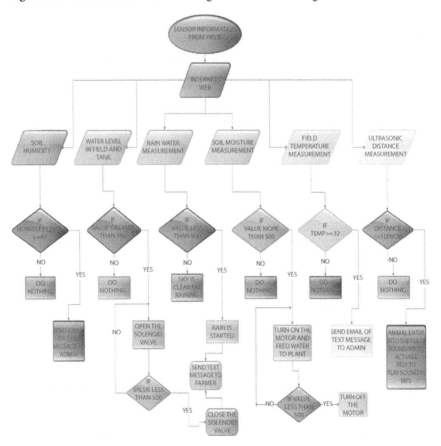

Figure 12.6 A flowchart which describes the complete operation of the proposed system.

farm. The things were easy by using this latest IoT project builder which consists of an androidapp for the Smartphone. The sensor like water level sensor measuring the water level of tank, rain drop sensor for alerting if there any raining or not, DHT22 sensor measures temperature and humidity of the field environment, soil moisture sensor measure the moisture level of the soil according to which the actuator like motor start or stop by feeding control signal to relay to activate. The solenoid valve is used to draw excess water from the field. The entire sensor feeds their value to the cayenne server and can be accessible via Smartphone and laptop. A flowchart that illustrates the whole operation of the proposed system is shown in Figure 12.6.

12.4.1 Animal Attack Control

Figure 12.7 illustrates the placement of the various sensors to avoid the animal attack in the field site. We use anultrasonic sensor which continuously giving fixed value by sending trigger pulses and obtaining echoes generated by striking the obstacle. If any wild animal invading through this path, then sensor value will suddenly change which will send a trigger signal to the Arduino and then Arduino will activate mp3 sound to threaten the invader animal. So that wild animal will leave the field and we are able to save our crop from destruction.

But to carry out the above process, this proposed model does not include any of the human physical appearance and the entire process can be managed remotely via IoT.

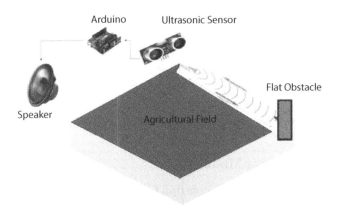

Figure 12.7 Placement of ultrasonic sensor with the Arduino to avoid the animal attack.

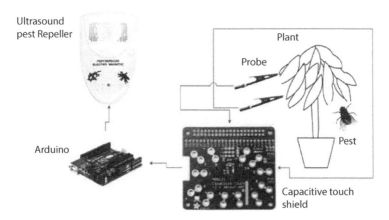

Figure 12.8 The probe connection of capacitive touch shield with Arduino to trigger ultrasound device to avoid pest attack.

12.4.2   Pest Attack Control

Pest is the main factor which is responsible for destroying the growth of the crop. Due to excessive use of pesticides, several deaths of consumers are happening. It contains toxic chemicals which directly enter our digestive system and cause various health related issues [21]. By using capacitive touch shield as illustrated in Figure 12.8, if any insect or pest comes in contact with leaves of the crop, it triggers a signal that will be generated which will activate the ultrasonic sound generator. Due to the low frequency (irritating to the small insect or pest) of ultrasound, the entire pest will stay away from the given area and thus we get rid of these things. So we can save crop as well as save human health-related issues.

12.4.3   DHT 11 Humidity & Temperature Sensor

Every DHT11 feature in the laboratory is specifically calibrated, which is extremely precise for calibration of the humidity [22]. The calibration coefficients are installed in the OTP storage as programs which are used in the internal signal detection process of the sensor. The serial interface with single-wire ensures device installation smooth and efficient.

12.4.4   Rain Sensor Module

The module rain sensor is a simple tool for measuring rain. This can also be used as switch whenever a drop of water passes via the rainy board and also to calculate the severity of the rainfall [23]. The system includes a rainfall panel and the separate control panel for more efficiency, an LED power detector and a potentiometer variable tolerance.

12.4.5   Soil Moisture Sensor

The sensor for soil moisture determines the moisture content in the soil. Measurement moisture in cultivation is crucial for helping farmers monitor their irrigation systems quite effectively [24]. Not only are farmers normally able to use less water to grow a crop however they are able to improve productivity and crop quality through improved soil moisture management during crucial plant growth phases.

12.5   Placement of Sensor in the Field

Netsim Simulation of the Architecture
We use NetSim network simulator to analyze the packet send by the various sensor which is placed in the field.

The graph of packet count versus various links ID is as shown in Figure 12.9 which is obtained from Table 12.3. From this, we get exact idea about how much information loss and transmitted to the cloud using various sensor places in the field.

All the values which are given by the sensor connected to the Arduino UNO, will be displayed by the cayenne dashboard. Cayenne dashboard

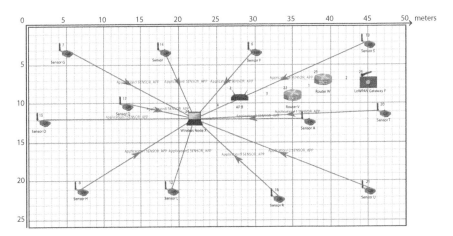

Figure 12.9 Screenshot of the various sensors placed at the field site by considering field size as 50 mm * 50 mm.

Table 12.3 The graph of packet count versus various links ID.

Link Id	Packets transmitted	Error packets	Collided packets	Bytes transmitted (Bytes)	Payload transmitted (Bytes)	Overhead transmitted (Bytes)
1	11,543	2	0	890,322	576,682	517,150
2	11,543	1	0	893,562	576,732	316,830
3	11,001	2	0	1,122,792	516,650	606,142
4	22,011	13	0	1,420,102	516,650	903,452
5	112,535	0	52,766	3,491,899	517,150	2,974,749

can be observed on the desktop (see Figure 12.10) as well as android app (see Figure 12.11).

A. Dashboard Snapshot of the Sensor Value in Desktop as Shown in Figure 12.10.
B. Dashboard Snapshot of the Sensor Value in the Android App as Shown in Figure 12.11.

If any value of the sensor is exceeded beyond its threshold value decided by the user, then according to the threshold value, trigger is generated.

• By sending email to the admin mailbox
• By sending text message to the admin mobile number
• By sending control trigger pulse to the respective actuator by using relay circuitry.

The hardware snapshot under working condition of the sensor as shown in the Figure 12.12.

Smart Farming using IoT is a hi-tech and effective way of doing agriculture in a sustainable way. Collecting data and monitoring for air humidity, air temperature, sunlight intensity and soil moisture, across multiple fields will definitely improve efficiency of water usage and crop yield of large as

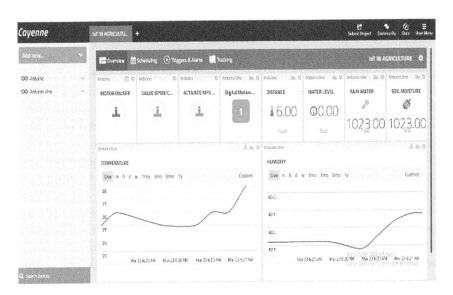

Figure 12.10 Dashboard snapshot of the sensor value in desktop.

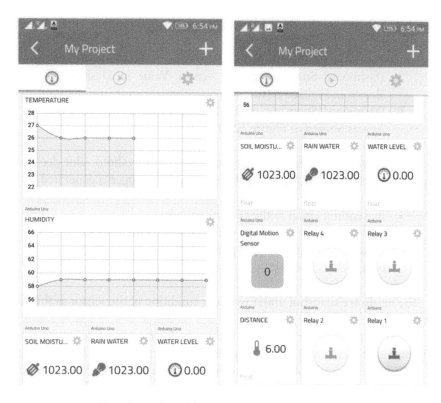

Figure 12.11 Dashboard snapshot of the sensor value in the android app.

well as local farms. Low cost sensors, data insights and IoT platforms will enable this increase in efficiency and production. Farmers can imagine production levels in real time and remotely to accelerate different decision making process. Precisely tracking production rates by field over a certain time allows for comprehensive predicting of future crop yield. Farmers can monitor multiple fields in several locations from any internet enable devices. Decisions can be made in real-time and from anywhere. Another advantage of using IoT is that farming equipment can be monitored and utilized according to labor effectiveness and production rates. Sensors are placed inside and outside of the agriculture fields. The entire IoT network is made up of sensors that can detect accurate weather conditions very accurately. Climate plays a very important role for the quality and quantity of the crop production. By using IoT solutions one can know the actual weather conditions. These sensors network monitors the real-time condition of the crops and try to compensate the different requirements which eventually increase the productivity.

Figure 12.12 Hardware snapshot of proposed system under working condition.

12.6 Conclusion

Optimized crop treatment such as watering, pesticide application, accurate planting, and harvesting directly affects the crop production rates. By using organized fashion of field structure and proper irrigation scheduling and providing them the early prediction of weather condition on their mobile directly, may save thousands of life. Now, by this technique farmers are able to produce crops in all three season effectively and losses will be minimized. So death toll ultimately decreased. For the pest control, we need to use ultrasound of various frequency which. When any pest interacts with any part of the plant, then by using capacitive touch shield, we can detect the presence of pest so an alert signal is generated by the ultrasound generator. For the supply of constant and continuous energy to the sensor, we need to set up a solar cell powered battery in the field. To reduce the consumption of the battery, we need to set up some logic to activate the sensor network at a particular time and other time, the sensor network remains idle. Incorporation of small exhaust fan as a heat sink to protect the sensor devices or drive circuitry from the excess heat of the sun so, the age of the sensor devices and circuitry will increase. The IoT enable Plane region step farming, animal and pest attack control a truly enhanced crop production rate.

References

1. Béné, C., Barange, M., Subasinghe, R., Pinstrup-Andersen, P., Merino, G., Hemre, G.I., Williams, M., Feeding 9 billion by 2050—Putting fish back on the menu. *Food Secur.*, 7, 2, 261–274, 2015.

2. Khanna, A. and Kaur, S., Evolution of Internet of Things (IoT) and its significant impact in the field of Precision Agriculture. *Comput. Electron. Agric.*, 157, 218–231, 2019.

3. Rigg, J., Salamanca, A., Phongsiri, M., Sripun, M., More farmers, less farming? Understanding the truncated agrarian transition in Thailand. *World Dev.*, 107, 327–337, 2018.

4. Sukhadeve, V. and Roy, S., Advance Agro Farm Design With Smart Farming, Irrigation and Rain Water Harvesting Using Internet of Things. *Management*, 1, 1, 33–45, 2016.

5. Bandyopadhyay, D. and Sen, J., Internet of things: Applications and challenges in technology and standardization. *Wireless Pers. Commun.*, 58, 1, 49–69, 2011.

6. Lynch, P., The origins of computer weather prediction and climate modeling. *J. Comput. Phys.*, 227, 7, 3431–3444, 2008.

7. Qin, Y., Sheng, Q.Z., Falkner, N.J., Dustdar, S., Wang, H., Vasilakos, A.V., When things matter: A survey on data-centric internet of things. *J. Netw. Comput. Appl.*, 64, 137–153, 2016.

8. Matta, P. and Pant, B., Internet of things: Genesis, challenges and applications. *J. Eng. Sci. Technol.*, 14, 3, 1717–1750, 2019.

9. Vieira, A.S., Beal, C.D., Ghisi, E., Stewart, R.A., Energy intensity of rainwater harvesting systems: A review. *Renewable Sustainable Energy Rev.*, 34, 225–242, 2014.

10. Hertel, T.W., The global supply and demand for agricultural land in 2050: A perfect storm in the making? *Am. J. Agric. Econ.*, 93, 2, 259–275, 2011.

11. White, T.A. and Snow, V.O., A modelling analysis to identify plant traits for enhanced water-use efficiency of pasture. *Crop Pasture Sci.*, 63, 1, 63–76, 2012.

12. Swathika, O.G. and Hemapala, K.T.M.U., IOT-Based Adaptive Protection of Microgrid, in: *International Conference on Artificial Intelligence, Smart Grid and Smart City Applications*, pp. 123–130, Springer, Cham, 2019, January.

13. Aswath, G.I., Vasudevan, S.K., Sundaram, R.M.D., Emerging security concerns for smart vehicles and proposed IoT solutions. *Int. J. Veh. Auton. Syst.*, 14, 2, 107–133, 2018.

14. Sitzia, T., Semenzato, P., Trentanovi, G., Natural reforestation is changing spatial patterns of rural mountain and hill landscapes: A global overview. *For. Ecol. Manage.*, 259, 8, 1354–1362, 2010.

15. Briner, S., Elkin, C., Huber, R., Grêt-Regamey, A., Assessing the impacts of economic and climate changes on land-use in mountain regions: A spatial dynamic modeling approach. *Agric. Ecosyst. Environ.*, 149, 50–63, 2012.

16. Pedrero, F., Kalavrouziotis, I., Alarcón, J.J., Koukoulakis, P., Asano, T., Use of treated municipal wastewater in irrigated agriculture—Review of some practices in Spain and Greece. *Agric. Water Manage.*, 97, 9, 1233–1241, 2010.
17. King, B.A., Stark, J.C., Neibling, H., Potato irrigation management, in: *Potato Production Systems*, pp. 417–446, Springer, Cham, 2020.
18. Savary, S., Horgan, F., Willocquet, L., Heong, K.L., A review of principles for sustainable pest management in rice. *Crop Prot.*, 32, 54–63, 2012.
19. Pluchinotta, I., Pagano, A., Giordano, R., Tsoukiàs, A., A system dynamics model for supporting decision-makers in irrigation water management. *J. Environ. Manage.*, 223, 815–824, 2018.
20. Goap, A., Sharma, D., Shukla, A.K., Krishna, C.R., An IoT based smart irrigation management system using Machine learning and open source technologies. *Comput. Electron. Agric.*, 155, 41–49, 2018.
21. Jaishankar, M., Tseten, T., Anbalagan, N., Mathew, B.B., Beeregowda, K.N., Toxicity, mechanism and health effects of some heavy metals. *Interdiscip. Toxicol.*, 7, 2, 60–72, 2014.
22. Dan-ao, H., Fei, W., Research application of the digital temperature and humidity sensor DHT11. *Electron. Des. Eng.*, 13, 2013.
23. Bangalore, V.L., U.S. Patent No. 7,966,153, U.S. Patent and Trademark Office, Washington, DC, 2011.
24. Haley, M.B. and Dukes, M.D., Validation of landscape irrigation reduction with soil moisture sensor irrigation controllers. *J. Irrig. Drain. Eng.*, 138, 2, 135–144, 2012.

Index

3D digital elevation model (DEM), 71, 78, 81
3D mapping, 76

Accelerometers, 78
Accuracy curve, 125, 143, 144
Actuators, 249
Advanced agriculture system, 250
Aerial drones, 80
Agribusiness incubators, 75–76, 77
Agricultural biodiversity, 69
Agricultural drones and IoT,
    COVID-19 problems in agriculture, 77–81
    functionalities of, 75–77
    overview, 68–69
    related work, 69–71
    smart production, 72–75
Agricultural internet of everything. *see* internet of things (IoT)
Agricultural informatics, 37–38
Agricultural robotization, 77
Agricultural system, 223, 226, 230, 232, 234, 238, 244–245
Agriculture, 89, 90–93, 117, 118, 128, 147–151, 153–154, 160, 166–167
    economy, 90
    precission, 91
Agripreneurship, 72, 73
Agro farm structure, 255
Agro IoT, 45–48
Animal attack control, 261
Arduino, 100, 107, 108, 110
Area monitoring, 253
Artificial neural networks, 2

Asian Development Bank, 73
Atmospheric pressure, 97
Augmentation, 131, 136, 138, 141
Automated data collection program, 77
Automation, 250

Batch normalization, 142, 143, 144
Bayesian networks, 8
Beaglebone black, 28, 29, 31
Big data, 90, 101, 102, 113
Big data analytics, 71
Blue snarfing, 112
Bluejacking, 112
Brushless DC (BLDC) motor, 197, 199, 200, 212, 214–216
Buzzer, 198

Canopy cover tracking, 77
Capacitive touch shield, 262
Carbon fibre, 196–199
Cayenne drag, 249
Cayenne IoT builder, 254
Centralized nodes, 252
Clasification, 117, 119–120, 121, 124, 128
Cloud
    computing, 71, 91, 148–149, 225–226, 237
    data storage, 91
    database, 91, 95
    storage, 106
CNN, 117–128
Cold storage facilities, 69, 73
Communication devices, 78, 79t

Compasses, 78
Confusion matrix, 122, 125–127
Continuous draw current, 212, 214
Convolutional layers, 120, 123–124
Coordination devices, 78, 79t
Cost–benefit model, 78
COTS (commercial off-the shelf)
    products, 78
Coverage area optimization, 173
Coverage problem, 180
Coverage ratio, 182
Coverage requirement, 181
COVID-19 problems in agriculture,
    77–81
    communication and networking
        mechanisms, 79–81
    implementation of drones, 77–79
    managing agricultural data safety
        and security, 81
Crop management, 238, 245
Crop scanning, 76
Crop spraying, 76
Crop tracking, 76–77
Cryptography, 242
Custering K-means, 104
Custom transducer system, 252

Data augmentation, 123
Data pre-processing, 139, 140
Database, 95, 98
Decision support system, 71
Decision tree structure for crop details
    prediction, 6
Decision trees, 5
Deep learning, 120–121, 123, 127–129,
    132, 137, 138, 139, 144, 145, 146
Deployment, 180
Depth-sensing camera (DSC) works,
    78
DHT 11 humidity & hemperature
    sensor, 262
DHT22 sensor, 261
Discharge rate, 215

Disease diagnosis, 120
Disease profiling software, 78
DoS, 94, 98, 99, 104, 105, 110, 112
Drainage mapping, 77
Drainage system, 256
Drones, 70, 71, 153–155, 167, 240,
    242–243. see also agricultural
    drones and IoT
    aerial, 80
    COTS-based, 78, 79
    engineering, 76
Dropout, 131, 142, 145
Drought, 77, 90
DSAS, 6

Eaves dropping, 98, 112
Economy, 89
Edge, 91
Education in agricultural informatics,
    51
Electronic speed controller (ESC),
    193–194, 197, 199–200, 214–216
Entomological modeling, 78
Entrepreneurial innovation, 68–69
Environment parameters, 89
Environmental informatics, 38
Evapotranspiration, 91
Evolutionary algorithms (EAs), 176

Farmers, 89, 90, 92, 113
Farming, 90, 113
Farming machinery, 252
Feature extraction, 134, 136
Feature maps, 123
Feed forward network, 102
Feed-forward back propagation, 3
Feeding control signal, 261
Fertility, 90
Fertilizer, 90, 103
Field water pond mapping, 77
Field-to-shelf monitoring
    management, 251
Fine-tuning, 142

FINKNN, 4
Fixed wing UAV, 190–192
Flight controller unit (FCU), 193,
   200–204
Follow-up monitoring, 80–81
Food and agriculture organization,
   75–76
Fully connected layers, 124
Furrow, 90, 91
Fuselage, 193–196, 201, 204, 210–211
Fuzzy, 92

GA, 95
GA algorithm, 174
GA-MWPSO, 177
Germination percentage measurement,
   77
Ghz, 94, 98
GPRS, 94, 99
GPS, 78–79
Greenhouse, 223, 228–229, 232
Ground control station (GSC),
   global positioning system, 193–194,
      196, 202, 204, 207
   radio telemetry, 193–194, 203–206
GSM, 95, 98, 104, 105
Gyroscopes, 78–79

Heat sink, 267
Hibrid optimization, 171
Hindrance, 256
Histogram oriented gradient, 25
Human participation in surveillance
   and monitoring, 74–75
Humidity, 91, 95, 97, 100, 108, 109
Hybrid algorithm (HA), 173
Hyperspectral irrigation, 76

Image annotation, 141
Image recognition, 76
Image processing, 20
Incubatvors, 75–77
Indian agriculture system, 172

Indian agritech startups, 73
Industrial monitoring, 253
Information fuzzy network, 4
Information intensive industry, 252
Informed decisions, 71
Integrated networks sensors, 73–74
Intelligent embedded excavators, 251
International finance corporation,
   75
Internet of Things (IoT), 41, 89–92, 94,
   111, 112, 147–149, 151, 153–154,
   167, 223–226, 228–229, 233–238,
   239–241, 244, 249
Intruders, 89
Intrusion detection, 21, 23
Invading, 249
Inventory measurement, 77
IoT in agriculture, 43–45
Irrigation, 89–92, 94, 112, 249
Irrigation indices, 259
Irrigation scheduling, 258
Irrigation techniques, 69

Jamming, 94, 98, 99, 104, 105, 110, 112

K-Means, 101, 107, 104, 112
Knowledge expert system, 3
kPa, 110
KV value, 212, 214

Landing gear, 193–194, 196
LDA, 95, 102, 108
Level detection sensor, 249
Lithium polymer battery (LiPo), 194,
   197–198, 213
Logarithmic loss, 125, 142
Loss curve, 125, 143, 144

MAC, 94
Machine learning, 1, 89, 90
Machine learning model, 2, 183
Man in the middle, 92
Markov chain model, 9

Max pooling, 124
Maximum take off weight (MTOW), 210
Mean best position (mbest), 178
MHz, 94
Microcontroller, 92
Monitoring devices, 147, 151
Multispectral irrigation, 76
My SQL, 100, 106, 107

Navigation devices, 78, 79t
Near-infrared camera, 78
Near-infrared image processing
    software, 78
Netsim simulation, 263
Neural networks, 120, 123, 128–129,
    131–134, 138, 144–146

Optical signal processing, 76
Over-irrigation, 259

Paddy field, 249
Pest attack, 249
Pest attack control, 262
pH, 91, 93, 102
pH sensor, 147, 155, 158, 160, 162, 166
Photogrammetric devices, 78, 79t
PIR sensor, 147, 155, 157, 160–161,
    163, 167
Plant breeding and plant species, 257
Plant density, 258
Plant disease, 117–121, 128–129
Plant seedling, 131, 132, 138, 139, 143,
    146
Post-disaster management, 78, 80–81
Power distribution board (PDB), 195
Precision agriculture, 70f, 78, 80f
Precision farming, 118
Principal component analysis, 8
Propeller,
    chord length, 199
    pitch, 199, 201–202, 210, 215
Protection devices, 78, 79t

Radio frequency identification (RFID),
    149, 154, 225, 235, 253
Rain detection sensor, 249
Rain sensor, 262
Raspberry Pi, 95, 147, 150–151, 156–
    157, 159–160, 162–163, 166–167
RBF, 95, 104, 108
Real-time,
    activities, 225
    data, 151, 165
    images, 154, 163, 167, 242–243
    monitoring, 223
    notifications, 152, 227
Real-time surveyed data collection and
    storage, 73–75
Regression, 95
Regression analysis, 6, 7
Reliability optimization, 179
Remote controller (RC), 190, 200–201,
    203, 205
Remote sensing, 77
Required thrust, 215–216
ResNet, 131, 133–135, 139, 142–145
RF, 95
RGB-D sensor, 147, 153, 155, 159,
    162–163, 165, 167
RL, 95
Robotics-based analysis, 251
Row spacing, 258

Satellite, 71
Satellite-based precision agriculture, 78
Scouting reports, 77
Security, 147–151, 155, 157, 162–163,
    166
    challenge, 233
    data, 244
    issues, 223, 226, 232, 240, 242
    mechanisms, 242
    problems, 230
    system, 224
    threats, 240–242
Self-guided cars, 75

Sensor, 16, 17, 147–155, 157–163,
165–167, 223–233, 235–236,
239–244
Sensor cloud, 108
Single rotor helicopter, 190–192
Smart agriculture, 225, 230–231, 234
Smart farming, 14, 67, 147–148, 154,
225–226, 232, 234–235, 241–243,
250
Smart security, 147, 151
Social property monitoring, 75
Soil moisture, 77, 108
sensors, 69
Soil moisture sensor, 263
Soil nutrient feed crops, 76
Soil parameters, 151, 162, 238
Solar radiation, 109
Solenoid valve, 261
Spoofing, 105, 110
State of the market, 251
Step farming, 249
Subsistence farmers, 77
Surface nutrient seeds, 76
SVR, 95

Temperature, 93, 95, 96, 100, 102,
103
TensorFlow, 124
Thermal irrigation, 76
Time series analysis, 8

UART, 100, 107, 108, 110
Ultrasonic sensor, 249

Under-irrigation, 259
Unmanned aerial vehicle (UAV), 70,
147, 153–155, 160, 163, 165–167
UV, 96, 101, 109

Value chain analysis, 68
Vision 2020, 71
Vision 2030, 71
Visual camera, 78

Water level indicator, 69
Water supply management, 21
Web 1.0, 72
Web 2.0, 72
Weed control, 21
Weed pressure mapping, 77
Weeds, 258
Wheat chlorophyll measurement, 77
Wi-Fi, 91, 94, 98, 105
Wind direction, 91, 93, 96, 97
Wind speed, 91, 93, 96, 97, 103
Wireless sensor networks (WSNs),
18, 71, 147, 149, 151–154, 171,
224–228, 231–232, 239, 241
World economic forum, 73
WSN framework, 252
WSN routing protocols, 175

Yield forecasting, 77

Zigbee, 105
ZigBee Pro/IEEE 802.15.4
communications protocol, 79